Decoding the TOEFL® iBT

Intermediate

LISTENING

INTRODUCTION

For many learners of English, the TOEFL® iBT will be the most important standardized test they ever take. Unfortunately for a large number of these individuals, the material covered on the TOEFL® iBT remains a mystery to them, so they are unable to do well on the test. We hope that by using the *Decoding the TOEFL® iBT* series, individuals who take the TOEFL® iBT will be able to excel on the test and, in the process of using the book, may unravel the mysteries of the test and therefore make the material covered on the TOEFL® iBT more familiar to themselves.

The TOEFL® iBT covers the four main skills that a person must learn when studying any foreign language: reading, listening, speaking, and writing. The *Decoding the TOEFL® iBT* series contains books that cover all four of these skills. The *Decoding the TOEFL® iBT* series contains books with three separate levels for all four of the topics, and it also contains *Decoding the TOEFL® iBT Actual Test* books. These books contain several actual tests that learners can utilize to help them become better prepared to take the TOEFL® iBT. This book, *Decoding the TOEFL® iBT Listening Intermediate*, covers the listening aspect of the test. Finally, the TOEFL® iBT underwent a number of changes in August 2019. This book—and the others in the series—takes those changes into account and incorporates them in the texts and questions, so readers of this second edition can be assured that they have up-to-date knowledge of the test.

Decoding the TOEFL® iBT Listening Intermediate can be used by learners who are taking classes and also by individuals who are studying by themselves. It contains eight chapters, each of which focuses on a different listening question, and one actual test at the end of the book. Each chapter contains explanations of the questions and how to answer them correctly. It also contains passages of varying lengths, and it focuses on asking the types of questions that are covered in the chapter. The passages and question types in *Decoding the TOEFL® iBT Listening Intermediate* are slightly lower levels than those found on the TOEFL® iBT. Individuals who use *Decoding the TOEFL® iBT Listening Intermediate* will therefore be able to prepare themselves not only to take the TOEFL® iBT but also to perform well on the test.

We hope that everyone who uses *Decoding the TOEFL® iBT Listening Intermediate* will be able to become more familiar with the TOEFL® iBT and will additionally improve his or her score on the test. As the title of the book implies, we hope that learners can use it to crack the code on the TOEFL® iBT, to make the test itself less mysterious and confusing, and to get the highest score possible. Finally, we hope that both learners and instructors can use this book to its full potential. We wish all of you the best of luck as you study English and prepare for the TOEFL® iBT, and we hope that *Decoding the TOEFL® iBT Listening Intermediate* can provide you with assistance during the course of your studies.

Michael A. Putlack
Stephen Poirier
Maximilian Tolochko

TABLE
OF
CONTENTS

ABOUT THE TOEFL® iBT LISTENING SECTION

Changes in the Listening Section

TOEFL® underwent many changes in August of 2019. The following is an explanation of some of the changes that have been made to the Listening section.

Format

The Listening section contains either two or three parts. Before August 2019, each part had one conversation and two lectures. However, since the changes in August 2019, each part can have either one conversation and one lecture or one conversation and two lectures. In total, two conversations and three lectures (in two parts) or three conversations and four lectures (in three parts) can appear. The possible formats of the Listening section include the following:

Number of Parts	First Part	Second Part	Third Part
2	1 Conversation + 1 Lecture	1 Conversation + 2 Lectures	
	1 Conversation + 2 Lectures	1 Conversation + 1 Lecture	
3	1 Conversation + 1 Lecture	1 Conversation + 1 Lecture	1 Conversation + 2 Lectures
	1 Conversation + 1 Lecture	1 Conversation + 2 Lectures	1 Conversation + 1 Lecture
	1 Conversation + 2 Lectures	1 Conversation + 1 Lecture	1 Conversation + 1 Lecture

The time given for the Listening section has been reduced from 60-90 minutes to 41-57 minutes.

Passages and Questions

The lengths of the conversations and the lectures remain the same as before. The length of each conversation and lecture is 3 to 6 minutes.

It has been reported that some conversations have academic discussions that are of high difficulty levels, making them almost similar to lectures. For example, some questions might ask about academic information discussed between a student and a professor in the conversation. In addition, questions for both the conversations and the lectures tend to ask for more detailed information than before.

The numbers of questions remain the same. The test taker is given five questions after each conversation and six questions after each lecture. The time given for answering each set of questions is either 6.5 or 10 minutes.

Each conversation or lecture is heard only once. The test taker can take notes while listening to the passage and refer to them when answering the questions.

Question Types

TYPE 1 Gist-Content Questions

Gist-Content questions cover the test taker's basic comprehension of the listening passage. While they are typically asked after lectures, they are sometimes asked after conversations as well. These questions check to see if the test taker has understood the gist of the passage. They focus on the passage as a whole, so it is important to recognize what the main point of the lecture is or why the two people in the conversation are having a particular discussion. The test taker should therefore be able to recognize the theme of the lecture or conversation in order to answer this question correctly.

TYPE 2 Gist-Purpose Questions

Gist-Purpose questions cover the underlying theme of the passage. While they are typically asked after conversations, they are sometimes asked after lectures as well. Because these questions focus on the purpose or theme of the conversation or lecture, they begin with the word "why." They focus on the conversation or lecture as a whole, but they are not concerned with details; instead, they are concerned with why the student is speaking with the professor or employee or why the professor is covering a specific topic.

TYPE 3 Detail Questions

Detail questions cover the test taker's ability to understand facts and data that are mentioned in the listening passage. These questions appear after both conversations and lectures. Detail questions require the test taker to listen for and remember details from the passage. The majority of these questions concern major details that are related to the main topic of the lecture or conversation rather than minor ones. However, in some cases where there is a long digression that is not clearly related to the main idea, there may be a question about the details of the digression.

TYPE 4 Making Inferences Questions

Making Inferences questions cover the test taker's ability to understand implications made in the passage and to come to a conclusion about what these implications mean. These questions appear after both conversations and lectures. These questions require the test taker to hear the information being presented and then to make conclusions about what the information means or what is going to happen as a result of that information.

TYPE 5 Understanding Function Questions

Understanding Function questions cover the test taker's ability to determine the underlying meaning of what has been said in the passage. This question type often involves replaying a portion of the listening passage. There are two types of these questions. Some ask the test taker to infer the meaning of a phrase or a sentence. Thus the test taker needs to determine the implication—not the literal meaning— of the sentence. Other questions ask the test taker to infer the purpose of a statement made by one of the speakers. These questions specifically ask about the intended effect of a particular statement on the listener.

TYPE 6 Understanding Attitude Questions

Understanding Attitude questions cover the speaker's attitude or opinion toward something. These questions may appear after both lectures and conversations. This question type often involves replaying a portion of the listening passage. There are two types of these questions. Some ask about one of the speakers' feelings concerning something. These questions may check to see whether the test taker understands how a speaker feels about a particular topic, if a speaker likes or dislikes something, or why a speaker might feel anxiety or amusement. The other category asks about one of the speaker's opinions. These questions may inquire about a speaker's degree of certainty. Others may ask what a speaker thinks or implies about a topic, person, thing, or idea.

TYPE 7 Understanding Organization Questions

Understanding Organization questions cover the test taker's ability to determine the overall organization of the passage. These questions almost always appear after lectures. They rarely appear after conversations. These questions require the test taker to pay attention to two factors. The first is the way that the professor has organized the lecture and how he or she presents the information to the class. The second is how individual information given in the lecture relates to the lecture as a whole. To answer these questions correctly, test takers should focus more on the presentation and the professor's purpose in mentioning the facts rather than the facts themselves.

TYPE 8 Connecting Content Questions

Connecting Content questions almost exclusively appear after lectures, not after conversations. These questions measure the test taker's ability to understand how the ideas in the lecture relate to one another. These relationships may be explicitly stated, or you may have to infer them from the words you hear. The majority of these questions concern major relationships in the passage. These questions also commonly appear in passages where a number of different themes, ideas, objects, or individuals are being discussed.

HOW TO USE THIS BOOK

Decoding the TOEFL® iBT Listening Intermediate is designed to be used either as a textbook in a classroom environment or as a study guide for individual learners. There are 8 chapters in this book. Each chapter provides comprehensive information about one type of listening question. There are 5 sections in each chapter, which enable you to build up your skills on a particular listening question. At the end of the book, there is one actual test of the Listening section of the TOEFL® iBT.

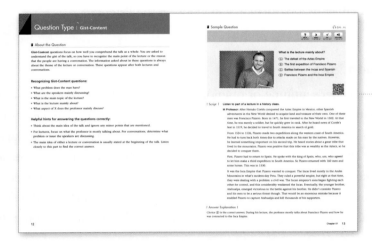

Question Type

This section provides a short explanation of the question type. It contains examples of typical questions so that you can identify them more easily and hints on how to answer the questions. There is also a short listening passage with one sample question and explanation.

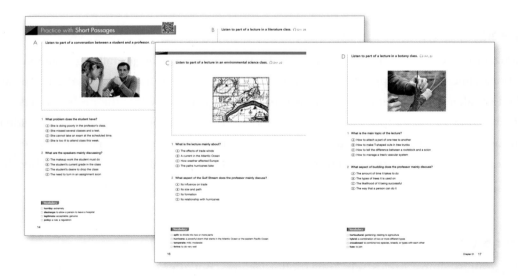

Practice with Short Passages

This section contains 4 passages. There are usually 2 conversations between 200 and 300 words long and 2 lectures between 400 and 500 words long. However, depending on the question type, there may be more conversations and fewer lectures or more lectures and fewer conversations. Each passage contains 2 questions of the type covered in the chapter and has a short vocabulary section.

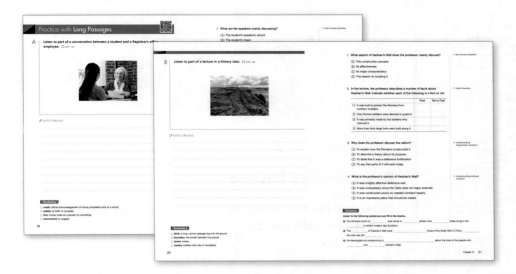

▮ Practice with Long Passages

This section contains 2 passages. There are normally 1 conversation between 350 and 450 words long and 1 lecture between 550 and 650 words long. However, depending on the question type, there may be either 2 conversations or 2 lectures. There is at least 1 question about the type of question covered in the chapter. The other questions are of various types. There are also a short vocabulary section and a dictation section to practice your listening skills.

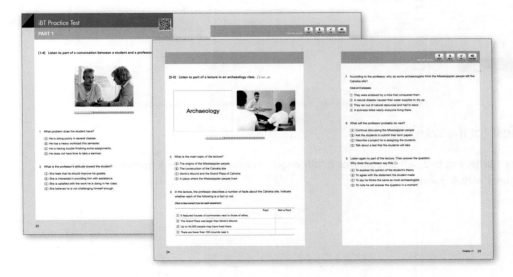

▮ iBT Practice Test

This section has 2 conversations between 500 and 550 words long with 4 questions and 3 lectures between 800 and 850 words long with 5 questions each.

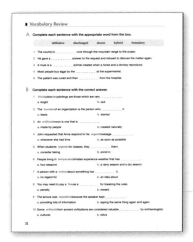

Vocabulary Review

This section has two vocabulary exercises using words that appear in the passages in the chapter.

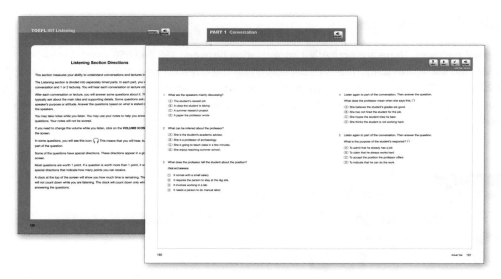

Actual Test (at the end of the book)

This section has 1 Listening test, which contains 2 full-length conversations with 5 questions and 3 full-length lectures with 6 questions.

Chapter **01**

Gist-Content

Question Type | Gist-Content

◼ About the Question

Gist-Content questions focus on how well you comprehend the talk as a whole. You are asked to understand the gist of the talk, so you have to recognize the main point of the lecture or the reason that the people are having a conversation. The information asked about in these questions is always about the theme of the lecture or conversation. These questions appear after both lectures and conversations.

Recognizing Gist-Content questions:

- What problem does the man have?
- What are the speakers mainly discussing?
- What is the main topic of the lecture?
- What is the lecture mainly about?
- What aspect of X does the professor mainly discuss?

Helpful hints for answering the questions correctly:

- Think about the main idea of the talk and ignore any minor points that are mentioned.
- For lectures, focus on what the professor is mostly talking about. For conversations, determine what problem or issue the speakers are discussing.
- The main idea of either a lecture or conversation is usually stated at the beginning of the talk. Listen closely to this part to find the correct answer.

What is the lecture mainly about?

(A) The defeat of the Aztec Empire

(B) The first expedition of Francisco Pizarro

(C) Battles between the Incas and Spanish

(D) Francisco Pizarro and the Inca Empire

| Script | Listen to part of a lecture in a history class.

M Professor: After Hernán Cortés conquered the Aztec Empire in Mexico, other Spanish adventurers in the New World desired to acquire land and treasure of their own. One of these men was Francisco Pizarro. Born in 1471, he first traveled to the New World in 1502. At that time, he was merely a soldier, but he quickly grew in rank. After he heard news of Cortés's feat in 1519, he decided to travel to South America in search of gold.

From 1524 to 1526, Pizarro made two expeditions along the western coast of South America. He had to turn back both times due to attacks made on his men by the natives. However, he learned something important on his second trip. He heard stories about a great tribe that lived in the mountains. Pizarro was positive that this tribe was as wealthy as the Aztecs, so he decided to conquer them.

First, Pizarro had to return to Spain. He spoke with the king of Spain, who, um, who agreed to let him make a third expedition to South America. So Pizarro returned with 160 men and some horses. This was in 1530.

It was the Inca Empire that Pizarro wanted to conquer. The Incas lived mostly in the Andes Mountains in what's modern-day Peru. They ruled a powerful empire, but right at that time, they were dealing with a problem: a civil war. The Incan emperor's sons began fighting each other for control, and this considerably weakened the Incas. Eventually, the younger brother, Atahualpa, emerged victorious in the battle against his brother. He didn't consider Pizarro and his men to be a serious threat though. That would be an enormous mistake because it enabled Pizarro to capture Atahualpa and kill thousands of his supporters.

| Answer Explanation |

Choice (D) is the correct answer. During his lecture, the professor mostly talks about Francisco Pizarro and how he was connected to the Inca Empire.

A   **Listen to part of a conversation between a student and a professor.** 🎧 CH1_2A

1 What problem does the student have?

(A) She is doing poorly in the professor's class.

(B) She missed several classes and a test.

(C) She cannot take an exam at the scheduled time.

(D) She is too ill to attend class this week.

2 What are the speakers mainly discussing?

(A) The makeup work the student must do

(B) The student's current grade in the class

(C) The student's desire to drop the class

(D) The need to turn in an assignment soon

| Vocabulary |

☐ **horribly:** extremely

☐ **discharge:** to allow a person to leave a hospital

☐ **legitimate:** acceptable; genuine

☐ **policy:** a rule; a regulation

B | **Listen to part of a lecture in a literature class.** 🎧 CH1_2B

1 **What is the lecture mainly about?**

   Ⓐ How the Grimm brothers developed their work
   Ⓑ When the Grimm brothers started their work
   Ⓒ Why the Grimm brothers collected stories
   Ⓓ Where the Grimm brothers got most of their stories

2 **What aspect of _Children's and Household Tales_ does the professor mainly discuss?**

   Ⓐ The titles of the stories in it
   Ⓑ The origins of the stories in it
   Ⓒ The number of stories in it
   Ⓓ The genres of the stories in it

Vocabulary

☐ **nationalism:** patriotism; love of one's country
☐ **key:** major; important
☐ **variation:** a difference
☐ **definitive:** final

C | Listen to part of a lecture in an environmental science class. 🎧 CH1_2C

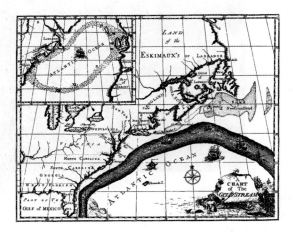

1 **What is the lecture mainly about?**

Ⓐ The effects of trade winds

Ⓑ A current in the Atlantic Ocean

Ⓒ How weather affected Europe

Ⓓ The paths hurricanes take

2 **What aspect of the Gulf Stream does the professor mainly discuss?**

Ⓐ Its influence on trade

Ⓑ Its size and path

Ⓒ Its formation

Ⓓ Its relationship with hurricanes

Vocabulary

☐ **split:** to divide into two or more parts

☐ **hurricane:** a powerful storm that starts in the Atlantic Ocean or the eastern Pacific Ocean

☐ **temperate:** mild; moderate

☐ **thrive:** to do very well

D   Listen to part of a lecture in a botany class. 🎧 CH1_2D

1   What is the main topic of the lecture?

Ⓐ How to attach a part of one tree to another

Ⓑ How to make T-shaped cuts in tree trunks

Ⓒ How to tell the difference between a rootstock and a scion

Ⓓ How to manage a tree's vascular system

2   What aspect of budding does the professor mainly discuss?

Ⓐ The amount of time it takes to do

Ⓑ The types of trees it is used on

Ⓒ The likelihood of it being successful

Ⓓ The way that a person can do it

Vocabulary

☐ **horticultural:** gardening; relating to agriculture

☐ **hybrid:** a combination of two or more different types

☐ **crossbreed:** to combine two species, breeds, or types with each other

☐ **fuse:** to join

A | **Listen to part of a conversation between a student and a Registrar's office employee.** 🎧 CH1_3A

✎ NOTE-TAKING

☐ **credit:** official acknowledgement of having completed work at a school

☐ **satisfy:** to fulfill; to complete

☐ **fine:** money owed as a penalty for something

☐ **recommend:** to suggest

1 What are the speakers mainly discussing?

← Gist-Content Question

    Ⓐ The student's academic record

    Ⓑ The student's major

    Ⓒ The student's unpaid tuition

    Ⓓ The student's course grades

2 Why does the employee tell the student about the school's policy?

← Understanding Function Question

    Ⓐ To say why she cannot answer a question

    Ⓑ To point out why the student cannot graduate

    Ⓒ To explain why the student owes money

    Ⓓ To disagree with the student's claim

3 What will the student probably do next?

← Making Inferences Question

    Ⓐ Request a copy of her transcript

    Ⓑ Visit the school library

    Ⓒ Make an appointment with her advisor

    Ⓓ Pay the employee some money

Dictation

Listen to part of the conversation again and fill in the blanks.

W1: Who's _____ _____ _____ . . . ? You can come over here, please . . . Ah, hello. How may I _____ _____ _____ today?

W2: Good afternoon. Uh, I'm a _____ and am going to be _____ next semester. Um, at least I _____ I'm going to be graduating. I was told that I need to come here to _____ _____ if I am going to have _____ _____ .

W1: Of course. We've been getting lots of students like you the past few days. Could you please give me your _____ _____ _____ ?

W2: Oh, yeah, sure. I've got it right, um . . . here. _____ _____ _____ .

B Listen to part of a lecture in a history class. 🎧 CH1_3B

✏ NOTE-TAKING

1 What aspect of Hadrian's Wall does the professor mainly discuss?

← Gist-Content Question

(A) The construction process

(B) Its effectiveness

(C) Its major characteristics

(D) The reason for building it

2 In the lecture, the professor describes a number of facts about Hadrian's Wall. Indicate whether each of the following is a fact or not.

← Detail Question

	Fact	Not a Fact
1 It was built to protect the Romans from northern invaders.		
2 Only Roman soldiers were allowed to guard it.		
3 It was primarily made by the soldiers who manned it.		
4 More than forty large forts were built along it.		

3 Why does the professor discuss the *vallum*?

← Understanding Organization Question

(A) To explain how the Romans constructed it

(B) To describe a theory about its purpose

(C) To state that it was a defensive fortification

(D) To say that parts of it still exist today

4 What is the professor's opinion of Hadrian's Wall?

← Understanding Attitude Question

(A) It was a highly effective defensive wall.

(B) It was unnecessary since the Celts were not major enemies.

(C) It was constructed poorly so needed constant repairs.

(D) It is an impressive place that should be visited.

| Dictation |

Listen to the following sentences and fill in the blanks.

❶ The Romans built it to _____ their lands in _____ Britain from _____ tribes living in the _____ in what's modern-day Scotland.

❷ The _____ of Hadrian's Wall were _____ _____ those of the Great Wall of China. _____ the wall was still _____.

❸ Archaeologists are endeavoring to _____ _____ _____ about the lives of the people who _____ and _____ Hadrian's Wall.

[1-4] **Listen to part of a conversation between a student and a professor.** 🎧 CH1_4A

1 What problem does the student have?

    (A) He is doing poorly in several classes.

    (B) He has a heavy workload this semester.

    (C) He is having trouble finishing some assignments.

    (D) He does not have time to take a seminar.

2 What is the professor's attitude toward the student?

    (A) She feels that he should improve his grades.

    (B) She is interested in providing him with assistance.

    (C) She is satisfied with the work he is doing in her class.

    (D) She believes he is not challenging himself enough.

3   What does the professor suggest that the student do?

   Ⓐ Stop participating in so many after-school activities

   Ⓑ Focus only on one of his majors

   Ⓒ Ask his professors for more time to do their assignments

   Ⓓ Continue working but stop playing sports

4   Listen again to part of the conversation. Then answer the question.
    What can be inferred about the student when he says this: 🎧

   Ⓐ He had a job the previous semester.

   Ⓑ His work interferes with his studies.

   Ⓒ He cannot afford to pay for school.

   Ⓓ His grades at school are good.

[5-9] Listen to part of a lecture in an archaeology class. 🎧 CH1_4B

Archaeology

5   What is the main topic of the lecture?

  Ⓐ The origins of the Mississippian people

  Ⓑ The construction of the Cahokia site

  Ⓒ Monk's Mound and the Grand Plaza of Cahokia

  Ⓓ A place where the Mississippian people live

6   In the lecture, the professor describes a number of facts about the Cahokia site. Indicate whether each of the following is a fact or not.

Click in the correct box for each statement.

	Fact	Not a Fact
① It featured houses of commoners next to those of elites.		
② The Grand Plaza was larger than Monk's Mound.		
③ Up to 40,000 people may have lived there.		
④ There are fewer than 100 mounds near it		

7 According to the professor, why do some archaeologists think the Mississippian people left the Cahokia site?

Click on 2 answers.

1 They were enslaved by a tribe that conquered them.

2 A natural disaster caused their water supplies to dry up.

3 They ran out of natural resources and had to leave.

4 A sickness killed nearly everyone living there.

8 What will the professor probably do next?

(A) Continue discussing the Mississippian people

(B) Ask the students to submit their term papers

(C) Describe a project he is assigning the students

(D) Talk about a test that the students will take

9 Listen again to part of the lecture. Then answer the question.
Why does the professor say this: 🎧

(A) To express his opinion of the student's theory

(B) To agree with the statement the student made

(C) To say he thinks the same as most archaeologists

(D) To note he will answer the question in a moment

[10-14] **Listen to part of a lecture in a geology class.** 🎧 CH1_4C

Geology

lakes

10 What is the lecture mainly about?

    Ⓐ How lakes can be created

    Ⓑ What lakes are used for

    Ⓒ How natural lakes compare to artificial ones

    Ⓓ Which countries have the most lakes

11 Based on the information in the lecture, indicate which method of lake formation the statements refer to.

Click in the correct box for each statement.

	Glacial Action	Plate Tectonics
1 Creates large cracks into which water flows		
2 Is the way that Lake Baikal was created		
3 Can block valleys with material and therefore form lakes		
4 Is responsible for most of the lakes in the Northern Hemisphere		

12 Why does the professor mention Lake Toba?

A To claim it is an oxbow lake

B To name a lake formed by a volcano

C To compare it in size to the Great Lakes

D To say it is the world's deepest lake

13 What does the professor imply about Lake Kariba?

A It is an artificial lake.

B It was made by beavers.

C It created the world's biggest lake.

D It is in danger of drying up.

14 Listen again to part of the lecture. Then answer the question.
What does the student mean when he says this: 🎧

A He did not do the assigned reading.

B He wants the professor to ask someone else.

C He is going to give the textbook definition.

D He is not positive about the answer.

[1-4] Listen to part of a conversation between a student and an information desk worker. 🎧 CH1_4D

1 What problem does the student have?

    Ⓐ He did not pay an entry fee for the expo.

    Ⓑ He arrived a day too late to attend the expo.

    Ⓒ He does not know the location of the expo.

    Ⓓ He failed to get any interviews at the expo.

2 Why does the woman ask the student about his résumé?

    Ⓐ To offer to help him check it over for mistakes

    Ⓑ To make sure that he has some copies of it with him

    Ⓒ To find out about the format that he wrote his in

    Ⓓ To advise him to print it on high-quality paper

3   What will the student probably do next?

   Ⓐ Go to Silas Hall to attend the expo

   Ⓑ Return to his dormitory to change into a suit

   Ⓒ Contact the expo organizers to ask them a question

   Ⓓ Give the woman his student identification card

4   Listen again to part of the conversation. Then answer the question.
What can be inferred about the woman when she says this: 🎧

   Ⓐ She thinks the student went to the wrong building.

   Ⓑ She cannot understand what the student is saying.

   Ⓒ She believes the student cannot attend the expo.

   Ⓓ She is surprised the student did not see a sign.

[5-9]   Listen to part of a lecture in a physiology class. 🎧 CH1_4E

Physiology

5   What aspect of hypnagogia does the professor mainly discuss?

 Ⓐ Some memories of it that people have

 Ⓑ Some ways people can enhance its effects

 Ⓒ The reasons only few people experience it

 Ⓓ The effects it has on the human body

6   According to the professor, when are there large amounts of theta waves in the brain?

    Ⓐ When a person has just woken up

    Ⓑ When a person is falling asleep

    Ⓒ When a person is sleeping deeply

    Ⓓ When a person is wide awake

7   Why does the professor mention Mary Shelley?

    Ⓐ To say how she got an idea for a book she wrote

    Ⓑ To praise the quality of writing in *Frankenstein*

    Ⓒ To comment on the research that she did on hypnagogia

    Ⓓ To state how hypnagogia negatively affected her

8   What comparison does the professor make between REM sleep and hypnagogia?

    Ⓐ The amount of time that each of them lasts

    Ⓑ The ability of people to act as they want in each of them

    Ⓒ The periods of sleep when people experience each of them

    Ⓓ The memories of each of them that people retain

9   Listen again to part of the lecture. Then answer the question.
    What does the professor mean when she says this: 🎧

    Ⓐ She does not remember any hypnagogic experiences she has had.

    Ⓑ She does not think that hypnagogia actually happens to people.

    Ⓒ She does not want to go through sleep paralysis during hypnagogia.

    Ⓓ She does not recall the most recent hypnagogic experience she had.

Vocabulary Review

A Complete each sentence with the appropriate word from the box.

definitive	discharged	dozen	hybrid	boundary

1 The country's _____ runs through the mountain range to the ocean.

2 He gave a _____ answer to the request and refused to discuss the matter again.

3 A mule is a _____ animal created when a horse and a donkey reproduce.

4 Most people buy eggs by the _____ at the supermarket.

5 The patient was cured and then _____ from the hospital.

B Complete each sentence with the correct answer.

1 **Vivid** colors in paintings are those which are very _____.
   a. bright   b. dull

2 The **founder** of an organization is the person who _____ it.
   a. leads   b. started

3 An **artificial** moon is one that is _____.
   a. made by people   b. created naturally

4 John requested that Anna respond to his **urgent** message _____.
   a. whenever she had time   b. as soon as possible

5 When students **register** for classes, they _____ them.
   a. consider taking   b. enroll in

6 People living in **temperate** climates experience weather that has _____.
   a. four seasons   b. a rainy season and a dry season

7 A person with a **notion** about something has _____ it.
   a. no regard for   b. an idea about

8 You may need to pay a **fine** as a _____ for breaking the rules.
   a. penalty   b. reward

9 The lecture was **repetitive** because the speaker kept _____.
   a. providing lots of information   b. saying the same thing again and again

10 Some **artifacts** from ancient civilizations are considered valuable _____ by archaeologists.
   a. cultures   b. relics

Chapter 02

Gist-Purpose

Question Type | Gist-Purpose

◼ About the Question

Gist-Purpose questions focus on the theme of the talk. You must determine why the conversation is taking place or why the professor is lecturing about a specific topic. These questions begin with "why." They do not ask about details. Instead, they ask about why the talk is taking place. These questions sometimes follow lectures but are more common after conversations.

Recognizing Gist-Purpose questions:

• Why does the student visit the professor?

• Why does the student visit the Registrar's office?

• Why did the professor ask to see the student?

• Why does the professor explain X?

Helpful hints for answering the questions correctly:

• Think about why the lecture or conversation is happening.

• For conversations, listen closely to the description of the problem the student has as well as the solution. Knowing both of them can help you determine why the student is speaking with the professor or visiting a certain office.

• In many instances, the student explains the reason he or she is visiting the professor or office at the beginning of the conversation. Always listen carefully to this part.

• In other instances, the student sums up the conversation at the end and therefore provides the answer to the question.

Why does the student visit the professor?

(A) To show an outline that she wrote

(B) To discuss the history of the Renaissance

(C) To ask about the topic she thought of

(D) To get some advice on a paper

| Script | Listen to part of a conversation between a student and a professor.

W1 Student: Professor Marlowe, I have a couple of questions for you. Are you still having office hours?

W2 Professor: Well, technically, they finished half an hour ago, but I don't mind talking to you. You're in my Renaissance history class, aren't you?

W1: Yes, that's correct. Thanks for remembering.

W2: So what can I do for you?

W1: Um . . . you assigned a paper for us to write in class today, but, uh, this is the first college paper I've ever had to write. So, um . . . I'm not really sure what I should do.

W2: Ah, okay . . . We've been studying the origins of the Renaissance in Europe lately. So why don't you pick a topic related to that?

W1: And then I just write about it?

W2: Not exactly. You need to come up with some sort of thesis. You know, uh, make an argument about something related to the origins of the Renaissance. Then, include historical facts to defend your thesis.

W1: Okay, I think I can do that. I was planning to write an outline first. Is it okay if I show you the outline tomorrow before I start writing? I don't want to make any mistakes.

| Answer Explanation |

Choice (D) is the correct answer. The student tells the professor, "You assigned a paper for us to write in class today, but, uh, this is the first college paper I've ever had to write. So, um . . . I'm not really sure what I should do." So she visits the professor to get some advice on a paper that she has to write.

A

Listen to part of a conversation between a student and a student activities office employee. 🎧 CH2_2A

1 Why does the student visit the student activities office?

Ⓐ To ask about additional funding

Ⓑ To learn how to schedule an event

Ⓒ To find out how to become an official club

Ⓓ To get permission to go on a trip

2 Why does the employee explain the application process?

Ⓐ To state the consequences of doing something improperly

Ⓑ To contradict the explanation in the student activities booklet

Ⓒ To provide the student with detailed instructions

Ⓓ To correct a statement that the student made

Vocabulary

☐ **vague:** unclear

☐ **rent:** to pay money to use something for a limited amount of time

☐ **minimal:** small; tiny

☐ **grant:** money given to a person or group

Listen to part of a conversation between a student and a professor. 🎧 CH2_2B

1 Why does the student visit the professor?

Ⓐ To discuss attending graduate school

Ⓑ To ask her to be his advisor

Ⓒ To request a letter of recommendation

Ⓓ To talk to her about her class

2 Why does the student explain his actions in the professor's class?

Ⓐ To state why he did not work very hard

Ⓑ To say what he wants her to write about

Ⓒ To point out that he was a good student

Ⓓ To argue that his grade should have been higher

Vocabulary

☐ **require:** to need

☐ **focus:** to emphasize

☐ **participate:** to take part in; to contribute to

☐ **sealed:** closed

C | Listen to part of a conversation between a student and a Math Department office secretary. 🎧 CH2_2C

1 Why does the student visit the Math Department office?

- Ⓐ To inquire about the location of a professor
- Ⓑ To pick up a form to drop a class
- Ⓒ To submit homework for a class he is in
- Ⓓ To find out where Professor Goodwin's office is

2 Why does the secretary explain Professor Goodwin's schedule?

- Ⓐ To mention why he canceled his morning class
- Ⓑ To say that he has class the rest of the day
- Ⓒ To explain why he will not return today
- Ⓓ To tell the student why he is not in his office

Vocabulary

- ☐ **head:** a leader; a manager
- ☐ **form:** an official document
- ☐ **regulation:** a rule; a law
- ☐ **insist:** to demand

D Listen to part of a lecture in an astronomy class. 🎧 CH2_2D

1 Why does the professor explain about light pollution?

- Ⓐ To provide a short history of its origins
- Ⓑ To say it is worse than noise pollution
- Ⓒ To name some places where it is very bad
- Ⓓ To show how it affects astronomers

2 Why does the professor explain about low-pressure sodium wavelength lights?

- Ⓐ To compare them with other types of lights
- Ⓑ To talk about their cost and development
- Ⓒ To describe their effectiveness in Tucson
- Ⓓ To argue that they do not work very well

Vocabulary

- ☐ **glare:** a harsh, bright light
- ☐ **telescope:** an instrument used to see distant objects in space
- ☐ **emit:** to give off
- ☐ **strict:** severe

A Listen to part of a conversation between a student and a professor. 🎧 CH2_3A

✏ NOTE-TAKING

_____

_____

_____

_____

_____

_____

_____

_____

Vocabulary

☐ **efficient:** well-organized

☐ **syllabus:** a written plan for a course

☐ **cover:** to study; to go over

☐ **pique:** to interest

1 Why does the student visit the professor? ← Gist-Purpose Question

    Ⓐ To discuss an aspect of archaeology

    Ⓑ To inquire about an upcoming exam

    Ⓒ To get information about an assignment

    Ⓓ To ask when some homework is due

2 What is the professor's opinion of the student? ← Understanding Attitude Question

    Ⓐ He thinks she could study harder.

    Ⓑ He believes she pays attention in class.

    Ⓒ He considers her an excellent writer.

    Ⓓ He is impressed by her hard work.

3 What does the professor give the student? ← Detail Question

    Ⓐ A syllabus

    Ⓑ A paper

    Ⓒ A book

    Ⓓ A study sheet

Dictation

Listen to part of the conversation again and fill in the blanks.

W: Professor Burgess, do you have some time to _____ _____ me about our paper?

M: Paper? We don't have a paper _____ until the end of the _____.

W: Yes, that's the _____ I'm talking about. I was hoping to start _____ _____ it as soon as possible.

M: I guess you _____ me by _____ since we're only in the _____ week of the semester. I _____ _____ that any student has ever asked me about doing a _____ paper until after the _____.

W: Oh, yeah. I _____ I see why you were a bit confused by my _____. In case you're curious, I've got a _____ _____ of classes this semester, and I also play on the _____ basketball team. So I'm basically trying to get _____ much work done _____ _____ now before practice begins.

B | Listen to part of a lecture in a zoology class. 🎧 CH2_3B

✏️ NOTE-TAKING

Vocabulary

☐ **fossil:** the preserved, hardened remains of a plant or animal

☐ **vegetation:** plant life

☐ **carnivorous:** relating to the eating of meat

☐ **stealth:** sneaky

1 **Why does the professor tell the students to look at their books?**

← Understanding Function Question

 Ⓐ To have them read a passage

 Ⓑ To show them some photographs

 Ⓒ To have them look at a chart

 Ⓓ To show them a diagram

2 **Why does the professor explain the nymph stage of the dragonfly?**

← Gist-Purpose Question

 Ⓐ To describe a part of its life cycle

 Ⓑ To state when it is in the most danger

 Ⓒ To note that it can fly at that time

 Ⓓ To claim it is a nymph for a short amount of time

3 **What will the professor probably do next?**

← Making Inferences Question

 Ⓐ Dismiss the class

 Ⓑ Ask some questions

 Ⓒ Take a break

 Ⓓ Continue lecturing

4 **Listen again to part of the lecture. Then answer the question. Why does the professor say this:** 🎧

← Understanding Function Question

 Ⓐ To state a new theory

 Ⓑ To point out a problem

 Ⓒ To make a comparison

 Ⓓ To give her opinion

Dictation

Listen to the following sentences and fill in the blanks.

❶ _____ _____ _____ _____ the dragonfly, which is one of the most interesting insects I've studied.

❷ _____ _____ dragonfly species spend the entire _____ stage in the _____.

❸ Dragonflies _____ _____ _____ flying in a sort of stealth mode. Thus they can _____ _____ _____ unaware insects, uh, even ones that are flying.

[1-4] **Listen to part of a conversation between a student and a librarian.** 🎧 CH2_4A

1 Why does the student visit the librarian?

Ⓐ To find out how to use the library's computer system

Ⓑ To ask about the locations of some journals

Ⓒ To get assistance in finding some research material

Ⓓ To discuss a project that she worked on before

2 How will the student get the journal articles she wants?

Ⓐ By visiting libraries in other locations

Ⓑ By downloading them from the Internet

Ⓒ By finding them on microfilm

Ⓓ By using the interlibrary loan system

3   Why does the librarian tell the student about Seaside College?

Ⓐ To suggest how to obtain the books she needs

Ⓑ To compare its library with the one they are in

Ⓒ To point out that it has outstanding research facilities

Ⓓ To say that it has the journals the student wants

4   What will the student probably do next?

Ⓐ Use the library's computer system

Ⓑ Make copies of some journal articles

Ⓒ Check out the books that she has

Ⓓ Make a card to use at another library

[5-9] Listen to part of a lecture in a physiology class. 🎧 CH2_4B

Physiology

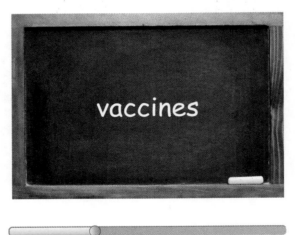

vaccines

5 Why does the professor explain some problems with vaccines?

    Ⓐ To argue that more research must be done on them

    Ⓑ To explain why he opposes their usage

    Ⓒ To show that they are not completely effective

    Ⓓ To warn against giving children too many of them

6 What does the professor imply about smallpox?

(A) Nobody has contracted it in recent times.

(B) It is the deadliest disease known to man.

(C) It affects children more than adults.

(D) Most of its victims lived in Europe and Asia.

7 What comparison does the professor make between smallpox and polio?

(A) The harm that they do to survivors

(B) The death rates for them

(C) The ages when most people get them

(D) The number of plagues they have caused

8 Based on the information in the lecture, indicate which person the statements refer to.

Click in the correct box for each statement.

	Edward Jenner	Jonas Salk
1 Tested his vaccine on a young boy		
2 Received widespread acceptance of his vaccine soon after his discovery		
3 Used a related form of a virus to make his vaccination		
4 Made one of the first vaccines ever		

9 Listen again to part of the lecture. Then answer the question.

What can be inferred about the professor when he says this: 🎧

(A) He hopes that the students submitted good work.

(B) He expects to return the papers by the next class.

(C) He does not give any tests in this class.

(D) He took a long time to grade the first reports.

[10-14] **Listen to part of a lecture in a meteorology class.** 🎧 CH2_4C

Meteorology

fog

10 What aspect of fog does the professor mainly discuss?

- Ⓐ What effects it has on the land
- Ⓑ How long it usually lasts
- Ⓒ Where it is most likely to get created
- Ⓓ How various types of it form

11 Why does the professor discuss advection fog?

    Ⓐ To mention how dangerous it can be for travelers

    Ⓑ To describe a type of fog that usually happens above water

    Ⓒ To contrast the way it dissipates with mountain fog

    Ⓓ To talk about the most common type of fog that appears

12 According to the professor, where does evaporation fog usually form?

Click on 2 answers.

    ① Above rivers

    ② Near mountains

    ③ Alongside oceans

    ④ Over lakes

13 Why does the professor explain how fog dissipates?

    Ⓐ To stress how it can happen very quickly

    Ⓑ To point out that it usually happens in the morning

    Ⓒ To show the effects of wind and heat on it

    Ⓓ To describe why fog forms on rare occasions

14 Listen again to part of the lecture. Then answer the question.
Why does the professor say this: 🎧

    Ⓐ To tell the students not to ask any questions yet

    Ⓑ To point out that a process can be complicated

    Ⓒ To say that fog dissipates at a slow rate

    Ⓓ To comment that the class is almost finished

[1-4]   **Listen to part of a conversation between a student and a physical fitness advisor.** 🎧 CH2_4D

1   Why does the student visit the physical fitness advisor?

    Ⓐ To ask about a class she is required to take

    Ⓑ To find out how to transfer to another class

    Ⓒ To inquire about how many credits she needs to take

    Ⓓ To learn when the date for signing up for classes is

2   According to the student, why does she want to take a class involving an indoor activity?

    Ⓐ She does not want to be outside during cold weather.

    Ⓑ She prefers indoor activities to outdoor ones.

    Ⓒ She heard that indoor classes do not last long.

    Ⓓ She enjoys playing sports that require a gym.

3 What can be inferred about the student?

   Ⓐ She has played racquet sports in the past.

   Ⓑ She is looking forward to studying with the man.

   Ⓒ She is uninterested in doing weightlifting.

   Ⓓ She is one of the school's top athletes.

4 Why does the physical fitness advisor tell the student about class enrollment?

   Ⓐ To indicate that she should not worry about any classes filling up

   Ⓑ To let her know that most classes limit the number of students

   Ⓒ To advise her to register quickly for the class she wants to take

   Ⓓ To answer her question about how many students can take each class

[5-9] Listen to part of a lecture in a history of technology class. 🎧 CH2_4E

History of Technology

the radio

5 How did Heinrich Hertz contribute to the development of the radio?

(A) He showed that radio waves could travel through the air.

(B) He came up with the idea of the electromagnetic spectrum.

(C) He devised the unit that is used to measure frequency.

(D) He managed to send a wireless transmission across an ocean.

6   What does the professor imply about Guglielmo Marconi?

  Ⓐ His work on the radio was more important than James Maxwell's.

  Ⓑ He was responsible for popularizing radio broadcasts.

  Ⓒ He should not be considered the real inventor of the radio.

  Ⓓ He insisted that a radio transmitter be put on the *Titanic*.

7   What is the professor's opinion of the effort to make radios smaller?

  Ⓐ It was important since it led to radios becoming more powerful.

  Ⓑ It made radios too expensive for most people to buy.

  Ⓒ It caused the development of the radio to slow down.

  Ⓓ It resulted in the radio becoming popular with many people.

8   Why does the professor explain the government's role in radio broadcasts?

  Ⓐ To show how it slowed the development of the radio

  Ⓑ To describe the licensing system that was created

  Ⓒ To complain about interference that closed some radio stations

  Ⓓ To mention why live sports broadcasts became so popular

9   How does the professor organize the information about the development of the radio that she presents to the class?

  Ⓐ By concentrating solely on the first and third stages of its creation

  Ⓑ By describing the important events in chronological order

  Ⓒ By going into detail on the theories that allowed it to be developed

  Ⓓ By focusing on the people who helped increase its popularity

◼ Vocabulary Review

A Complete each sentence with the appropriate word from the box.

participated	requirements	trap	emitting	efficient

1 _____ methods are those which require less time, energy, and money than others.

2 The soldiers hope to _____ the enemy when they enter the city.

3 More than 500 people _____ in the event held at city hall last night.

4 One of the _____ to work at the company is to have a college degree.

5 This device is _____ strange noises that nobody can explain.

B Complete each sentence with the correct answer.

1 When Janet **contracted** the illness, she suddenly _____.

   a. got healthy   b. became sick

2 A person **critical** to a company is someone who is very _____.

   a. well paid   b. important

3 Deborah's solution was **vague**, so she did not provide _____.

   a. many details   b. any information at all

4 Marconi's radio could **transmit** far, so he _____ radio waves across the ocean.

   a. sent   b. received

5 An **effective** teacher is someone who instructs students _____.

   a. very well   b. for many years

6 Lisa looked at John _____ because she was **skeptical** of his claims.

   a. happily   b. doubtfully

7 **Carnivorous** animals such as sharks and lions eat _____.

   a. plants   b. meat

8 Some predators use **stealth** to _____ while they are hunting.

   a. hide from other animals   b. chase other animals

9 Water **condenses** when it changes from its gaseous form into a _____.

   a. solid   b. liquid

10 Mr. Jenkins will discuss the _____ that were passed because of the new **regulations**.

   a. rules   b. issues

Chapter **03**

Detail

◼ About the Question

Detail questions focus on your ability to understand the facts that are mentioned in a talk. You must listen closely to the details and remember them. These questions cover major details, not minor ones. However, if a speaker talks about something not related to the main topic for a while, there may be a question about the details covered in it. These questions appear after both lectures and conversations.

Recognizing Detail questions:

1 Most Detail questions have four answer choices and one correct answer. These questions appear on the test like this:

- According to the professor, what is one way that X can affect Y?
- What are X?
- What resulted from the invention of the X?
- According to the professor, what is the main problem with the X theory?

2 Other detail questions have two or more correct answers. These questions either require you to click on two answer choices or ask you to check if several statements are true or not. These questions appear on the test like this:

- According to the professor, how did prehistoric humans get to Australia? [Click on 2 answers.]
- In the lecture, the professor describes a number of facts about earthquakes. Indicate whether each of the following is a fact about earthquakes. [Click in the correct box for each statement.]

Helpful hints for answering the questions correctly:

- Be sure to recognize the main idea or topic of the talk. Then, focus on any facts mentioned that are related to it. If you are not sure about the correct answer, select the answer choice closest to the main idea or topic of the talk.

- Ignore facts about minor details in the talk.

- The correct answers to these questions are often paraphrased from the talk. Be careful of answer choices that use the exact words from the talk. These are sometimes purposely misleading.

HELP NEXT OK VOLUME

According to the professor, what were ziggurats used for?

(A) They were palaces for their rulers.

(B) They were utilized as tombs for leaders.

(C) They were temples used to honor gods.

(D) They were storage places for grain.

| Script | **Listen to part of a lecture in an archaeology class.**

W Professor: The ancient Egyptian pyramids were constructed thousands of years ago. But there are impressive structures which were made even before they were. These buildings were constructed in nearby Mesopotamia. I'm referring to the ziggurats that the Sumerian, Babylonian, and Assyrian civilizations erected. Sadly, most of them have been destroyed. While there are a few exceptions, what we know about them primarily comes from ancient accounts.

M Student: I've heard of them before, but I'm not exactly sure what they are. They weren't tombs like the pyramids were, right?

W: That's correct. Ziggurats were ancient temples dedicated to the gods which the Mesopotamian people worshipped. We're not sure, but we think that every urban center in Mesopotamia had a ziggurat. Let me show you a couple of pictures. This is Chogha Zanbil . . . It's one of the few ziggurats remaining today. It's located in Iran. Here are the ruins of another . . . here . . . and here . . . This is an artist's reconstruction of a ziggurat . . . As I hope you saw, they weren't made of enormous blocks like the pyramids were. Instead, they were made of mud bricks. Ziggurats had bases that were square or rectangular in nature. They were at least thirty meters long on each side. However, some of the larger ones were around 100 meters long. They had several levels, so some attained great heights. We know of a few that were more than fifty meters high. As they got higher, the size of each level decreased. According to some reports, ziggurats could have up to eight levels. Some had stairs going up while others had ramps. We believe the top level of each ziggurat had a building in which priests worshipped gods.

| Answer Explanation |

Choice ⓒ is the correct answer. The professor comments, "Ziggurats were ancient temples dedicated to the gods which the Mesopotamian people worshipped," so she states that they were used to honor the gods of the Mesopotamians.

A **Listen to part of a conversation between a student and a student services office employee.** 🎧 CH3_2A

1 According to the student, what has happened to him recently? (Choose 2 answers.)

Ⓐ He has received some parking tickets.

Ⓑ He has been late for class due to parking problems.

Ⓒ He has started parking his car in a pay lot.

Ⓓ He has been unable to find parking spots at times.

2 How does the student decide to solve his problem?

Ⓐ By paying to park in any lot on campus

Ⓑ By parking on the city streets

Ⓒ By purchasing a new parking sticker

Ⓓ By stopping driving during the semester

Vocabulary

☐ **basically:** mostly; essentially

☐ **upgrade:** to advance to a higher level

☐ **access:** entry; admission

☐ **pocketbook:** a wallet; the money that one has

B | Listen to part of a lecture in a psychology class. 🎧 CH3_2B

1 In the lecture, the professor describes a number of facts about memory recall. Indicate whether each of the following is a fact or not.

	Fact	Not a Fact
☐1 Can allow people to focus on details during emotional events		
☐2 Is difficult to remember regular events		
☐3 Is related to strong feelings		
☐4 Lets people recall happy events well when they are sad		

2 According to the professor, what is encoding?

   Ⓐ The trigger that allows people to remember past events

   Ⓑ The ability to recall memories based on one's mood

   Ⓒ The manner that memories get erased from the brain

   Ⓓ The way that the brain records various events

Vocabulary

☐ **trigger:** to cause; to activate

☐ **prioritize:** to rank two or more things according to importance

☐ **retrieval:** recovery

☐ **terrifying:** frightening; causing great fear

Listen to part of a lecture in a physics class. 🎧 CH3_2C

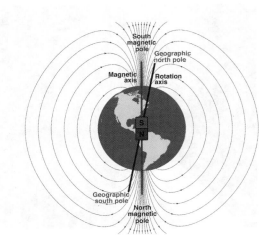

1   In the lecture, the professor describes a number of facts about the Earth's magnetic field. Indicate whether each of the following is a fact or not.

	Fact	Not a Fact
1 It has the shape of a perfect circle.		
2 Its poles are in a constant state of movement.		
3 It protects the planet from solar winds.		
4 Its north and south poles are not found at the geographic North and South poles.		

2   According to the professor, how does the dynamo theory state that the Earth's magnetic field is formed?

Ⓐ Through the interaction of the ozone layer and the core

Ⓑ Through the rotating of the Earth and its core

Ⓒ Through the action of basalt rocks in the core

Ⓓ Through the interaction of the atmosphere and solar winds

Vocabulary

☐ **subsequently:** then; afterward

☐ **slightly:** somewhat; a little

☐ **flip:** to turn over

☐ **vice versa:** in reverse order of what was stated

D **Listen to part of a lecture in an art history class.** 🎧 CH3_2D

1 **According to the professor, what is a characteristic of Minimalist art? (Choose 2 answers.)**

   Ⓐ It was intended to be art with no hidden meaning.
   Ⓑ Both straight and curved lines were commonly used.
   Ⓒ Primary colors and basic materials were used to make it.
   Ⓓ Artists utilized simple figures to create symbolism.

2 **Who was Donald Judd?**

   Ⓐ The founder of the Minimalist Movement
   Ⓑ A practitioner of Abstract Expressionism
   Ⓒ A Minimalist artist
   Ⓓ A partner of Frank Stella

Vocabulary

☐ **pare:** to trim; to cut
☐ **elaborate:** fancy; decorate; ornate
☐ **pretentious:** showy; having an exaggerated outward appearance
☐ **sculptor:** a person who makes sculptures or statues

A

Listen to part of a conversation between a student and a professor. 🎧 CH3_3A

✎ NOTE-TAKING

| Vocabulary |

☐ **chemist:** a person who studies or does chemistry

☐ **miss:** not to attend or go to something, such as a class

☐ **submit:** to turn in

☐ **post:** to put online

1   **What can be inferred about the professor?**

Making Inferences Question

   (A) He and Professor Kenwood are in different departments.

   (B) He is the student's academic advisor.

   (C) He has attended a conference with Professor Kenwood.

   (D) He takes off points when students do not attend his class.

2   **What will the student do at the event?**

   (A) Attend a workshop

   (B) Present a paper

   (C) Submit an application

   (D) Do some networking

3   **Listen again to part of the conversation. Then answer the question. What is the purpose of the professor's response?** 🎧

Understanding Function Question

   (A) To agree to the student's request

   (B) To promise to make an introduction

   (C) To give the name of the student's partner

   (D) To announce a change in plans

Dictation

Listen to part of the conversation again and fill in the blanks.

M2: You need to _____ _____ _____ acquire the notes from the classes you miss from someone you _____ . Those two lessons are going to be _____ _____ for your upcoming midterm.

M1: I, uh, I don't _____ _____ anyone in the class. Is there a student you _____ _____ that I speak with to _____ _____ _____ ?

M2: Hmm . . . I'll talk to David Greenwood since he is one of the _____ _____ in the class. Just be sure to _____ _____ when you return.

M1: I really _____ that.

B Listen to part of a lecture in a geology class. 🎧 CH3_3B

✏ NOTE-TAKING

1 **What can be inferred about the professor?**

← Making Inferences Question

(A) He intends to end the class in a few minutes.

(B) He has seen tsunamis hit the shore in person.

(C) He encourages the students to participate in class.

(D) He thinks tsunamis are deadlier than hurricanes.

2 **According to the professor, what causes tsunamis the most often?**

← Detail Question

(A) Volcanic eruptions

(B) Ice breaking off from glaciers

(C) Landslides

(D) Earthquakes

3 **In the lecture, the professor describes a number of facts about tsunamis. Indicate whether each of the following is a fact or not.**

← Detail Question

	Fact	Not a Fact
1 They become faster when they reach shallow water.		
2 They move in a single direction once they form.		
3 They can travel vast distances across oceans.		
4 They can be caused when objects from space hit oceans.		

4 **Why does the professor mention Krakatoa?**

← Understanding Organization Question

(A) To show how warning systems kept people safe from a tsunami

(B) To give an example of a volcano causing a tsunami

(C) To compare it with the earthquake in Japan in 2011

(D) To point out how much damage its erupting caused

Dictation

Listen to the following sentences and fill in the blanks.

❶ A tsunami is an _____ _____ larger than normal that can _____ coastlines and cause a great amount of _____ .

❷ There have also been tsunamis _____ _____ massive volcanic _____ above the ocean's surface.

❸ _____ _____ , in 2011, a tsunami in Japan caused by a powerful _____ killed nearly 16,000 people _____ numerous efforts to _____ them _____ the approaching danger.

[1-4] Listen to part of a conversation between a student and a professor. 🎧 CH3_4A

1 What are the speakers mainly discussing?

   Ⓐ An internship the student was offered

   Ⓑ Summer school courses

   Ⓒ The student's summer activities

   Ⓓ An assignment in the professor's class

2 Why does the professor ask the student about her plans after graduation?

   Ⓐ To learn which field she wants to work in

   Ⓑ To determine if she will work or attend graduate school

   Ⓒ To find out where in the country she is going to live

   Ⓓ To advise her to delay graduating until she knows what she will do

3 What is the professor's opinion of internships?

Ⓐ They do not pay enough money to students.

Ⓑ They can provide experience for future jobs.

Ⓒ They require a great deal of hard work.

Ⓓ They are not worth the amount of time invested in them.

4 What does the professor recommend that the student do?

Click on 2 answers.

1 Transfer to another department

2 Search for a job

3 Attend summer school

4 Apply for an internship

[5-9] Listen to part of a lecture in an archaeology class. 🎧 CH3_4B

Archaeology

glass

5 According to the professor, why did people believe that the Mesopotamians invented glass first?

(A) Many ancient glassmakers are known to have come from there.

(B) Ancient sites had many pieces of glass in them.

(C) Mesopotamian texts explain how they made glass.

(D) They were known to export glass to many areas.

6 Why does the professor mention soda ash?

   Ⓐ To name an ingredient needed to make glass

   Ⓑ To describe its chemical formula

   Ⓒ To explain how it gives glass its color

   Ⓓ To say that it contains a large amount of silica

7 How did the Egyptians make glass?

Click on 2 answers.

   ☐1 By using the process of glassblowing

   ☐2 By adding obsidian to the ingredients

   ☐3 By using the drawing method

   ☐4 By utilizing the process called casting

8 What comparison does the professor make between the Egyptians and Phoenicians?

   Ⓐ The period of time when they first made glass

   Ⓑ The ways in which they utilized glass

   Ⓒ The methods they used to create glass

   Ⓓ The different colors of glass they made

9 What will the professor probably do next?

   Ⓐ Answer any questions the students have

   Ⓑ Have the students watch a video

   Ⓒ Show some samples of ancient glass to the students

   Ⓓ Demonstrate the art of glassblowing

[10-14] Listen to part of a lecture in an economics class. 🎧 CH3_4C

Economics

K-waves

10 What is the main topic of the lecture?

Ⓐ A theory on economic cycles

Ⓑ The life of Nikolai Kondratiev

Ⓒ A comparison between two economic theories

Ⓓ The reasons that recessions happen

11 How does the professor organize the information about the way the K-wave cycle works that she presents to the class?

    Ⓐ By talking about information from a student's presentation

    Ⓑ By drawing on the board as she speaks

    Ⓒ By making an extensive comparison

    Ⓓ By providing a definition from a book

12 What is the professor's opinion of K-waves?

    Ⓐ They do not exist at all.

    Ⓑ They are mostly accurate on the economy.

    Ⓒ They cannot account for some economic activity.

    Ⓓ They are able to predict the future.

13 In the lecture, the professor describes a number of facts about K-waves. Indicate whether each of the following is a fact or not.

Click in the correct box for each statement.

	Fact	Not a Fact
① Show that economies behave in sixty-year cycles		
② Often feature wars during the second phase		
③ Can be used to show economic activity in ancient times		
④ Have shown that there are at least five economic waves since the 1800s		

14 Listen again to part of the lecture. Then answer the question.
Why does the professor say this: 🎧

    Ⓐ To mention that World War II did not belong to the third wave

    Ⓑ To show that not all K-wave cycles last the same amount of time

    Ⓒ To claim that the third wave had poor economic activity

    Ⓓ To indicate that the end of the K-wave cycle lasted a long time

[1-4] **Listen to part of a conversation between a student and a professor.** 🎧 CH3_4D

1   What are the speakers mainly discussing?

   Ⓐ A class that the student is currently taking

   Ⓑ An internship that the student will apply for

   Ⓒ A paper that the student has to write

   Ⓓ The student's plans for the coming months

2   What is the professor's opinion of Mercy Hospital?

   Ⓐ It has excellent doctors working at it.

   Ⓑ It is in need of improving its facilities.

   Ⓒ It does not treat its student interns very well.

   Ⓓ It is a place that the student should avoid.

3   What is the student concerned about?

Click on 2 answers.

1   Having his grades go down

2   Being forced to work on weekends

3   Not being able to earn any money

4   Having to pay for the internship

4   Listen again to part of the conversation. Then answer the question.
    What can be inferred from the student's response to the professor? 🎧

    Ⓐ The professor is the student's academic advisor.

    Ⓑ The student is planning to take a Psychology class.

    Ⓒ The professor teaches classes in the sciences.

    Ⓓ The student is majoring in Chemistry.

[5-9] **Listen to part of a lecture in an art history class.** 🎧 CH3_4E

Art History

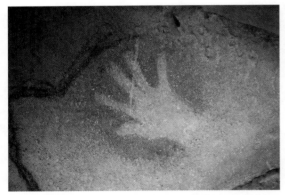

a painting from a French cave © Claude Valette

a painting by Gao Qipei

5   What aspect of finger-painting does the professor mainly discuss?

   Ⓐ Various techniques utilized by artists

   Ⓑ Famous paintings using that method

   Ⓒ How it has been practiced over time

   Ⓓ Who the most famous finger-painters are

6 According to the professor, what are finger flutings?

Ⓐ Impressions of fingers in clay that have hardened

Ⓑ Outlines of hands that are painted on cave walls

Ⓒ Primitive paintings done by hand and by using simple paints

Ⓓ Any type of painting that is made by using the fingers

7 Why does the professor discuss Gao Qipei?

Ⓐ To go into detail on the artists he trained to do finger-painting

Ⓑ To name some of the famous works of art that he created

Ⓒ To claim that he helped spread finger-painting around the world

Ⓓ To describe his role in promoting finger-painting in China

8 What did Ruth Shaw do?

Ⓐ She came up with the idea of using fingers to paint on walls.

Ⓑ She traveled around the world to promote finger-painting.

Ⓒ She developed the methods of finger-painting used in modern times.

Ⓓ She held several exhibitions of works made by finger-painting.

9 What is the professor's opinion of finger-painting?

Ⓐ It is a sophisticated method for all kinds of artists.

Ⓑ It provides a number of benefits for children.

Ⓒ It is something she is not particularly interested in.

Ⓓ It mostly results in childish paintings being made.

◢ Vocabulary Review

A Complete each sentence with the appropriate word from the box.

determine	submit	vice versa	byproduct	periodic

1 The students should _____ their essays to the professor by Friday.

2 There are _____ rains in the desert, but they happen mostly during the summer months.

3 It is not possible to _____ the cause of the accident at this time.

4 While role-playing, the regular workers pretended to be managers and _____.

5 One _____ of photosynthesis is oxygen, which plants create and release into the air.

B Complete each sentence with the correct answer.

1 Thanks to Edison's **innovations**, people have used his _____ for decades.
   a. inventions   b. methods

2 Glen hopes to attend _____ college like one of the **prestigious** institutes in the big city.
   a. a respected   b. an expensive

3 As soon as Jason gained **access** to the laboratory, he _____ it and began doing work.
   a. considered   b. entered

4 **Prehistoric** people lived _____ during times when there was no recorded history.
   a. a while ago in the past   b. thousands of years ago

5 The **landslide** caused extensive damage when lots of _____ fell down the mountain.
   a. snow   b. rocks

6 The **terrifying** images of victims during the pandemic _____ most people.
   a. frightened   b. disgusted

7 The **elaborate** plan that Jim came up with failed because it was too _____.
   a. simple   b. complex

8 I ran into the person **by accident**, so I told him that I _____.
   a. suffered an injury   b. did not mean to do that

9 To **popularize** a toy, it often takes a big marketing effort to make children _____ it.
   a. like   b. ignore

10 They will **detonate** some dynamite and hope the _____ creates a big hole.
   a. explosion   b. fire

Chapter 04

Making Inferences

Question Type | Making Inferences

About the Question

Making Inferences questions focus on your ability to understand the implications that are made in a talk. You are asked to determine the meanings of these implications. These are sometimes replay questions, or you may need to make a conclusion based on the information in a talk. These questions appear after both lectures and conversations.

Recognizing Making Inferences questions:

- What does the professor imply about X?
- What will the student probably do next?
- What can be inferred about X?
- What does the professor imply when he says this: (replay)

Helpful hints for answering the questions correctly:

- Learn how to read between the lines to understand what implications the speakers are making. Don't focus on the literal meanings of some sentences.
- For replay questions, listen to all of the excerpted sentences since they often provide context clues and hints. They can help you find the correct answer.
- Pay close attention to the end of a talk. That is when the student or professor often mentions what is going to happen next.

What can be inferred about the professor?

Ⓐ He commonly gives extensions to students.

Ⓑ He wants the student to turn in a printed report.

Ⓒ He assigns the students two papers each semester.

Ⓓ He teaches in the Anthropology Department.

| Script | Listen to part of a conversation between a student and a professor.

M1 Student: Professor Reynolds, I wonder if I can get an extension on the paper which we have to turn in this Thursday.

M2 Professor: You need to have a really good excuse, Ken. Why should I give you extra time to complete the project? How would that be fair to the other students?

M1: Um . . . I've got three other major assignments due this week, sir. I have to complete papers in my international relations class and my anthropology class. And I've also got to make a presentation in my economics class.

M2: Hmm . . . That does seem like a lot of work. When do you propose to submit the paper?

M1: I can hand in a printed version of it first thing on Monday morning. Or I can email it by Sunday night.

M2: All right. I suppose I can give you until Monday. But this had better be a very good paper. I'm going to grade it harder than all of the other ones.

M1: That's totally understandable. Thank you very much, sir.

M2: You're welcome. Okay, you've got a busy week. You'd better get going. And make sure that paper is in my hands no later than nine in the morning.

| Answer Explanation |

Choice Ⓑ is the correct answer. The student tells the professor, "I can hand in a printed version of it first thing on Monday morning. Or I can email it by Sunday night." In response, the professor says, "I suppose I can give you until Monday." Since the professor wants the paper on Monday, it can be inferred that he wants the student to turn in a printed report.

A

Listen to part of a conversation between a student and a study abroad office employee. 🎧 CH4_2A

1 **What can be inferred about the student?**

Ⓐ He is enrolled in an Italian class.

Ⓑ He has visited Asia before.

Ⓒ He cannot speak German well.

Ⓓ He prefers to study in Japan.

2 **What will the student probably do next?**

Ⓐ Take a look at some brochures

Ⓑ Leave the office

Ⓒ Sign up for a program

Ⓓ Look at some information online

Vocabulary

☐ **strong:** excellent; outstanding

☐ **appealing:** attractive; interesting

☐ **lacking:** absent; missing

☐ **dig up:** to find

Listen to part of a lecture in an archaeology class. 🎧 CH4_2B

1   What can be inferred about the winter solstice?

Ⓐ It was an important day in some ancient societies.

Ⓑ Ancient people had big celebrations then.

Ⓒ It was believed to be the coldest day of the year.

Ⓓ Important decisions were sometimes made on it.

2   What will the professor probably do next?

Ⓐ Let the students ask some questions

Ⓑ Give the students a quick quiz

Ⓒ Show some pictures to the students

Ⓓ Talk more about the Newgrange passage grave

Vocabulary

☐ **approximately:** around; about

☐ **precision:** exactness

☐ **align:** to be in a straight line

☐ **engraving:** a carving or etching

C **Listen to part of a lecture in an environmental science class.** 🎧 CH4_2C

1 What can be inferred about the Bay of Fundy?

Ⓐ It has some of the world's largest salt marshes.

Ⓑ Few migratory birds live in its mudflats.

Ⓒ The rivers flowing to it move slowly.

Ⓓ Its mudflats freeze during the winter months.

2 What will the professor probably do next?

Ⓐ Assign homework to the students

Ⓑ Let the students go home

Ⓒ Tell the students about a test

Ⓓ Allow the students to take a break

Vocabulary

☐ **sandbar:** an area in water with a large amount of sand that is visible at low tide

☐ **ecosystem:** a unique environment formed by the organic and nonorganic elements in it

☐ **flock:** a large group of birds

☐ **marsh:** a wetland that has various plants growing in it; a swamp

D | **Listen to part of a lecture in an economics class.** 🎧 CH4_2D

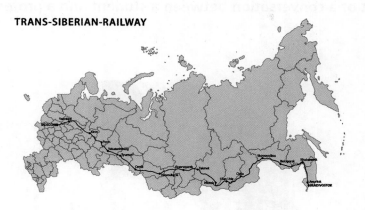

TRANS-SIBERIAN-RAILWAY

1 **What does the professor imply about Russia?**

Ⓐ It built the Trans-Siberian Railway to help fight the Germans.

Ⓑ More people live in its eastern part than its western part.

Ⓒ Traveling to its eastern part was difficult in the 1800s.

Ⓓ It has fought several wars with China during its history.

2 **Listen again to part of the lecture. Then answer the question. What does the professor imply when he says this:** 🎧

Ⓐ Russia went into debt to build the railway.

Ⓑ No other country has built a similar railway.

Ⓒ The railway has benefitted Russia financially.

Ⓓ There are plans to construct more railways in Russia.

Vocabulary

☐ **terminus:** an end

☐ **link:** a connection

☐ **temporary:** short-term; lasting a limited amount of time

☐ **fortune:** a very large amount of money

A   **Listen to part of a conversation between a student and a professor.** 🎧 CH4_3A

✏ NOTE-TAKING

| Vocabulary |

☐ **prepared:** ready

☐ **specific:** detailed

☐ **individually:** alone; by oneself

☐ **point:** an opinion

1 What problem does the student have?

← Gist-Content Question

    Ⓐ She got a poor grade on her most recent paper.

    Ⓑ She is unable to do work on an assignment.

    Ⓒ She does not understand the work she must do.

    Ⓓ She is unhappy with her laboratory partner.

2 What does the professor imply about the student?

← Making Inferences Question

    Ⓐ She is not prepared to take his course.

    Ⓑ She needs to submit her work on time.

    Ⓒ She is not working as hard as she should.

    Ⓓ She made a poor choice for her partner.

3 Listen again to part of the conversation. Then answer the question. What is the purpose of the professor's response? 🎧

← Understanding Function Question

    Ⓐ To tell the student to wait a few weeks

    Ⓑ To encourage the student to do something else

    Ⓒ To reject the student's suggestion

    Ⓓ To praise the student for her quick thinking

Dictation

Listen to part of the conversation again and fill in the blanks.

W: So . . . what _____ we _____ _____ do? Is there _____ _____ we can change lab partners? Uh, I mean, Kevin and I _____ _____ _____. But maybe it would be better if we had partners with schedules _____ _____ each of ours.

M: Well, that _____ _____ _____ a good idea two or three weeks ago. But the other groups _____ _____ _____ _____ good work on their projects. So I don't _____ _____ I can ask any of them to _____ _____ their work for you two.

W: Is there _____ _____ we can do?

M: There's really only one thing I can _____ _____ . . . You're going to have to do work on the project _____.

Listen to part of a lecture in a geology class. 🎧 CH4_3B

✏ NOTE-TAKING

Vocabulary

☐ **landscape:** the appearance of an area of land

☐ **melt:** to change from a solid to a liquid

☐ **steep:** vertical; having sides that go up and down rather than left to right

☐ **flood:** to cover dry land with water

1 What aspect of glaciers does the professor mainly discuss?

← Gist-Content Question

    Ⓐ Their retreat after the last ice age

    Ⓑ The land formations that they create

    Ⓒ The amount of land that they cover

    Ⓓ The manner in which they move forward

2 According to the professor, how does an arête form?

← Detail Question

    Ⓐ Glaciers move forward and push earth and rock in front of them.

    Ⓑ Two glaciers cut land on different sides yet never touch.

    Ⓒ Several glaciers erode an area of land around a mountain.

    Ⓓ A glacier cuts through a mountain and opens a passage to the sea.

3 What will the professor probably do next?

← Making Inferences Question

    Ⓐ Show a picture to the students

    Ⓑ Ask the students some questions

    Ⓒ Give the students a short quiz

    Ⓓ Have the students submit their reports

4 Listen again to part of the lecture. Then answer the question.
What is the purpose of the professor's response? 🎧

← Understanding Attitude Question

    Ⓐ To request that the student be patient

    Ⓑ To answer the student's question

    Ⓒ To indicate he will not give an answer

    Ⓓ To grant the student permission

Dictation

Listen to the following sentences and fill in the blanks.

❶ _____ _____ glaciers are moving rivers of ice that _____ massive amounts.

❷ Valleys _____ _____ glaciers are usually U-shaped and have _____ floors and _____, nearly vertical sides.

❸ _____ a glacier's melting water washes the earth and rock away. _____ _____, it doesn't.

[1-4]   **Listen to part of a conversation between a student and a chemistry laboratory instructor.** 🎧 CH4_4A

1   What are the speakers mainly discussing?

    Ⓐ Why the student should study harder

    Ⓑ Which class the student should take

    Ⓒ How the student can improve his study habits

    Ⓓ What the student can do to get a higher grade

2   What does the laboratory instructor imply about the student's lab report?

    Ⓐ Several sections of it were not filled out.

    Ⓑ The student conducted the wrong experiment for it.

    Ⓒ It should have received a lower grade than it did.

    Ⓓ She took points off because it was turned in late.

3   In the conversation, the laboratory instructor describes a number of facts about Professor Glassman's class. Indicate whether each of the following is a fact or not.

Click in the correct box for each statement.

	Fact	Not a Fact
1 The students in it can conduct lab experiments.		
2 There are more than fifty students in it.		
3 There is still space in it for students to join.		
4 The professor encourages the students to ask questions during his lectures.		

4   What does the laboratory instructor offer to do for the student?

Ⓐ Conduct an experiment with him

Ⓑ Provide him with some tutoring

Ⓒ Show him how to write a lab report

Ⓓ Introduce him to a professor

[5-9]   Listen to part of a lecture in a zoology class. 🎧 CH4_4B

Zoology

nests

5   What is the lecture mainly about?

Ⓐ The best nests for laying eggs in

Ⓑ The reasons that birds build nests

Ⓒ The manner in which nests protect birds

Ⓓ The kinds of nests birds build

6 What can be inferred about ostriches, pheasants, and quail?

   (A) They are often killed by animals in their nests.

   (B) They may build two different types of nests.

   (C) They only lay one or two eggs at a time.

   (D) They lay eggs which are the color of their nests.

7 What is the professor's opinion of burrow nests?

   (A) They protect eggs very well.

   (B) They make efficient use of space.

   (C) They take a long time to make.

   (D) They are easy for predators to find.

8 What kind of birds make platform nests?

   (A) Birds that live in cold environments

   (B) Birds that prefer high altitudes

   (C) Birds that live near the water

   (D) Birds that are smaller than normal

9 Based on the information in the lecture, indicate which type of nest the statements refer to.

Click in the correct box for each statement.

	Cavity Nest	Cup Nest	Suspended Nest
1 Is used by woodpeckers, owls, and parrots			
2 Has a small hole for birds to enter and leave			
3 Can be made with grass, twigs, mud, and saliva			
4 May also be called a saucer nest due to its appearance			

[10-14]   Listen to part of a lecture in a history class. 🎧 CH4_4C

History

shoguns

10 What does the professor imply about Japanese emperors during the time of the shoguns?

    Ⓐ They had armies of samurai.

    Ⓑ They wanted to open Japan to the West.

    Ⓒ They had no real power.

    Ⓓ They tried modernizing the army.

11 Why does the professor mention Commodore Matthew Perry?

    Ⓐ To discuss how he fought some battles against the Japanese

    Ⓑ To name the person responsible for opening Japanese ports

    Ⓒ To say that he was an assistant to the Japanese emperor

    Ⓓ To describe his role in the events of the Meiji Restoration

12 Why does the professor explain the events of the Meiji Era?

    Ⓐ To cover the battles of the rebellion in detail

    Ⓑ To show how Japan modernized so quickly

    Ⓒ To express his opposition to the actions of the Japanese

    Ⓓ To compare them with events in other countries

13 How did the Japanese emperor help reform Japan?

Click on 2 answers.

    1️⃣ By having all the samurai arrested

    2️⃣ By making its military more modern

    3️⃣ By having automobiles built in the country

    4️⃣ By requiring children to be educated

14 Listen again to part of the lecture. Then answer the question.

What does the professor imply when he says this: 🎧

    Ⓐ He will continue lecturing to the class.

    Ⓑ He wants to discuss another topic now.

    Ⓒ He is going to give the students a break.

    Ⓓ He needs to talk about a class assignment.

[1-4] Listen to part of a conversation between a student and an art museum curator. 🎧 CH4_4D

1   What are the speakers mainly discussing?

(A) An art auction to be held at the museum

(B) A special display of student work that just ended

(C) Preparations for an upcoming art exhibition

(D) Renovations to one wing of the art museum

2   According to the student, who should pay admission?

(A) University students

(B) Faculty and staff members

(C) All attendees

(D) People not associated with the university

3   What does the woman imply about the university?

   (A) It has less money to spend these days.

   (B) It refuses to permit students to display their work.

   (C) It is considering closing down the art museum.

   (D) It provides a lot of support for art students.

4   Listen again to part of the conversation. Then answer the question.
     What is the purpose of the woman's response? 🎧

   (A) To give approval to the student's idea

   (B) To tell the student she needs time to think

   (C) To reject the student's suggestion

   (D) To commend the student for his idea

[5-9] **Listen to part of a lecture in a sociology class.** 🎧 CH4_4E

Sociology

5　What aspect of fast food does the professor mainly discuss?

　　Ⓐ Its start during ancient times

　　Ⓑ Its benefits and disadvantages

　　Ⓒ Its effects on people's health

　　Ⓓ Its development over time

6   What was the automat?

   Ⓐ A place where people could buy food from machines

   Ⓑ A place which sold food cooked on the premises

   Ⓒ A place which was the first to use fast-food assembly lines

   Ⓓ A place where diners sat down and ordered from a menu

7   Why does the professor discuss White Castle?

   Ⓐ To compare the food that it served with that served at KFC

   Ⓑ To claim that it imitated Roman street sellers in its style

   Ⓒ To describe its contributions to the fast-food industry

   Ⓓ To point out how its prices led to an increase in its popularity

8   According to the professor, how did the automobile affect the fast-food industry?

   Ⓐ It made dining at fast-food restaurants a big event for families.

   Ⓑ It helped people living in suburbs get easy access to fast food.

   Ⓒ It let large groups of people dine at fast-food restaurants.

   Ⓓ It resulted in people taking their food to their homes to eat it.

9   What will the professor probably do next?

   Ⓐ Assign the students some homework

   Ⓑ Continue lecturing to the students

   Ⓒ Let the students take a short break

   Ⓓ Answer any questions the students have

◪ Vocabulary Review

A Complete each sentence with the appropriate word from the box.

aligned	appealing	sophomore	proceeds	steep

1 Truck drivers must be careful when they are driving down _____ mountains.

2 The statues are _____ so that no shadows fall on them during the day.

3 Irene is entering her second year of school, so she is now a _____.

4 All _____ from the event will be donated to local charities.

5 Because the chance to travel abroad was so _____, Linda decided to leave at once.

B Complete each sentence with the correct answer.

1 General Wilson's army **defeated** the enemy, so the other country _____ the war.
   a. won   b. lost

2 The manager agreed to make an **exception** and to _____ to happen.
   a. allow something uncommon   b. permit an illegal act

3 Dennis lost his entire family **fortune** when he _____.
   a. quit his job   b. spent all of his money

4 When Mr. Roberts asks for a **specific** device, he wants to receive _____.
   a. any tool available   b. exactly what he asked for

5 The animals are **thriving** in their new environment and _____ a lot.
   a. reproducing   b. migrating

6 The hurricane **flooded** the entire valley, so it was _____.
   a. destroyed by winds   b. covered with water

7 The officials **embraced** the changes and _____ everything.
   a. eagerly accepted   b. completely rejected

8 A rainforest _____ is an **ecosystem** that is both hot and wet.
   a. environment   b. geography

9 The **pristine** forest contains land that has _____ by humans.
   a. been explored   b. not been touched

10 Because Chester refused to _____, he was unable to **adapt** to the foreign culture.
   a. work hard   b. change

Chapter 05

Understanding Function

◢ About the Question

Understanding Function questions focus on your ability to understand the basic meaning of what the speakers are saying in a talk. You are asked to infer the meaning of a phrase or sentence said by a person in a talk. Or you must determine why a speaker brings up a particular topic or discusses a certain matter. These questions appear after both lectures and conversations.

Recognizing Understanding Function questions:

1   Some Understanding Function questions ask about what the speaker is inferring. These are often replay questions. They may appear like this:

  - What does the professor imply when he says this: (replay)
  - What can be inferred from the professor's response to the student? (replay)

2   Other Understanding Function questions ask about the purpose of a statement or a topic in the talk. These may be regular questions or replay questions. They may appear like this:

  - What is the purpose of the woman's response? (replay)
  - Why does the student say this: (replay)
  - Why does the professor ask the student about his grades?
  - Why does the man tell the student about the library?

Helpful hints for answering the questions correctly:

- Do not think about the literal meaning of what is being said. Instead, try to read between the lines to determine the real meaning by understanding what a person is implying. Think about what the effect of a particular statement is on the listener.

- When professors interact with students in lectures, pay close attention to what both of them are saying. This dialog is often used for replay questions.

- While replay questions ask about one sentence in particular, three or four sentences are usually excerpted for them. Listen carefully to all of these sentences since they can provide context clues that will help you find the correct answer.

◼ Sample Question

Listen again to part of the conversation. Then answer the question.

What can be inferred from the student's response to the woman?

- (A) He will return to the store tomorrow.
- (B) He will file a complaint with the manager.
- (C) He will give her his phone number.
- (D) He will go to his part-time job soon.

| Script | **Listen to part of a conversation between a student and a bookstore employee.**

M Student: Hello. You're the manager of the store, right? The man over there told me that I should speak with you.

W Bookstore Employee: Yes, I'm the manager on duty now. Is there something I can help you with?

M: I sure hope so. I'm looking for a couple of books for my psychology class. Apparently, they have been sold out for a week. But the professor said in class this morning that the books which were ordered should be here by now. Unfortunately, uh . . .

W: They're not on the shelves, are they?

M: No. I just checked, but I couldn't find the books anywhere on the shelves. And I looked everywhere, um, for at least ten minutes.

W: Which class is this for?

M: It's Psychology 58. It's Professor Gordon's class.

W: Okay, a big shipment of books just arrived here about half an hour ago. The books are likely in that pile. However, it's going to take us a couple of hours to go through everything. How about giving me your number? I'll call you when we find them. And I'll set aside copies for you to make sure you get them.

M: That sounds like it'll work. Thanks a lot.

| Answer Explanation |

Choice ⓒ is the correct answer. When the student says, "That sounds like it'll work," he is agreeing with the woman's suggestion. It can therefore be inferred that he will give the woman his phone number since she plans to call him when the books he wants are available.

A **Listen to part of a conversation between a student and a professor.** 🎧 CH5_2A

1 Why does the professor tell the student about the bookstores near campus?

Ⓐ To emphasize that they have cheap prices

Ⓑ To say that she saw the textbook at one of them

Ⓒ To state they have the most recent edition of the textbook

Ⓓ To suggest where she can buy the textbook

2 Listen again to part of the conversation. Then answer the question.
What does the professor imply when she says this: 🎧

Ⓐ She thinks the student is not serious about class.

Ⓑ She is surprised by the student's comment.

Ⓒ She did not know the book was sold out.

Ⓓ She wants the student to read the book.

| Vocabulary |

☐ **sold out:** unavailable because all of the items have been bought

☐ **checked out:** having been borrowed from a library

☐ **fairly:** quite

☐ **option:** a choice

Listen to part of a conversation between a student and a student housing office employee. 🎧 CH5_2B

1   Listen again to part of the conversation. Then answer the question.
    What is the purpose of the man's response? 🎧

    Ⓐ To agree with the student

    Ⓑ To admit his job is difficult

    Ⓒ To indicate that he needs a break

    Ⓓ To get the student to say why she is there

2   Listen again to part of the conversation. Then answer the question.
    Why does the student say this: 🎧

    Ⓐ To laugh at the man's joke

    Ⓑ To argue that she does not have time

    Ⓒ To express her disbelief

    Ⓓ To refuse the man's demand

Vocabulary

☐ **possession:** an item owned by a person

☐ **hazard:** a danger

☐ **remove:** to take out or away

☐ **bind:** a difficult position

C Listen to part of a lecture in a zoology class. 🎧 CH5_2C

1 Why does the professor tell the students about the hunting index?

    Ⓐ To describe an indirect counting method

    Ⓑ To question how effective it is

    Ⓒ To state that it is the most reliable counting method

    Ⓓ To mention which places it is often used at

2 Listen again to part of the lecture. Then answer the question.
Why does the professor say this: 🎧

    Ⓐ To argue that sample counting should not be used

    Ⓑ To compare sample counting with total counting

    Ⓒ To point out that sample counting has flaws

    Ⓓ To note that sample counting takes too much time

Vocabulary

☐ **habitat:** the area where an animal lives

☐ **advisable:** prudent: sensible

☐ **herd:** a large group of animals that lives together

☐ **mobility:** movement; flexibility

D Listen to part of a lecture in an architecture class. 🎧 CH5_2D

1 Listen again to part of the lecture. Then answer the question.
  What does the professor imply when he says this: 🎧

  Ⓐ Many students know the answer to his question.

  Ⓑ He is glad that the students ask questions in class.

  Ⓒ Several students have visited the castle in person.

  Ⓓ The students are graded on class participation.

2 Listen again to part of the lecture. Then answer the question.
  What can be inferred from the professor's response to the student? 🎧

  Ⓐ He is disappointed by the student's lack of knowledge.

  Ⓑ He is pleased that the student asked the question.

  Ⓒ He will discuss Romanesque Revival at a later time.

  Ⓓ He wants the student to find the information herself.

Vocabulary

☐ **inspiration:** a motivation; a stimulus

☐ **ruins:** the destroyed remains of a building

☐ **elongated:** lengthened; longer than normal

☐ **arch:** an opening that curves upward

Practice with Long Passages

A **Listen to part of a conversation between a student and the dean of students.**

🎧 CH5_3A

✏ NOTE-TAKING

Vocabulary

☐ **annual:** yearly

☐ **extracurricular:** relating to something done after school

☐ **stipend:** a small salary

☐ **solely:** only

1 What are the speakers mainly discussing?

← Gist-Content Question

    Ⓐ The student's grades and extracurricular activities

    Ⓑ The manner in which the student will pay his tuition

    Ⓒ A scholarship the student hopes to receive

    Ⓓ An interview the student needs to prepare for

2 What does the student say about his family?

← Detail Question

    Ⓐ They live in the same city as he does.

    Ⓑ He provides financial assistance for them.

    Ⓒ His sisters will attend college soon.

    Ⓓ His father is currently working two jobs.

3 Listen again to part of the conversation. Then answer the question. Why does the student say this: 🎧

← Understanding Function Question

    Ⓐ To note why he needs more money

    Ⓑ To mention why he wants to get a job

    Ⓒ To state his interest in winning a scholarship

    Ⓓ To explain his desire to get a higher grade

Dictation

Listen to part of the conversation again and fill in the blanks.

W: _____ _____ _____ select you and not the other nominees?

M: Oh, good question. Well, I believe my academic record _____ _____ _____ . I've also been deeply _____ in both school life and the local community.

W: Yes, but _____ _____ _____ _____ .

M: I realize that. However, I think my family circumstances should be _____ , too. Since I was ten, it has _____ my father, my two younger sisters, and me. I've _____ my dad _____ my sisters, and I've _____ my family financially by _____ since I was eleven.

W: Are you _____ doing that now?

M: Yes, ma'am. I send home _____ _____ _____ of the money I earn each month to _____ _____ my little sisters, _____ _____ _____ are attending high school.

B | Listen to part of a lecture in an environmental science class. 🎧 CH5_3B

✏ NOTE-TAKING

Vocabulary

☐ **coniferous:** relating to a tree that does not lose its leaves and which has needles for leaves

☐ **deciduous:** relating to a tree that loses its leaves in fall and has broad leaves

☐ **assumption:** a guess; a supposition

☐ **bark:** the hard outer covering of a tree

1 Based on the information in the lecture, indicate which type of tree the statements refer to.

← Connecting Content Question

	Coniferous Trees	Deciduous Trees
1 Typically grow in the southern areas of the taiga		
2 Can perform photosynthesis any time of the year		
3 Grow well in the acidic soil of the taiga		
4 Have thick bark that can resist forest fires		

2 What similarity do all of the mammals living in the taiga have?

← Detail Question

Ⓐ White hair

Ⓑ Great speed

Ⓒ Thick fur

Ⓓ The ability to hibernate

3 Why does the professor tell the students about birds living in the taiga?

← Understanding Function Question

Ⓐ To name some of the species that reside there

Ⓑ To say that their breeding grounds are there

Ⓒ To claim there are more birds than other animals there

Ⓓ To explain why they stay there in summer

4 Listen again to part of the lecture. Then answer the question. Why does the professor say this: 🎧

← Understanding Attitude Question

Ⓐ To praise the student despite his incorrect guess

Ⓑ To tell the student he should reconsider his statement

Ⓒ To thank the student for the question that he asked

Ⓓ To encourage the student to consider why he is wrong

Dictation

Listen to the following sentences and fill in the blanks.

❶ Oh, uh, _____ _____ _____ _____ , another name for a taiga forest is a boreal forest.

❷ It's a _____ assumption to make, so you're thinking the _____ _____ , but that's not what happens _____ _____ .

❸ They usually flock there in huge numbers in summertime. _____ _____ _____ _____ there are many bogs and swamps in the taiga.

[1-4] **Listen to part of a conversation between a student and a language center employee.** 🎧 CH5_4A

1   What are the speakers mainly discussing?

    Ⓐ The most popular foreign languages

    Ⓑ Future summer employment

    Ⓒ A mutual acquaintance of theirs

    Ⓓ The student's current part-time job

2   How does the student know the language center has jobs available?

    Ⓐ He saw an advertisement in the newspaper.

    Ⓑ One of his professors told him about them.

    Ⓒ A former tutor informed him about the positions.

    Ⓓ There was an announcement made on a website.

3   Why does the employee tell the student about the Italian Language Department?

    Ⓐ To say that he will provide tutoring services there

    Ⓑ To tell him where he should go next

    Ⓒ To request a recommendation letter from a professor there

    Ⓓ To mention who will conduct a language test

4   Listen again to part of the conversation. Then answer the question.
    What is the purpose of the woman's response? 🎧

    Ⓐ To encourage the student to learn another language

    Ⓑ To reject the student's request for a job

    Ⓒ To respond negatively to the student's statement

    Ⓓ To propose that the student reconsider his thoughts

[5-9] **Listen to part of a lecture in a history class.** 🎧 CH5_4B

History

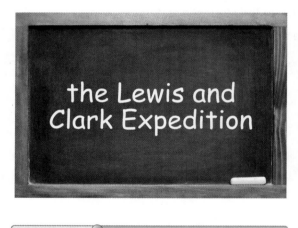

the Lewis and Clark Expedition

5 What aspect of the Lewis and Clark Expedition does the professor mainly discuss?

Ⓐ What scientific discoveries were made by the group

Ⓑ Why the group was sent to explore the Louisiana Territory

Ⓒ Which difficulties the group managed to overcome

Ⓓ How the group managed to attain most of its objectives

6   Why does the professor tell the students to open their books?

   (A) To show them some pictures

   (B) To have them look at a map

   (C) To get them to read a passage from it

   (D) To assign some reading to them

7   Why does the professor discuss the Continental Divide?

   (A) To explain the lack of a water route to the Pacific Ocean

   (B) To point out that it runs through the Yellowstone area

   (C) To say that Sacajawea led the group past it

   (D) To mention that Fort Mandan was built near it

8   What is the professor's opinion of the Lewis and Clark Expedition?

   (A) It took too long to complete its mission.

   (B) It was very lucky at times.

   (C) It was mostly unsuccessful.

   (D) It was filled with brave men.

9   Listen again to part of the lecture. Then answer the question.
    What does the professor imply when he says this: 🎧

   (A) The natives were not usually interested in helping the expedition.

   (B) The expedition members had trouble talking to the natives.

   (C) The expedition did a poor job of following its orders at times.

   (D) The natives helped the members of the expedition a great deal.

[10-14] Listen to part of a lecture in a geology class. 🎧 CH5_4C

Geology

plate tectonics

10 Why does the professor discuss plate tectonics?

ⓐ To answer a question asked by a student

ⓑ To review material that many students do not understand

ⓒ To discuss why there are earthquakes and volcanoes

ⓓ To point out how some plates are large while others are small

11 Why does the professor mention the Andes Mountains?

- (A) To describe how they were formed
- (B) To claim that they have several active volcanoes
- (C) To talk about a powerful earthquake there
- (D) To say they are a highly active part of the Ring of Fire

12 In the lecture, the professor describes a number of facts about the Ring of Fire. Indicate whether each of the following is a fact or not.

Click in the correct box for each statement.

	Fact	Not a Fact
1 Contains some of the Earth's deepest trenches		
2 Has more volcanoes in its western part than its eastern part		
3 Has fewer than half of the planet's volcanoes		
4 Is comprised solely of the Pacific Plate		

13 According to the professor, how have the Japanese prepared for earthquakes?

- (A) By passing strict construction laws
- (B) By encouraging people to be ready for them
- (C) By building large numbers of seawalls
- (D) By banning construction along fault lines

14 Listen again to part of the lecture. Then answer the question.
Why does the student say this? 🎧

- (A) To say that the professor made a mistake
- (B) To ask the professor to be more specific
- (C) To refute the professor's argument
- (D) To request that the professor repeat herself

[1-4] **Listen to part of a conversation between a student and a professor.** 🎧 CH5_4D

1   Why does the student visit the professor?

   Ⓐ To show the professor the work she has done

   Ⓑ To get some assistance with an assignment

   Ⓒ To ask some questions about a lecture

   Ⓓ To discuss doing a project for bonus points

2 What is the professor's attitude toward the student being on the basketball team?

- Ⓐ He is supportive of her not attending some of his classes.
- Ⓑ He understands why she does not have very much time.
- Ⓒ He believes that she should quit the team to study more.
- Ⓓ He thinks that it is making her focus much less on school.

3 According to the professor, what do trusses do?

Click on 2 answers.

- ☐ Protect bridges from rain, wind, and snow
- ☐ Allow bridges that are long to be constructed
- ☐ Add strength to the wires on suspension bridges
- ☐ Support a large amount of weight

4 Why does the professor ask the student what covered bridges are made of?

- Ⓐ To see if she has really seen any before
- Ⓑ To prove that she can make a model of one
- Ⓒ To have her answer her own question
- Ⓓ To show her that they cannot support much weight

[5-9] **Listen to part of a lecture in a biology class.** 🎧 CH5_4E

Biology

- monocular vision
- binocular vision

camouflage

5 What is the main topic of the lecture?

Ⓐ Experiments on the eyesight of animals

Ⓑ Various aspects of animal vision

Ⓒ How camouflage works on vision

Ⓓ Differences between color and black and white vision

6 What effect does monocular vision have on animals?

(A) It permits them to see only in black and white.

(B) It allows them to have color vision.

(C) It gives them good vision in the front.

(D) It lets them see well to either side.

7 Why does the professor tell the students about color vision in animals?

(A) To focus on the outstanding eyesight of bees

(B) To respond to a question a student asks

(C) To describe how the color spectrum works

(D) To explain how rods and cones in the eyes work

8 Why does the professor mention zebras?

(A) To claim that they can see predators from far away

(B) To state that their poor vision makes them prey animals

(C) To point out how their stripes affect predators' vision

(D) To note that they can see in the ultraviolet range of light

9 What does the professor imply about monkeys?

(A) They are unable to remember things that they have seen.

(B) They are only able to see the same things that humans can see.

(C) They cannot tell the difference between two objects of the same type.

(D) They have poor vision in general but have other stronger senses.

◾ Vocabulary Review

A Complete each sentence with the appropriate word from the box.

extracurricular	notable	assumption	checked out	distinguish

1 The art historian can _____ fake paintings from real ones.

2 Most students at the high school are involved in at least one _____ activity.

3 The doctor made a(n) _____ that the patient would take all of the medicine.

4 One _____ speaker at the conference is the CEO of a multinational company.

5 Carla visited the library and _____ several books she needed for her research.

B Complete each sentence with the correct answer.

1 Sally had a **legitimate** reason for missing work, so her manager _____ her excuse.
   a. accepted   b. rejected

2 Once Mark _____ the painting, he will have **acquired** ten of that artist's works.
   a. looks at   b. purchases

3 The building can **withstand** powerful earthquakes, so it _____ during one.
   a. will not fall down   b. will likely collapse

4 Because there are many **hazards** on the island, it is too _____ for people to go there.
   a. distant   b. dangerous

5 Fred _____ a bow and arrows, so he became **proficient** at archery.
   a. purchased   b. improved his skills at using

6 The ancient **ruins** in the city include some _____ and temples.
   a. beautiful scenery   b. destroyed buildings

7 The **camouflage** which polar bears use allows them to _____ prey they are hunting.
   a. search for   b. hide from

8 The robot has a lot of **mobility**, which means that it can _____ well.
   a. move around   b. do many tasks

9 The _____ of a tree is known as the **bark**.
   a. underground part   b. outer covering

10 Clarice's **objective** is to fulfill every _____ of hers at work by the end of the year.
   a. goal   b. chore

Chapter **06**

Understanding Attitude

About the Question

Understanding Attitude questions focus on your ability to recognize the attitudes or opinions of speakers. You are asked to recognize how speakers feel about particular topics, to determine if speakers like or dislike something, or to understand why speakers are experiencing particular emotions. You are also asked to recognize speakers' opinions on various topics. These questions appear after both lectures and conversations.

Recognizing Understanding Attitude questions:

1 Some Understanding Attitude questions ask about speakers' feelings. These may be regular questions or replay questions. They may appear like this:

- What is the professor's attitude toward X?
- What is the professor's opinion of X?
- What does the woman mean when she says this: (replay)

2 Other Understanding Attitude questions ask about speakers' opinions. These may be regular questions or replay questions. They may appear like this:

- What can be inferred about the student?
- What can be inferred about the student when she says this: (replay)
- What does the professor imply about the student's paper?

Helpful hints for answering the questions correctly:

- The tone of voice that a speaker uses can be helpful in finding the correct answer.
- When speakers give their opinions on topics, pay close attention. Be sure to differentiate between the facts stated by speakers and their opinions.
- You may need to read between the lines to answer these questions correctly. The literal meanings of sentences may not be their actual meanings.
- When there are replay questions, pay close attention to all of the excerpted sentences rather than only the sentence the question asks about. The excerpted sentences provide context clues and hints that can help you find the correct answer.

■ Sample Question

HELP   NEXT   OK   VOLUME

What is the professor's opinion of the Embargo Act of 1807?

Ⓐ It helped keep the country out of war.

Ⓑ It caused the economy to become bad.

Ⓒ It led to the start of a war against France.

Ⓓ It ended a depression in the United States.

| Script | **Listen to part of a lecture in an economics class.**

M Professor: Everyone's familiar with the Great Depression, right . . . ? It began in the late 1920s and lasted throughout the 1930s. However, you may not be aware that there have been many other depressions in the history of the United States. There were several in the 1800s. I'd like to talk about the first one in that century. It started in 1807 and didn't end until 1814.

First, it's important to understand the historical situation then. In the first decade of the 1800s, Europe was involved in the wars of Napoleon. The United States, as a relatively new and fairly weak country, had no interest in getting involved on either side of the war. However, the French and English constantly interfered with American shipping in the Atlantic Ocean. To make matters worse, the English often boarded American ships and took some of the sailors. They claimed the sailors were English, uh, even though they were American. Then, they forced those men to serve on English warships.

Well, in response, President Thomas Jefferson encouraged the passing of the Embargo Act of 1807. It forbade the exporting of all products from the United States. It was, to put it simply, a disaster. The shipping industry was, of course, hit hard. But as trade came to a halt, industries across the country suffered. Yes, there was smuggling, but it was relatively minor. The main result of the new law was that the country went into an economic depression. I'd say this was easily the worst mistake of Jefferson's presidency. To make matters worse, the country was eventually forced to go to war against England. So the embargo didn't even keep the country neutral. But let me tell you about the effects of the depression before we get to the War of 1812.

| Answer Explanation |

Choice Ⓑ is the correct answer. The professor comments, "Well, in response, President Thomas Jefferson encouraged the passing of the Embargo Act of 1807. It forbade the exporting of all products from the United States. It was, to put it simply, a disaster. The shipping industry was, of course, hit hard. But as trade came to a halt, industries across the country suffered. Yes, there was smuggling, but it was relatively minor. The main result of the law was that the country went into an economic depression." So he clearly believes that the Embargo Act of 1807 caused the American economy to become bad.

Practice with **Short Passages**

A **Listen to part of a conversation between a student and a professor.** CH6_2A

1 What can be inferred about the student?

- Ⓐ She took a summer school class with Professor Radcliffe.
- Ⓑ She is going to start her senior year next semester.
- Ⓒ She is thinking of becoming an Art History major.
- Ⓓ She prefers Professor Radcliffe to Professor Tauber.

2 Listen again to part of the conversation. Then answer the question.
What does the student mean when she says this:

- Ⓐ She will enroll in the professor's class.
- Ⓑ She is planning to attend summer school.
- Ⓒ She is pleased the professor will be her advisor.
- Ⓓ She will do her best in the class.

Vocabulary

- ☐ **clue:** an idea
- ☐ **inform:** to tell something to someone
- ☐ **limit:** to restrict
- ☐ **drop-off:** a decline; a decrease

124

Listen to part of a conversation between a student and an admissions office employee. 🎧 CH6_2B

1   What is the student's attitude toward her job?

   Ⓐ She believes it is an important job on campus.

   Ⓑ She wants to learn it as well as possible.

   Ⓒ She is working solely to make money.

   Ⓓ She thinks she will get a lot of experience.

2   **Listen again to part of the conversation. Then answer the question.**
   What can be inferred about the student when she says this: 🎧

   Ⓐ She cannot answer the man's question.

   Ⓑ She has never been to Asbury Hall.

   Ⓒ She thinks she should lead tours soon.

   Ⓓ She has a class in Asbury Hall.

Vocabulary

☐ **campus:** the land and buildings occupied by a school

☐ **close:** careful

☐ **observer:** a person who watches, often carefully

☐ **comprehensive:** detailed

C Listen to part of a lecture in an environmental science class. 🎧 CH6_2C

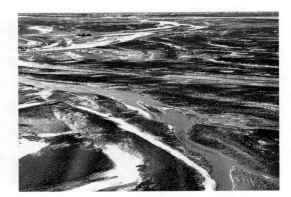

1 What is the professor's opinion of future melting of permafrost?

- (A) It would make many animals lose their homes.
- (B) It would open new lands to exploration.
- (C) It would enable people to live on those lands.
- (D) It could cause problems around the world.

2 Listen again to part of the lecture. Then answer the question.
What does the professor mean when he says this: 🎧

- (A) The student missed something that was important.
- (B) The student figured out the answer to her own question.
- (C) The student ought to change the question she asked.
- (D) The student needs to consider some other factors.

Vocabulary

- ☐ **polar:** relating to the Arctic or Antarctic
- ☐ **patch:** a small area
- ☐ **shade:** a place that is somewhat dark because it is blocked from the sun's light
- ☐ **thaw:** to be freed from the physical effects of being frozen

D Listen to part of a lecture in an astronomy class. 🎧 CH6_2D

1 What is the professor's opinion of solar flares?

Ⓐ They have been studied enough by astronomers.

Ⓑ They are less dangerous than coronal mass ejections.

Ⓒ They can cause a great number of problems.

Ⓓ They should be tracked to see how they affect the solar system.

2 Listen again to part of the lecture. Then answer the question.
What can be inferred about the professor when she says this: 🎧

Ⓐ She is aware that few sunspots have formed lately.

Ⓑ She considers the sun's magnetic field to be weak.

Ⓒ She thinks magnetic forces create all sunspots.

Ⓓ She believes it is possible sunspots form for another reason.

Vocabulary

☐ **rim:** the outer edge of a circular object

☐ **cycle:** a complete series of events that repeats itself

☐ **peak:** having the greatest intensity

☐ **spew:** to eject, often with great force

A **Listen to part of a conversation between a student and a professor.** 🎧 CH6_3A

✏️ NOTE-TAKING

Vocabulary

☐ **sophomore:** a second-year student

☐ **return:** to give back

☐ **lend:** to let someone borrow something

☐ **habit:** a custom; a routine

1 What problem does the student have?

← Gist-Content Question

    (A) His grades in the professor's class are low.

    (B) He cannot come up with a topic for a paper.

    (C) The course material is too hard for him.

    (D) He lacks enough time to do his homework.

2 In the conversation, the student and professor describe a number of facts about the student's study habits. Indicate whether each of the following is a fact or not.

← Detail Question

	Fact	Not a Fact
1 He takes comprehensive notes in class.		
2 He asks questions when he does not understand something.		
3 He seldom reviews his class notes.		
4 He does not read the assigned material.		

3 Listen again to part of the conversation. Then answer the question. What can be inferred about the professor when she says this: 🎧

← Understanding Attitude Question

    (A) She dislikes giving students extra assignments.

    (B) She wants to discuss a topic other than extra credit.

    (C) She thinks the student is not focusing enough.

    (D) She believes the student's grade is acceptable.

Dictation

Listen to part of the conversation again and fill in the blanks.

M: My name's Jason Wilcox, and I'm a _____. I'm here because, well, uh . . . I got a C+ on the most _____ exam, and I only got a B- on the _____ you returned to us today. I was, you know, _____ _____ hoping to get a higher grade, but that _____ _____.

W: All right. Would you like to know _____ _____ _____ your grade?

M: Yes, absolutely. I also _____ um . . . can I do an _____ assignment or something to help my grade?

W: We can _____ that in a bit. But let's _____ _____ your performance first.

M: Sure. So . . . what _____ _____ _____ I should do?

Listen to part of a lecture in an economics class. 🎧 CH6_3B

✏ NOTE-TAKING

| Vocabulary |

☐ **barter:** to trade goods for one another without using money

☐ **temple:** a religious building where people can worship

☐ **precious:** valuable

☐ **wane:** to decrease in size or amount

1 **What is the lecture mainly about?**

← Gist-Content Question

   Ⓐ Ancient ideas for modern banking

   Ⓑ The origins of banking

   Ⓒ European banking concepts

   Ⓓ The evolution of banking laws

2 **What is the female student's opinion of banking in ancient times?**

← Understanding Attitude Question

   Ⓐ She thinks it was primitive.

   Ⓑ She finds it very interesting.

   Ⓒ She says it was inefficient.

   Ⓓ She thinks it was advanced for its time.

3 **What comparison does the professor make between Mesopotamia and the Roman Empire?**

← Connecting Content Question

   Ⓐ The type of material they bartered with

   Ⓑ The laws they passed regarding banking

   Ⓒ The manner in which they minted coins

   Ⓓ The metals they used to make coins with

4 **Listen again to part of the lecture. Then answer the question. What does the professor mean when he says this:** 🎧

← Understanding Attitude Question

   Ⓐ The Templars and Hospitallers were Europe's first bankers.

   Ⓑ Banking in Europe originated due to the Crusades.

   Ⓒ The European religious orders had a great idea for banking.

   Ⓓ European Crusaders were responsible for new banking laws.

Dictation

Listen to the following sentences and fill in the blanks.

❶ _____ , the two _____ _____ storage sites were temples and palaces. _____ had sound structures _____ _____ _____ guards to protect the priests and rulers.

❷ There's also _____ _____ certain families back then were in the _____ of making loans and storing grain and coins _____ _____ .

❸ Their contribution to banking was _____ _____ , uh, I'd say.

[1-4] **Listen to part of a conversation between a student and a professor.** 🎧 CH6_4A

1   What is the professor's attitude toward the student?

    Ⓐ He enjoys being the student's advisor.

    Ⓑ He believes the student is knowledgeable.

    Ⓒ He is displeased with the student's decision.

    Ⓓ He thinks the student should choose another job.

2   What does the student say about the internship?

    Ⓐ It does not provide a salary.

    Ⓑ It involves working full time.

    Ⓒ It is only for graduate students.

    Ⓓ It will last for an entire year.

3   What will the professor do for the student?

Click on 2 answers.

- ☐1   Contact a museum employee
- ☐2   Select an independent research topic
- ☐3   Write a letter of recommendation
- ☐4   Assist the student in filling out his application

4   Listen again to part of the conversation. Then answer the question.

What can be inferred about the professor when he says this: 🎧

- Ⓐ   He believes the student is mistaken.
- Ⓑ   He doubts the student's comment.
- Ⓒ   He would like to do research with the student.
- Ⓓ   He wants to hear an explanation.

[5-9] Listen to part of a lecture in an economics class. 🎧 CH6_4B

Economics

Reconstruction

5 What is the lecture mainly about?

    (A) The effects of Reconstruction on the South

    (B) The reasons the Civil War was fought

    (C) Agriculture in the South during Reconstruction

    (D) Northern involvement in Reconstruction

6   What is the professor's opinion of Reconstruction?

   Ⓐ It was an illegal act by the Union.

   Ⓑ It made the South better than it was before the war.

   Ⓒ It was very hard on the Southern states.

   Ⓓ It caused feelings of resentment to go away.

7   According to the professor, who were carpetbaggers?

   Ⓐ Sharecroppers who were freed slaves

   Ⓑ Southerners who made money during Reconstruction

   Ⓒ Farmers who rented the land they grew crops on

   Ⓓ Northerners who took advantage of Southerners

8   What does the professor imply about cotton farmers in the South?

   Ⓐ They sold most of their crops to Northerners after the Civil War.

   Ⓑ They gave up growing it in favor of crops such as corn and wheat.

   Ⓒ They made more money before the Civil War than after it.

   Ⓓ They could not make any money without the use of slave labor.

9   Listen again to part of the lecture. Then answer the question.

   What can be inferred about the professor when he says this: 🎧

   Ⓐ He is disappointed by the students' reactions.

   Ⓑ He made a mistake while he was speaking.

   Ⓒ He will define some terms for the students.

   Ⓓ He believes he has covered an idea in detail.

[10-14] **Listen to part of a lecture in a history class.** 🎧 CH6_4C

History

Timbuktu

10 Why does the professor mention the market in Timbuktu?

- (A) To point out that it was destroyed in an invasion
- (B) To talk about a major feature of the city
- (C) To discuss its unique architecture
- (D) To go over its nearness to the city's mosques

11 In the lecture, the professor describes a number of facts about Timbuktu. Indicate whether each of the following is a fact or not.

Click in the correct box for each statement.

	Fact	Not a Fact
① Served as the capital of the Mali Empire for a time		
② Became a noted place of Islamic learning		
③ Started as a center of trade near the Sahara Desert		
④ Had thousands of students studying at its schools		

12 Why does the professor tell the students about the Moroccan involvement in Timbuktu?

Ⓐ To note when the city began to go into decline

Ⓑ To say when many manuscripts were brought there

Ⓒ To remark that its population reached its height then

Ⓓ To argue that more than half its residents were killed

13 What does the professor think should be done with the manuscripts in Timbuktu?

Ⓐ They should be placed in private collections.

Ⓑ They ought to be copied and then put on the Internet.

Ⓒ They need to be kept in Timbuktu by its residents.

Ⓓ They would be better off in museums around the world.

14 Listen again to part of the lecture. Then answer the question.
What does the professor mean when she says this: 🎧

Ⓐ She does not want to cover a topic yet.

Ⓑ She forgot what she was going to say.

Ⓒ She is going to provide some background information.

Ⓓ She wants the students to understand something.

[1-4] **Listen to part of a conversation between a student and a librarian.** 🎧 CH6_4D

1   What is the student's problem?

   Ⓐ She is unable to put recalls on some library books.

   Ⓑ The reference material she needs has been lost.

   Ⓒ She cannot find some books that should be available.

   Ⓓ Some books she wants have been checked out.

2   Why does the librarian explain the importance of copyrights?

   Ⓐ To tell the student that she may need to visit some used bookstores

   Ⓑ To point out that the student can get some books for low prices

   Ⓒ To advise the student that some books are no longer in print

   Ⓓ To inform the student on why some used books are hard to find

3   What is the likely outcome of the student visiting the website the librarian tells her about?

   Ⓐ She will be able to acquire some material for her class.

   Ⓑ She will receive information on how to download e-books.

   Ⓒ She will find out about some alternative sources of information.

   Ⓓ She will get to learn about advances in archaeology.

4   Listen again to part of the conversation. Then answer the question.
   What does the student mean when she says this? 🎧

   Ⓐ She prefers e-books to printed books.

   Ⓑ She is willing to read an e-book.

   Ⓒ She recently purchased her first e-book.

   Ⓓ She is very familiar with e-books.

[5-9] **Listen to part of a lecture in a zoology class.** 🎧 CH6_4E

Zoology

birds of prey

5 What is the professor's opinion of the hunting method of owls?

Ⓐ It is only effective for small animals.

Ⓑ It lets them catch animals efficiently.

Ⓒ It requires them to hunt in the dark.

Ⓓ It utilizes their sense of smell well.

6   Why does the professor explain how good the eyesight of bald eagles is?

     Ⓐ To point out that it lets them see in color

     Ⓑ To mention why they fly so high in the air

     Ⓒ To note why they can hunt prey at night

     Ⓓ To state why they are such good hunters

7   What is the likely outcome of a golden eagle spotting a goose flying in the air?

     Ⓐ It will attack the goose from above.

     Ⓑ It will fly at the goose from behind.

     Ⓒ It will go to the goose from the ground.

     Ⓓ It will fly at the goose from the front.

8   How is the lecture organized?

     Ⓐ The professor shows videos of hunting methods while analyzing them.

     Ⓑ The professor contrasts the life cycles of several species of birds.

     Ⓒ The professor discusses the hunting methods of each species separately.

     Ⓓ The professor focuses upon some unique species of birds.

9   Based on the information in the lecture, indicate which bird of prey the statements refer to.

Click in the correct box for each statement.

	Owl	Eagle	Hawk
① Usually takes its prey to high places in order to eat it			
② May hunt animals as they leave their dens			
③ Mostly hunts at night			
④ Has four primary ways in which it hunts			

▪ Vocabulary Review

A Complete each sentence with the appropriate word from the box.

drop-off	symmetrical	rim	amendment	waned

1 All the figures in the painting have _____ bodies because of the artist's skill.

2 The country's constitution may only be changed by passing a(n) _____.

3 There was a _____ in attendance when the weather suddenly became warmer.

4 The effects of the virus _____ as the patient regained his health.

5 They looked down into the valley from atop the _____ surrounding it.

B Complete each sentence with the correct answer.

1 Because the copyright has **expired**, the author's claim to the work _____.

   a. must be respected   b. is no longer valid

2 Whenever ice **thaws**, it goes from a frozen state to a _____ one.

   a. liquid   b. gaseous

3 The professor's **comprehensive** lecture provided a great _____ on the topic.

   a. amount of detail   b. number of pictures

4 One of the museum's biggest **donors** just _____ the institution some valuable items.

   a. bought   b. gave

5 The editor read the entire _____ after Julie submitted the **manuscript**.

   a. contract   b. book

6 Susan **lent** her friend some money and expects the _____ to be paid back by December.

   a. gift   b. loan

7 The **vertical** stripes on the animal go _____ over most of its body.

   a. up and down   b. back and forth

8 There was _____ at the store due to the **shortage** caused by the famine.

   a. plenty of food   b. little food

9 People in ancient times **bartered** by _____ things they had for those they wanted.

   a. trading   b. selling

10 This **advanced** technology is many years _____ everything else created so far.

   a. ahead of   b. behind

Chapter **07**

Understanding
Organization

◢ About the Question

Understanding Organization questions focus on your ability to determine how a talk is organized. You are asked to notice how the professor organizes the lecture or presents certain information to the class. Or you may be asked to determine how specific information relates to the lecture as a whole. These questions usually appear after lectures.

Recognizing Understanding Organization questions:

1   Some Understanding Organization questions ask how the material in the professor's lecture is organized. They may appear like this:

  - How does the professor organize the information about X that he presents to the class?
  - How is the discussion organized?

2   Other Understanding Organization questions ask about the information that is presented in the talk. They may appear like this:

  - Why does the professor discuss X?
  - Why does the professor mention X?

Helpful hints for answering the questions correctly:

- Consider how the professor organizes the lecture. Common ways are by using chronological order, by providing a cause and an effect, by comparing and contrasting, by categorizing, by describing a problem and a solution, by giving examples, and by using sequence.

- The professor may explain the purpose of the lecture at the beginning or end of the talk. Pay close attention to these parts of the lecture.

- When the professor talks about something not related to the main topic of the lecture, consider why the professor did that.

- For specific facts, think about the professor's purpose in mentioning them.

HELP NEXT OK VOLUME

Why does the professor mention the Gothic style?

Ⓐ To compare it with a style Donatello used later

Ⓑ To contrast the works of Donatello and Michelangelo

Ⓒ To say that Donatello used it in his later years

Ⓓ To state that she prefers it to the classical style

| Script | **Listen to part of a lecture in an art history class.**

W Professor: Okay, let's settle down. We're really busy today as we need to study several Renaissance artists. The first one we're going to cover was one of the greatest sculptors of the Renaissance and was from Florence. Does anyone know who I'm talking about? Martin?

M Student: It's got to be Michelangelo.

W: Well, yes, he was a great sculptor and came from Florence, but we're discussing him next class. In fact, we'll spend the entire day talking about Michelangelo. Does anyone else know who I'm referring to . . . ? No guesses . . . ? Okay, it's Donatello, who was Florence's second-greatest sculptor. He was born in 1475 and lived until 1564. He was arguably the most influential artist in Italy during the fifteenth century. He was also a great influence on Michelangelo.

Let me show you some of his work. Look up here, please. This is *David*. Uh, it's the first statue named *David* he made. It's not his most famous one. This is *St. Mark* . . . And this is *St. John the Evangelist* . . . They're beautiful, aren't they? Here's another statue named *David* . . . This is, um, I'd say, his most famous work.

I hope you recognized the Gothic style of the first statue. See here . . . and here . . . However, over time, Donatello developed his own style. It was more realistic and featured figures with strong emotions on their faces. Notice the classical influence on Donatello. Here's a statue from ancient Rome . . . And here's one of Donatello's works . . . The influence, I think, is quite clear. And that's how Donatello affected the world of Italian art. He studied the art of Rome in his thirties, and that made him completely change his sculpting style. Let me show you the second *David* up close. You'll see exactly what I'm talking about. Look here . . .

| **Answer Explanation** |

Choice Ⓐ is the correct answer. The professor says, "I hope you recognized the Gothic style of the first statue. See here . . . and here . . . However, over time, Donatello developed his own style. It was more realistic and featured figures with strong emotions on their faces." In doing so, she compares the Gothic style of Donatello's early work with a style he used later.

Practice with **Short Passages**

A

Listen to part of a conversation between a student and a professor. 🎧 CH7_2A

1 Why does the student discuss Dwight Arnold?

- Ⓐ To explain how he plans to get the information he missed
- Ⓑ To argue that he is one of the top students in the class
- Ⓒ To praise his accomplishments in the field of astronomy
- Ⓓ To tell the professor that Dwight has been tutoring him

2 Why does the professor mention the test?

- Ⓐ To say that the student did poorly on it
- Ⓑ To tell the student that he must take it
- Ⓒ To note which chapters it will cover
- Ⓓ To state that it will be worth 100 points

Vocabulary

- ☐ **roommate:** a person who lives with another individual
- ☐ **borrow:** to use something belonging to another person for a short period of time
- ☐ **trust:** to believe
- ☐ **exempt:** not having to do something

Listen to part of a lecture in a history class. 🎧 CH7_2B

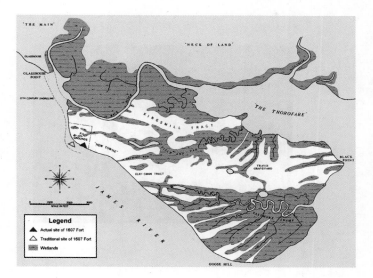

1 How does the professor organize the information about Jamestown that he presents to the class?

Ⓐ By presenting the information chronologically

Ⓑ By telling it from the point of view of the natives

Ⓒ By showing slides and then lecturing on events

Ⓓ By focusing on the successes the colonists had

2 Why does the professor mention the background of the Jamestown settlers?

Ⓐ To explain why they decided to leave England

Ⓑ To show how they were poorly suited for doing work

Ⓒ To compare them with colonists from other countries

Ⓓ To say that most of them had military backgrounds

Vocabulary

☐ **charter:** a written contract

☐ **peninsula:** a piece of land surrounded by water on three sides

☐ **brackish:** salty

☐ **chief:** the leader of a tribe

Listen to part of a lecture in an archaeology class. 🎧 CH7_2C

1 How does the professor organize the information about the Moras cave paintings that she presents to the class?

    Ⓐ By talking about the paintings in the order they were made

    Ⓑ By lecturing as she shows pictures of the paintings

    Ⓒ By first talking about animal paintings and then about hand stencils

    Ⓓ By stressing the methods used to make the paintings

2 Why does the professor discuss calcite?

    Ⓐ To go into detail on its relationship with uranium

    Ⓑ To explain its importance in dating cave paintings

    Ⓒ To point out that it is responsible for cave popcorn

    Ⓓ To claim it proves the caves are thousands of years old

▌Vocabulary

☐ **cave:** a hollow opening in the ground or a mountain

☐ **depict:** to show; to feature

☐ **prehistoric:** relating to something before recorded history

☐ **confident:** sure about; positive of

D | **Listen to part of a lecture in an anthropology class.** 🎧 CH7_2D

1 How is the lecture organized?

  (A) The professor provides several examples to prove his point.

  (B) The professor discusses various theories based on language.

  (C) The professor covers all of the information in chronological order.

  (D) The professor talks about the theory that he believes in the most.

2 Why does the professor mention Egyptian hieroglyphics?

  (A) To compare it with the writing of the Indus River Valley civilization

  (B) To state that some hieroglyphics resemble modern-day Dravidian writing

  (C) To argue that the Dravidian language was influenced by it

  (D) To claim that it was the first form of writing that humans invented

Vocabulary

☐ **dialect:** a variety of a language that is slightly different from what is commonly used
☐ **remnant:** something that remains from another thing that was destroyed
☐ **obstacle:** something blocking or hindering another thing
☐ **extant:** surviving; existing

A **Listen to part of a lecture in an education class.** 🎧 CH7_3A

🖊 NOTE-TAKING

☐ **rote:** repetition; memorization

☐ **reform:** change intended to improve something

☐ **compulsory:** mandatory; required to be done

☐ **curriculum:** a course of study at a school

1 Why does the professor mention King Frederick the Great of Prussia?

← Understanding Organization Question

(A) To explain how war influenced his thoughts on education

(B) To argue that he was the best educated of all Prussian kings

(C) To say that he sent his children to regular schools

(D) To credit him with establishing Prussian mass education

2 Why does the professor explain the gymnasium?

← Gist-Purpose Question

(A) To comment on what the students who attended it learned

(B) To make sure students do not misinterpret her comments

(C) To show how it was similar to modern-day middle schools

(D) To point out the most important feature of Prussian mass education

3 According to the professor, why did some people in Prussia oppose mass education? (Choose 2 answers.)

← Detail Question

(A) They were afraid that educated people would rebel.

(B) They preferred to hire tutors for their children.

(C) They wanted their children to do farm work instead.

(D) They thought many people had no need to be educated.

4 Based on the information in the lecture, indicate which period of mass education in Prussia the statements refer to.

← Connecting Content

	Mass Education before 1819	Mass Education after 1819
1 Required instructors to be trained		
2 Focused mostly on reading and writing		
3 Obliged students to pass tests to move on to higher levels		
4 Was heavily influenced by feelings of nationalism		

Dictation

Listen to the following sentences and fill in the blanks.

❶ The system _____ _____ _____ under the rule of King Frederick the Great of Prussia.

❷ Now, uh, don't _____ . The gymnasium wasn't a physical education center like you may be _____ .

❸ Many teachers became _____ of German nationalism and _____ a strong _____ _____ the futures of their students.

B   Listen to part of a lecture in a chemistry class.   🎧 CH7_3B

🖊 NOTE-TAKING

Vocabulary

☐ **density:** mass; thickness

☐ **miniscule:** very small; tiny

☐ **potential:** possible; having the possibility of doing something in the future

☐ **ban:** to prohibit the use of; to make illegal

1 Why does the female student ask the professor about plutonium?

← Understanding Function Question

    Ⓐ To say she thought it was artificial

    Ⓑ To learn how it can be made in a lab

    Ⓒ To ask him to provide more details

    Ⓓ To check on a statement that he made

2 What comparison does the professor make between cadmium and mercury? (Choose 2 answers.)

← Connecting Content Question

    Ⓐ The type of harm that they can do

    Ⓑ The amount needed to injure humans

    Ⓒ The parts of the body in which they are found

    Ⓓ The types of animals they concentrate in

3 What is the professor's opinion of banning heavy metals?

← Understanding Attitude Question

    Ⓐ The government should do that immediately.

    Ⓑ It would often not provide any benefits.

    Ⓒ Enforcing a ban would be simple to do.

    Ⓓ The environment would become cleaner immediately.

4 How is the lecture organized?

← Understanding Organization Question

    Ⓐ The professor defines heavy metals and then discusses their effects on people.

    Ⓑ The professor explains the positive and negative aspects of heavy metals.

    Ⓒ The professor talks about the different ways heavy metals can enter the environment.

    Ⓓ The professor talks about the harm heavy metals can do and then explains what they are.

Dictation

Listen to the following sentences and fill in the blanks.

❶ For example, um, _____ classifications are based on density, _____ on atomic number, and _____ on atomic weight.

❷ I'm sorry, but did you _____ _____ _____ plutonium is an artificial element? I _____ it appears in nature.

❸ Well, it's not _____ _____ _____ you may think. Heavy metals have _____ uses in a wide variety of industries, so it would be _____ impossible to make them _____ to use.

[1-4] **Listen to part of a conversation between a student and a Drama Department employee.** 🎧 CH7_4A

1   According to the student, what is going to happen next week?

    (A) A play is going to be staged by some students.

    (B) The performers are going to choose their costumes.

    (C) Rehearsals for a performance are going to begin.

    (D) Some repairs are going to be made at the theater.

2   Why does the student mention the curtains?

    (A) To remark that they make noise when they open

    (B) To say that they cannot be closed anymore

    (C) To complain that they are too dirty

    (D) To state that they keep falling onto the stage

3 What will the student probably do next?

Ⓐ Return to the Drama Department

Ⓑ Describe another problem at the theater

Ⓒ Accompany the man to the theater

Ⓓ Learn how to get funding for repairs

4 Listen again to part of the conversation. Then answer the question.
   What does the student imply when she says this: 🎧

Ⓐ She did not attend the recent performance.

Ⓑ She is surprised by the man's comment.

Ⓒ She thought the last play had bad acting.

Ⓓ She believes the performance was a bit strange.

[5-9] **Listen to part of a lecture in a zoology class.** 🎧 CH7_4B

Zoology

horns and antlers

5 What can be inferred about female deer?

   Ⓐ They are larger than males.

   Ⓑ They have no antlers.

   Ⓒ Their horns are straight.

   Ⓓ Their bodies lack keratin.

6   Why does the professor tell the students about rhino horns?

    Ⓐ To describe how they form

    Ⓑ To compare them with caribou antlers

    Ⓒ To respond to a student's inquiry

    Ⓓ To say that they are made of ivory

7   Based on the information in the lecture, indicate which type of appendage the statements refer to.

Click in the correct box for each statement.

	Horns	Antlers
1 Fall off every year and then regrow the next year		
2 Are common in most males and females of certain species		
3 Have velvet that grow on them at times		
4 Grow branches like those trees have		

8   According to the professor, how are females' horns different from males' horns?

    Ⓐ They are made of stronger material.

    Ⓑ They are straighter and narrower.

    Ⓒ They are not made from keratin.

    Ⓓ They are easily broken during fights.

9   How does the professor organize the information about horns and antlers that she presents to the class?

    Ⓐ She compares and contrasts the two of them.

    Ⓑ She shows pictures of each and then describes them.

    Ⓒ She brings examples to class and lectures on them.

    Ⓓ She focuses on antlers first and then talks about horns.

Listen to part of a lecture in a physics class.  CH7_4C

Physics

Lord Kelvin

10 What aspect of Lord Kelvin does the professor mainly discuss?

(A) His scientific achievements

(B) His influence on later scientists

(C) His major written works

(D) His university experiments

11 Why does the professor discuss absolute zero?

   Ⓐ To say that it will likely never be achieved

   Ⓑ To describe how it would affect humans

   Ⓒ To explain how it applies to the Kelvin scale

   Ⓓ To state what it is on the Fahrenheit scale

12 What was the mirror galvanometer used for?

   Ⓐ Detecting pulses of light

   Ⓑ Navigating on oceans

   Ⓒ Measuring temperatures

   Ⓓ Determining the positions of stars

13 Listen again to part of the lecture. Then answer the question.
Why does the professor say this: 🎧

   Ⓐ He will wait until a student answers his question.

   Ⓑ He is disappointed by the lack of a response.

   Ⓒ He expected the students to make a guess.

   Ⓓ He thought nobody would recognize the name.

14 Listen again to part of the lecture. Then answer the question.
What does the professor imply when he says this: 🎧

   Ⓐ The students will be tested on the material.

   Ⓑ He is going to let the students leave soon.

   Ⓒ He wants to go into detail on Lord Kelvin's life.

   Ⓓ The students should ask any questions they have.

[1-4] **Listen to part of a conversation between a student and a professor.** 🎧 CH7_4D

squid

1 What problem does the student have?

- Ⓐ He does not have enough time to complete an assignment.
- Ⓑ His partner is not doing some work on a project.
- Ⓒ He dislikes the topic he was given by the professor.
- Ⓓ His schedule is making it hard for him to do an assignment.

2   Why does the professor ask the student about squid?

    Ⓐ To find out why he dislikes them

    Ⓑ To determine what he knows about them

    Ⓒ To see how prepared he is for the exam

    Ⓓ To confirm that he did the lab work on them

3   Why does the professor mention sperm whales?

    Ⓐ To emphasize how well some squid can fight

    Ⓑ To suggest an alternative research topic

    Ⓒ To argue that they can be larger than giant squid

    Ⓓ To say that they are capable of sinking small boats

4   What does the professor tell the student to do?

    Ⓐ Work together on the project with another student

    Ⓑ Consider doing some onsite research during summer

    Ⓒ Focus on the intelligence of squid in his paper

    Ⓓ Watch some videos on squid to learn more about them

[5-9]   Listen to part of a lecture in an art history class. 🎧 CH7_4E

Art History

5   What is the main topic of the lecture?

　Ⓐ The primary artists in the Vorticist and Futurist movements

　Ⓑ The influence which Vorticism had on Futurism

　Ⓒ The two most influential art movements of the 1900s

　Ⓓ Two art movements that were influenced by Cubism

6   Why does the professor mention Ezra Pound?

    (A) To claim that he was a member of the Futurists

    (B) To argue that he was a founder of the Vorticist movement

    (C) To say that he helped write an art manifesto

    (D) To state that he came up with the name Vorticism

7   According to the professor, what caused Vorticism to die out as a movement?

Click on 2 answers.

    1   Many of its members stopped doing radical art.

    2   Most people who practiced it turned to Futurism.

    3   It lost popularity due to the failure of the magazine *Blast*.

    4   Some of its followers died in battle.

8   Based on the information in the lecture, indicate which art movement the statements refer to.

Click in the correct box for each statement.

	Vorticism	Futurism
1 Featured dynamism as one of its major themes		
2 Had two waves that were separated by World War I		
3 Featured art with bold colors and harsh lines		
4 Had members in the art, dance, film, and music industries		

9   How is the lecture organized?

    (A) The professor covers Vorticism and Futurism together in chronological order.

    (B) The professor discusses one art movement and then covers another one.

    (C) The professor shows examples of art from two movements and compares them.

    (D) The professor goes into detail on the manifestos published by both movements.

◢ Vocabulary Review

A   Complete each sentence with the appropriate word from the box.

stab	obstacles	brackish	banned	confident

1   The government _____ people from polluting the environment for any reason.

2   Many fish lay their eggs in the _____ waters of estuaries.

3   Swordfish often _____ other fish when they are hunting for food.

4   Several _____ were blocking the path, so we left the trail and walked through the forest.

5   Mr. Carter is _____ that he can improve the company's financial situation.

B   Complete each sentence with the correct answer.

1   The probability of success is **miniscule**, so there is a _____ chance.
    a. small   b. big

2   It is rude to **interrupt** a conversation by _____ when others are speaking.
    a. asking for help   b. trying to talk

3   Please be **precise** and tell the customer the _____ amount she owes.
    a. approximate   b. exact

4   **Compulsory** events are those which everyone at the company _____ .
    a. knows about   b. must attend

5   Because I **trust** you, I _____ everything you said about the problem.
    a. believe   b. respect

6   The group's members **rebelled** and attempted to _____ their rights.
    a. fight for   b. ask about

7   A **spontaneous** cheer _____ arose from the fans in the stadium.
    a. naturally occurring   b. extremely loud

8   Lions are **aggressive** animals that _____ others when they are hunting.
    a. search for   b. attack

9   The person **responsible** for cleaning the factory must _____ .
    a. resign at once   b. do his duty

10 Because the window is **transparent**, light _____ .
    a. can pass through it   b. is blocked by it

Chapter 08

Connecting Content

Question Type | Connecting Content

◢ About the Question

Connecting Content questions focus on your ability to recognize how ideas or topics in a talk relate to one another. You are asked to notice what their connections are. These connections may be stated overtly, or you may have to infer them. These questions usually appear in talks where different ideas, people, places, themes, or objects are discussed. These questions almost always appear after lectures.

Recognizing Connecting Content questions:

1   Many Connecting Content questions appear as charges or tables. They have four sentences or phrases, and you need to match them with various themes, ideas, causes, effects, problems, solutions, objects, or individuals. They may appear like this:

- Based on the information in the lecture, indicate which . . . the statements refer to.
  [Click in the correct box for each statement.]

	X	Y
1 [sentence or phrase]		
2 [sentence or phrase]		
3 [sentence or phrase]		
4 [sentence or phrase]		

2   Other Connecting Content questions ask you to make inferences based on the relationships mentioned in the talk. They may appear like this:

- What is the likely outcome of doing procedure X before procedure Y?
- What can be inferred about X?
- What does the professor imply about X?
- What comparison does the professor make between X and Y?

Helpful hints for answering the questions correctly:

- When a professor discusses multiple individuals, themes, places, ideas, or objects in a lecture, it is likely that a chart question will appear. Pay attention to the important details the professor mentions.

- Pay close attention when a professor makes comparisons in a lecture.

- Think about possible future results of actions or events that the professor describes. You may sometimes need to predict a future result, come to a conclusion, or determine the effect of a cause.

? HELP	> NEXT	✓ OK	◀)) VOLUME

Based on the information in the lecture, indicate which type of eclipse the statements refer to.

Click in the correct box for each statement.

	Solar Eclipse	Lunar Eclipse
① Lasts for a few minutes		
② Happens when the moon moves in front of the sun		
③ Takes place more often than the other type of eclipse		
④ May result in the moon turning a red color		

| Script | Listen to part of a lecture in an astronomy class.

M Professor: Before we finish class, I'd like to discuss tomorrow's upcoming big event. I'm referring to the eclipse that's happening. It's going to be a solar eclipse. There hasn't been one here in quite a while, so I encourage you to observe it. Now, let me go into detail on eclipses.

An eclipse happens when one large body in space blocks the light of the sun from reaching another large body. There are two types of eclipses: solar eclipses and lunar eclipses. What's a solar eclipse? It's simple . . . Basically, the moon passes in front of the sun and therefore obstructs the sun's light. A shadow is then cast over a part of the Earth. That's what's going to take place sometime around noon tomorrow. The moon will move in front of the sun for a few minutes, so it's going to turn dark. We're getting a total eclipse, which only happens once every eighteen months or so. And the next one won't take place here either. It's going to happen halfway around the world. There are partial eclipses as well. This happens roughly two times each year. As the name suggests, the moon doesn't completely cover the sun. So it doesn't get totally dark. It's still a fascinating phenomenon to experience.

For a lunar eclipse to happen, the Earth needs to obstruct the sun's light from reaching the moon. This happens at night. Typically, the moon takes on a reddish appearance. Lunar eclipses are more common than solar eclipses, but they don't happen on a monthly basis due to the moon's orbit around the Earth. They're also visible to many more people than solar eclipses. When a lunar eclipse happens, if it's dark in your area, you can see it.

| Answer Explanation |

Solar Eclipse: ①, ②   Lunar Eclipse: ③, ④   About solar eclipses, the professor says, "The moon will move in front of the sun for a few minutes, so it's going to turn dark." He also comments, "Basically, the moon passes in front of the sun and therefore obstructs the sun's light." As for lunar eclipses, the professor notes, "Lunar eclipses are more common than solar eclipses," and, "Typically, the moon takes on a reddish appearance."

A   **Listen to part of a conversation between a student and a professor.** 🎧 CH8_2A

1   What can be inferred about the professor's class?

     Ⓐ It is a requirement for all students to take.

     Ⓑ The students must write three papers for it.

     Ⓒ She has been teaching it for several years.

     Ⓓ All freshmen are required to take it.

2   What comparison does the professor make between high school and college?

     Ⓐ The difficulty level

     Ⓑ The number of classes

     Ⓒ The quality of the instructors

     Ⓓ The number of assignments

Vocabulary

☐ **excuse:** a reason for not doing something

☐ **essentially:** basically; for the most part

☐ **fail:** to do very poorly at something, such as a class

☐ **encourage:** to inspire a person to do well

Listen to part of a lecture in an astronomy class. 🎧 CH8_2B

1 **What comparison does the professor make between the moons of Mars and Europa and Io?**

   Ⓐ How they are shaped

   Ⓑ What their orbits are

   Ⓒ When they were first seen

   Ⓓ How close to their planets they are

2 **Based on the information in the lecture, indicate which moon of Mars the statements refer to.**

	Phobos	Deimos
☐1 Is located closer to Mars		
☐2 Takes about thirty hours to orbit Mars		
☐3 Is the bigger of the two moons		
☐4 Has a diameter of roughly twelve kilometers		

Vocabulary

☐ **rotate:** to spin in a circle

☐ **deviation:** a variance from what is normal

☐ **spherical:** round; globular

☐ **asteroid:** a small, rocky body that orbits the sun but has not been captured by a planet's gravity

Listen to part of a lecture in a botany class. 🎧 CH8_2C

1 What is the likely outcome of sprinkling the soil around a pine tree with lime?

- (A) The tree will not produce any pine cones.
- (B) The tree will become stronger.
- (C) The tree will grow faster than before.
- (D) The tree will not grow very well.

2 What can be inferred about calcium?

- (A) It is of little use to plants.
- (B) It has a high pH level.
- (C) It is not normally found in soil.
- (D) It forms acidic compounds.

Vocabulary

- ☐ **crucial:** vital; important
- ☐ **toxic:** poisonous
- ☐ **leech:** to remove; to drain from
- ☐ **decompose:** to decay; to break down and rot

Listen to part of a lecture in a zoology class. 🎧 CH8_2D

1 Based on the information in the lecture, indicate which type of bear the statements refer to.

	Black Bear	Grizzly Bear
1 Has front claws shorter than five centimeters in length		
2 Starts mating when it is four years old		
3 Has a face that appears to be straight		
4 Is normally larger than the other		

2 What comparison does the professor make between grizzly bears and black bears?

Ⓐ The hunting methods they use

Ⓑ The food they consume

Ⓒ The dens they make

Ⓓ The habitats in which they live

> **Vocabulary**

- ☐ **diet:** the food an animal eats on a regular basis
- ☐ **omnivore:** an animal that eats both plant matter and meat
- ☐ **hibernate:** to sleep for an extended period of time, especially during winter
- ☐ **offspring:** babies born to an animal

Practice with Long Passages

A

Listen to part of a conversation between a student and a student activities office employee. 🎧 CH8_3A

✏ NOTE-TAKING

Vocabulary

☐ **sanctioned:** officially approved

☐ **consume:** to take up something such as time or money

☐ **intensive:** demanding

☐ **sheet:** a piece of paper

1 Why does the student visit the student activities office?

    (A) To inquire about taking part in intramural sports

    (B) To learn how to start her own club

    (C) To ask when a club is going to start meeting

    (D) To find out about extracurricular activities

← Gist-Purpose Question

2 What comparison does the man make between the student newspaper and the history club?

    (A) The amount of time each of them requires

    (B) The number of people involved with them

    (C) The fees students must pay to join them

    (D) The amount of funding each of them receives

← Connecting Content Question

3 What does the student express an interest in?

    (A) The hiking club

    (B) The computer club

    (C) The chess club

    (D) Intramural sports

← Detail Question

Dictation

Listen to part of the conversation again and fill in the blanks.

M: There are _____ clubs that meet once a week for an hour or so _____ there are _____ that might only meet once _____ two weeks.

W: That sounds _____. Do you happen to know which clubs meet _____ _____?

M: Sure. I've got a sheet _____ everything right here. Look here . . . The hiking club meets _____ _____ _____ on Saturday, but its members may hike for several hours at a time.

W: I'll _____. I'm not into that kind of physical activity. _____ _____ is there?

M: Let's see . . . _____ _____ the chess club, the computer club, or the history club? _____ _____ _____ only meets once every two weeks.

W: I love computers. When does that club meet again?

M: You're _____ _____. Its members are getting together tonight, so you can attend the meeting and _____ _____.

Listen to part of a lecture in a meteorology class. 🎧 CH8_3B

✏ NOTE-TAKING

| Vocabulary |

☐ **illuminate:** to brighten; to make light

☐ **horizontal:** even; level

☐ **visible:** able to be seen

☐ **sphere:** a globe; an orb

1 How is the lecture organized?

← Understanding Organization Question

Ⓐ The professor discusses several types of lightning individually.

Ⓑ The professor covers only the most dangerous types of lightning.

Ⓒ The professor describes the types of lightning he has seen.

Ⓓ The professor talks only about lightning that frequently occurs.

2 Based on the information in the lecture, indicate which type of lightning the statements refer to.

← Connecting Content Question

	Cloud-to-Ground Lightning	Internal Cloud Lightning	Ball Lightning
1 Is also called sheet lightning			
2 Is no explanation for why it occurs yet			
3 Looks like it is one single bolt			
4 Is the most common type of lightning			

3 What comparison does the professor make between anvil crawler lightning and bead lightning?

← Connecting Content Question

Ⓐ How many bolts they have

Ⓑ How dangerous they are

Ⓒ What they look like in the sky

Ⓓ What conditions they need

4 Listen again to part of the lecture. Then answer the question. What does the professor mean when he says this: 🎧

← Understanding Attitude Question

Ⓐ The lightning they are observing looks impressive.

Ⓑ Sprites are the rarest type of lightning to occur.

Ⓒ He prefers the red lightning to the blue lightning.

Ⓓ He has never seen sprites or jets in person.

Dictation

Listen to the following sentences and fill in the blanks.

❶ Lightning is _____ _____ _____ which direction it travels, its location in the sky, and the shape and branching of its bolts.

❷ _____ of them. The _____ _____ _____ of lightning is internal cloud lightning.

❸ All right, so those are the _____ types. But there are some other, um, _____ _____ ones.

[1-4] **Listen to part of a conversation between a student and a professor.** CH8_4A

1 What problem does the student have?

   Ⓐ He was unable to complete his homework on time.

   Ⓑ He received a poor grade on the midterm exam.

   Ⓒ His GPA is lower than he had expected.

   Ⓓ He does not understand the course material.

2 What is the professor's opinion of David Parker?

   Ⓐ He is doing a poor job as a teaching assistant.

   Ⓑ He is the best tutor for his students.

   Ⓒ He grades all of the exams fairly.

   Ⓓ He needs to work harder during tutoring sessions.

3 Based on the information in the conversation, indicate which study method the statements refer to.

Click in the correct box for each statement.

	Tutor	Study Group
1 May be unable for the student to learn very quickly		
2 Might not have meeting times that match the student's schedule		
3 Will be able to have all the student's questions answered		
4 Might study with someone not serious about learning		

4 What will the professor probably do next?

Ⓐ Go over the day's lesson with the student

Ⓑ Tell the student how to join a study group

Ⓒ Make a phone call to David Parker

Ⓓ Give the student some tips on studying

[5-9] **Listen to part of a lecture in a history class.** 🎧 CH8_4B

History

---

5   What is the lecture mainly about?

(A) The wars between Carthage and Rome

(B) The Mediterranean world in ancient times

(C) The colonies of the Phoenician Empire

(D) The seafaring voyages of the Phoenicians

6   Based on the information in the lecture, indicate which Phoenician colonies the statements refer to.

Click in the correct box for each statement.

	Colonies in Spain	Carthage
1 Consisted of small places independent of one another		
2 Relied upon trading for wealth		
3 Took over Malta, Sardinia, and parts of Sicily		
4 Obtained wealth from gold and other minerals		

7 What was the result of the fighting between Carthage and Greece in Sicily?

Click on 2 answers.

1 Neither side managed to defeat the other.

2 Carthage lost control of several islands.

3 Carthage lost access to valuable minerals.

4 The Greeks did not control all of Sicily.

8 Why does the professor mention Hamilcar Barca?

(A) To call him the teacher of Hannibal

(B) To say that he won the First Punic War

(C) To talk about his role in Carthage's wars

(D) To blame him for losing the war against Greece

9 What will the professor probably do next?

(A) Have the students look at a map

(B) Discuss a war Carthage fought

(C) Begin talking about Roman colonization

(D) Allow the students to take a break

Listen to part of a lecture in a musicology class. 🎧 CH8_4C

a lyre

a cithara

an aulos

10 What kind of instrument was the cithara similar to?

Ⓐ A harp

Ⓑ A lyre

Ⓒ A horn

Ⓓ A drum

11 What comparison does the professor make between the aulos and the syrinx?

    Ⓐ The country in which they originated

    Ⓑ The manner in which they were made

    Ⓒ The occasions when they were played

    Ⓓ The type of music they could create

12 Based on the information in the lecture, indicate which type of musical instrument the statements refer to.

Click in the correct box for each statement.

	String Instrument	Wind Instrument	Percussion Instrument
1 Was very popular in Greece and Rome			
2 Had holes of different lengths cut into it			
3 Was often partially made from animal skin			
4 Sometimes used a sound box that was a turtle shell			

13 What can be inferred about music in the ancient world?

    Ⓐ More people sang than played instruments.

    Ⓑ It was only made by professionals.

    Ⓒ It sounded like some modern music.

    Ⓓ Few people listened to it for enjoyment.

14 How is the lecture organized?

    Ⓐ The professor describes various types of instruments and their uses.

    Ⓑ The professor talks about instruments that were rare in ancient times.

    Ⓒ The professor focuses on instruments that have been excavated at dig sites.

    Ⓓ The professor shows some real instruments and then lectures on them.

[1-4] **Listen to part of a conversation between a student and a professor.** 🎧 CH8_4D

1 Why did the professor ask to see the student?

    (A) To advise her that she is on academic probation

    (B) To discuss the low results of her midterm exam

    (C) To find out why she did not turn in some work

    (D) To ask her about her poor class attendance

2 Why does the professor tell the student about his 8:30 AM class?

    (A) To state that he understands why some students miss it

    (B) To suggest that the student should start taking it

    (C) To point out that he has to go downtown to teach it

    (D) To say that the students in it have to give a presentation

3   What does the professor tell the student to do?

   Ⓐ Give him a signed note from the director

   Ⓑ Attend all of his classes from now on

   Ⓒ Complete her work for his class on time

   Ⓓ Share her notes with another student in class

4   What can be inferred about the professor?

   Ⓐ He normally takes off points when students skip his class.

   Ⓑ He is teaching a class in the Drama Department this semester.

   Ⓒ He gives a large number of written assignments in his classes.

   Ⓓ He will see *Twelfth Night* performed at the theater on Friday.

[5-9] Listen to part of a lecture in an astronomy class. 🎧 CH8_4E

Astronomy

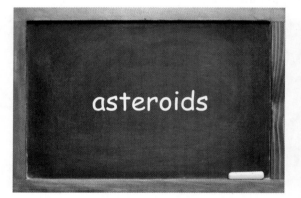

asteroids

Lagrange points

5 According to the professor, what prevented a planet from forming between Mars and Jupiter?

Click on 2 answers.

1. The great mass of Jupiter
2. The lack of material located there
3. The strength of Jupiter's gravity
4. The quick orbit around the sun of Mars

6   What does the professor imply about Vesta?

   Ⓐ An impact on a moon of Jupiter formed it.

   Ⓑ It orbits the sun from inside the asteroid belt.

   Ⓒ Most astronomers consider it a dwarf planet.

   Ⓓ There is a chance it could collide with the Earth.

7   Why does the professor mention Lagrange points?

   Ⓐ To explain why Trojan asteroids do not collide with planets

   Ⓑ To state that most asteroids pass through them during their orbits

   Ⓒ To say that B-type and C-type asteroids can be found in them

   Ⓓ To claim that astronomers have not identified all of them yet

8   What comparison does the professor make between asteroids and meteoroids?

   Ⓐ Why each of them has unstable orbits

   Ⓑ How large each of them is

   Ⓒ What damage each can cause to the Earth

   Ⓓ How quickly each of them orbits the sun

9   Listen again to part of the lecture. Then answer the question.
   What does the professor imply when he says this: 🎧

   Ⓐ Most asteroids are too small to be seen from the Earth.

   Ⓑ There are few astronomers actively trying to find asteroids.

   Ⓒ So many asteroids exist that some will hit the Earth in the future.

   Ⓓ There are more than a million asteroids in the solar system.

■ Vocabulary Review

A   Complete each sentence with the appropriate word from the box.

| toxic | encouraged | sanctioned | significant | fragments |

1   A club must be _____ by the school for it to use rooms in the main building.

2   The discovery of the temple was a _____ event for the archaeologists.

3   Chlorine gas is _____, so you should not breathe it.

4   The vase burst into tiny _____ when he dropped it.

5   Ms. Hand _____ all of the members of her team to reach their goals.

B   Complete each sentence with the correct answer.

1   The Roman Empire paid **tribute** to some barbarian tribes by giving them _____.
   a. advice on various topics   b. large amounts of gold

2   Two cars **collided** at the intersection when one of them _____ the other.
   a. ran into   b. avoided

3   **Attendance** at the speech is mandatory, so the employees will all _____.
   a. be there   b. listen in

4   Jupiter and Mars are both **spheres** that are shaped like _____.
   a. squares   b. balls

5   When the Earth _____, it **rotates** on its axis.
   a. orbits the sun   b. spins around in a circle

6   The ground was suddenly **illuminated** when Arthur turned on _____.
   a. the lights   b. the speakers

7   The **outcome** of the game is still in doubt, so nobody knows _____.
   a. where it will be played   b. what will happen

8   Animals such as bears and squirrels that _____ are said to **hibernate**.
   a. store food for winter   b. sleep during winter

9   _____ animals such as whales can weigh a **massive** amount.
   a. Enormous   b. Warm-blooded

10 Jessica looked at her **transcript** to check out her _____.
   a. schedule   b. grades

Actual Test

Listening Section Directions

This section measures your ability to understand conversations and lectures in English.

The Listening section is divided into separately timed parts. In each part, you will listen to 1 conversation and 1 or 2 lectures. You will hear each conversation or lecture only one time.

After each conversation or lecture, you will answer some questions about it. The questions typically ask about the main idea and supporting details. Some questions ask about a speaker's purpose or attitude. Answer the questions based on what is stated or implied by the speakers.

You may take notes while you listen. You may use your notes to help you answer the questions. Your notes will not be scored.

If you need to change the volume while you listen, click on the **VOLUME ICON** at the top of the screen.

In some questions, you will see this icon: 🎧 This means that you will hear, but not see, part of the question.

Some of the questions have special directions. These directions appear in a gray box on the screen.

Most questions are worth 1 point. If a question is worth more than 1 point, it will have special directions that indicate how many points you can receive.

A clock at the top of the screen will show you how much time is remaining. The clock will not count down while you are listening. The clock will count down only while you are answering the questions.

🎧 AT01

1   What are the speakers mainly discussing?

    Ⓐ The student's newest job

    Ⓑ A class the student is taking

    Ⓒ A summer research project

    Ⓓ A paper the professor wrote

2   What can be inferred about the professor?

    Ⓐ She is the student's academic advisor.

    Ⓑ She is a professor of archaeology.

    Ⓒ She is going to teach class in a few minutes.

    Ⓓ She enjoys teaching summer school.

3   What does the professor tell the student about the position?

Click on 2 answers.

    1   It comes with a small salary.

    2   It requires the person to stay at the dig site.

    3   It involves working in a lab.

    4   It needs a person to do manual labor.

4   Listen again to part of the conversation. Then answer the question.

What does the professor mean when she says this: 🎧

   Ⓐ She believes the student's grades are good.

   Ⓑ She has not hired the student for the job.

   Ⓒ She hopes the student tries his best.

   Ⓓ She thinks the student is not working hard.

5   Listen again to part of the conversation. Then answer the question.

What is the purpose of the student's response? 🎧

   Ⓐ To admit that he already has a job

   Ⓑ To claim that he always works hard

   Ⓒ To accept the position the professor offers

   Ⓓ To indicate that he can do the work

AT02

History of
Technology

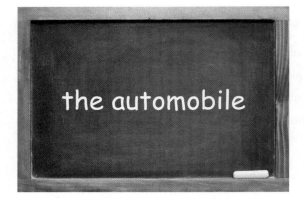

Benz's car made in 1885

6 What is the lecture mainly about?

    Ⓐ The most famous car manufacturers

    Ⓑ The development of the automobile

    Ⓒ European contributions to the automobile

    Ⓓ The man who invented the car

7 According to the professor, what did Robert Anderson do?

    Ⓐ He mass-produced automobiles.

    Ⓑ He designed the internal combustion engine.

    Ⓒ He created an early steam engine.

    Ⓓ He invented the electric car.

8 How does the professor organize the information about the car made by Karl Benz that he presents to the class?

    Ⓐ By comparing it with the car made by Gottlieb Daimler

    Ⓑ By focusing solely on the way that its engine operated

    Ⓒ By having the students look at pictures as he describes it

    Ⓓ By going over the development process in detail

9   Based on the information in the lecture, indicate which type of car the statements refer to.

Click in the correct box for each statement.

	Steam Car	Electric Car	Gas Car
1 Could not travel much faster than people who were walking			
2 Was mass-produced by Henry Ford			
3 Was displayed at the Paris World's Fair			
4 Relied upon heavy batteries to run			

10   Listen again to part of the lecture. Then answer the question.

What can be inferred about the professor when he says this: 🎧

A He thinks people should do more research on steam engines.

B He wants the students to pay close attention to him.

C He considers the earliest cars fairly inefficient.

D He believes that he is stating a little-known fact.

11   Listen again to part of the lecture. Then answer the question.

What is the purpose of the professor's response? 🎧

A To say he has already answered the student's question

B To comment that the student is incorrect

C To show he agrees with the student

D To ask the student to repeat her question

AT03

Astronomy

12 What is the main topic of the lecture?

(A) The early years of the manned space program

(B) Research on how space would affect animals

(C) Animals that were sent into outer space

(D) The space race between the Americans and the Soviets

13 Why does the professor explain the Karman Line?

(A) To say that there is no gravity past it

(B) To mention the extreme temperatures there

(C) To point out where the atmosphere ends

(D) To comment on the radiation that exists there

14 What does the professor imply about the flight Albert II went on?

(A) It completed an orbit of the Earth.

(B) It traveled past the Karman Line.

(C) It was the first in which an animal survived.

(D) It was launched after *Sputnik*.

15 Why does the professor discuss *Sputnik*?

    Ⓐ To name the types of animals that were launched with it

    Ⓑ To mention the successful results of the satellite launch

    Ⓒ To say why it was poorly designed and therefore had problems

    Ⓓ To show how it influenced the Soviets to put a man in orbit

16 What resulted from the flight that Ham took into space?

    Ⓐ It was decided to stop sending animals into space.

    Ⓑ The Americans put an animal in orbit for the first time.

    Ⓒ It was learned that work could be done while weightless.

    Ⓓ Scientists were able to shield creatures from radiation.

17 Based on the information in the lecture, indicate which space program the statements refer to.

Click in the correct box for each statement.

	Soviet Space Program	American Space Program
① Sent the first live animals across the Karman Line		
② Launched animals into space with V-2 rockets		
③ Mainly sent dogs into space		
④ Sent the first animals to complete an orbit of the Earth		

AT04

1 Why does the student visit the Registrar's office?

   Ⓐ To complain about one of her professors

   Ⓑ To discuss why she is failing her classes

   Ⓒ To ask about withdrawing from school

   Ⓓ To receive a form her advisor told her about

2 Why is the student going to Argentina?

   Ⓐ To do volunteer work

   Ⓑ To go on a family vacation

   Ⓒ To study at a school there

   Ⓓ To visit a friend of hers

3 Why does the employee tell the student she will get F's in her classes?

   Ⓐ To get the student to start studying much harder

   Ⓑ To tell the student that she should take her tests

   Ⓒ To discourage the student from dropping out of school

   Ⓓ To explain what will happen if a form is not submitted

HELP NEXT OK VOLUME

HIDE TIME 00:06:30

4 What will the student probably do next?

(A) Fill out a form

(B) Visit the dean of students

(C) Meet her advisor

(D) Get a signature

5 Listen again to part of the conversation. Then answer the question.

What does the student imply when she says this:

(A) She has changed her mind about leaving.

(B) She forgot to bring a pen with her.

(C) She does not want to fill out the form.

(D) She cannot get her advisor's signature.

AT05

Architecture

the Colosseum

6 What aspect of the Colosseum does the professor mainly discuss?

  (A) The events held in it

  (B) Its influence on Rome

  (C) The construction process

  (D) Its primary features

7 Why does the professor mention the statue of Emperor Nero?

  (A) To say it was erected since Nero funded the Colosseum

  (B) To remark that it used to be located inside the Colosseum

  (C) To explain how the Colosseum received its name

  (D) To note its influence on the building of the Colosseum

8 In the lecture, the professor describes a number of facts about the Colosseum. Indicate whether each of the following is a fact or not.

Click in the correct box for each statement.

	Fact	Not a Fact
1 Was a free-standing building unlike most ancient amphitheaters		
2 Had different types of columns on each of its tiers		
3 Took more than ten years to build		
4 Was able to hold around 50,000 people at one time		

9 Why does the professor tell the students about the dimensions of the Colosseum?

   Ⓐ To explain why it took so long to build it

   Ⓑ To respond to an inquiry by a student

   Ⓒ To emphasize how large it was

   Ⓓ To note why large battles could be fought in it

10 According to the professor, what was beneath the main floor of the Colosseum?

Click on 2 answers.

   1　Large water tanks

   2　Rooms for gladiators

   3　Training areas

   4　Lifts for raising and lowering things

11 Listen again to part of the lecture. Then answer the question.

What does the professor mean when she says this: 🎧

   Ⓐ The Romans had many professionally trained engineers.

   Ⓑ Roman engineering skills were better than those in modern times.

   Ⓒ It required great skill to bring ships into the Colosseum.

   Ⓓ The ships the Romans built were impressive works of engineering.

Authors

Michael A. Putlack

- MA in History, Tufts University, Medford, MA, USA
- Expert test developer of TOEFL, TOEIC, and TEPS
- Main author of the Darakwon *How to Master Skills for the TOEFL® iBT* series and *TOEFL® MAP* series

Stephen Poirier

- Candidate for PhD in History, University of Western Ontario, Canada
- Certificate of Professional Technical Writing, Carleton University, Canada
- Co-author of the Darakwon *How to Master Skills for the TOEFL® iBT* series and *TOEFL® MAP* series

Maximilian Tolochko

- BA in History and Education, University of Oklahoma, USA
- MS in Procurement and Contract Management, Florida Institute of Technology, USA
- Co-author of the Darakwon *TOEFL® MAP* series

Decoding the TOEFL® iBT
LISTENING Intermediate NEW TOEFL® EDITION

Publisher Chung Kyudo
Editor Kim Minju
Authors Michael A. Putlack, Stephen Poirier, Maximilian Tolochko
Proofreader Michael A. Putlack
Designers Koo Soojung, Park Sunyoung

First published in November 2020
By Darakwon, Inc.
Darakwon Bldg., 211, Munbal-ro, Paju-si, Gyeonggi-do 10881
Republic of Korea
Tel: 82-2-736-2031 (Ext. 250)
Fax: 82-2-732-2037

ISBN 978-89-277-0881-0 14740
    978-89-277-0875-9 14740 (set)

www.darakwon.co.kr

Photo Credits
p. 74 Claude Valette / Wikimedia Commons
https://commons.wikimedia.org/wiki/File:06_
MainN%C3%A9gativeFineEtPetite.jpg#/media/File:06_
MainNégativeFineEtPetite.jpg

Components Student Book / Answer Book
12 11 10 9 8 7 6   24 25 26 27 28

Decoding the TOEFL® iBT

Answers
Scripts
Explanations

Intermediate

LISTENING

🦋 DARAKWON

Decoding the TOEFL® iBT

Intermediate

LISTENING

Answers
Scripts
Explanations

Practice with Short Passages
p. 14

A

Answers 1 Ⓑ 2 Ⓐ

| Script |

Listen to part of a conversation between a student and a professor.

M Professor: Hello, Teresa. I haven't seen you in a couple of weeks. Did you decide to drop my class? You didn't show up for the test we had yesterday. What's going on?

W Student: Er, hi, Professor Jacobs. Actually, um, that's why I need to speak with you. You see, uh, I've been horribly ill lately. I was hospitalized for a few days two weeks ago, and after I got discharged, I just stayed in my dorm room for a week or so.

M: That's terrible. If you don't mind my asking, what happened?

W: Um, the doctors aren't quite sure yet. All I know is that I felt awful and didn't have any energy at all. Fortunately, I'm feeling better now. So . . . about the exam . . .

M: Ah, yes, the exam. Since it appears as though you have a legitimate excuse, you won't be counted as absent from any of the classes you missed. When do you think you can make up the exam?

W: Oh, great. I'm so glad I can do that. How about this week?

M: Do you think you can get caught up on the material? You missed at least four lectures.

W: Oh, right . . . Well, one of my friends is in the class, so I'll borrow his notes. I think I can review everything and be ready by, uh, next Monday or Tuesday. How does that sound?

M: I'm not at school on Monday, so let's do it on Tuesday right after class ends. Oh, and you'll need to provide a doctor's note. Sorry to request that, but it's school policy.

W: No problem. I'll give it to you when I take the test. Thanks, sir.

Answer Explanations

1 Ⓑ The professor tells the student, "I haven't seen you in a couple of weeks. Did you decide to drop my class? You didn't show up for the test we had yesterday." So she missed several classes and a test.

2 Ⓐ The student and professor mostly talk about the makeup exam that the student must take for the professor's class.

B

Answers 1 Ⓐ 2 Ⓒ

| Script |

Listen to part of a lecture in a literature class.

W Professor: *Grimm's Fairy Tales* is perhaps the best-known collection of children's stories in the world. I'm sure every one of you either read them or had them read to you as children. The collection includes classics such as *Little Red Riding Hood, Cinderella, Snow White, Hansel and Gretel,* and *Rapunzel.* Interestingly, the Grimm brothers, Jacob and Wilhelm, wrote the collection of stories not so much to entertain people but to increase awareness of German nationalism. The two brothers were born in the late 1700s during a time of turmoil in Europe. I'm referring, of course, to the French Revolution. In addition, at that time, Germany was divided into many small states. In 1806, Napoleon defeated Prussia, the most powerful of those states, and began exerting a strong influence over most of the other German states. One result of this was the growth of German nationalism. The Grimm brothers played a key role in that.

Jacob and Wilhelm were librarians. In 1806, German writer Clemens Brentano asked them to help him collect fairy tales for a collection he planned to publish. Brentano, however, later set aside his plans. But the Grimms still collected the stories. Most of them were stories that had been circulating throughout the German states for many years. They were commonly known, but nobody had ever written them down. And each story had variations that reflected the local culture of where it was told. The Grimm brothers set out to make definitive versions of each story. They also wanted to make sure that the stories reflected German culture. They added parts, changed sections, and improved the stories to make them more Germanic.

M Student: Didn't many of the stories actually originate in France and other places?

W: That's correct. A couple are even thought to have come from China originally. But the Grimms changed so much that the origins are hard to determine for large numbers of them. The brothers, you see, collected stories from a wide variety of sources. For example, family members, servants who worked for them, and even passing travelers told them stories. They sought anyone who had a story to tell. The brothers listened carefully, wrote down everything they heard, and then went to work changing the stories to suit their purposes.

Between 1806 and 1812, they collected eighty-six stories.

They published those stories in a collection called *Children's and Household Tales* in 1812. Over the next several decades, they published more tales and edited the ones in the first volume. Many of the original stories had aspects of violence and romance that people later considered unsuitable for children. These elements were toned down or removed. The final collection has more than 200 tales. It's considered a classic of literature today.

Answer Explanations

1 Ⓐ The professor mostly talks about how the Grimm brothers developed their work.

2 Ⓒ The professor focuses on the number of stories in the work in stating, "Between 1806 and 1812, they collected eighty-six stories. They published those stories in a collection called *Children's and Household Tales* in 1812. Over the next several decades, they published more tales and edited the ones in the first volume. Many of the original stories had aspects of violence and romance that people later considered unsuitable for children. These elements were toned down or removed. The final collection has more than 200 tales."

C

Answers   1 Ⓑ   2 Ⓑ

| Script |

Listen to part of a lecture in an environmental science class.

M Professor: The most important current in the Atlantic Ocean is the Gulf Stream. It extends from the Gulf of Mexico in the south to an area north of Norway. It's a warm-water current, and because of that, it has a great amount of influence on the weather in the regions it passes. In fact, it's generally believed that without the influence of the Gulf Stream on certain lands, historical weather patterns might have been very different. I'll explain what I mean in a moment, but, uh, first, let me go over some facts about the Gulf Stream.

Look at the map on the screen up here . . . It shows the path the Gulf Stream takes. It's formed by warm water flowing across the Atlantic from Africa. Near the equator, trade winds push the water westward. It hits the northern coast of South America and is pushed into the Gulf of Mexico here . . . Then, it curves northeast . . . and flows into the Atlantic by Florida . . . Next, it pushes in a northeasterly direction along the North American coast . . . At the Grand Banks, uh, near Newfoundland . . . it moves east across the Atlantic. Then, it splits into several currents. One curves south past the Canary Islands here . . . while the main branch moves north past Ireland and Britain. It eventually ends north of Norway in the Arctic Ocean. The northern branch, by the way, is called the North Atlantic Drift.

W Student: That path looks similar to how hurricanes travel.

M: An excellent observation. You're right. Many hurricanes do follow the current's path. So you can use the current's path to predict where some hurricanes will wind up.

Now, uh, back to the Gulf Stream . . . It's about 100 to 200 kilometers wide. The widest part is in the south. It narrows as it moves north. It extends underwater to a depth of between, oh, 800 and 1,200 meters. It moves at a rate ranging from six to nine kilometers per hour. The temperature varies throughout it. It's around twenty-five degrees Celsius where it begins. But the water gets cooler and denser as it moves into northern regions.

Now, uh, what about my comment on the Gulf Stream and historical weather patterns . . . ? Well, it carries warm water to Northern Europe. This causes the temperature in Europe to be about five degrees warmer than it would be without the current. So despite its northern latitude, Europe has a relatively temperate climate. This allowed Europeans to thrive at northern latitudes that are hostile to humans in other parts of the world. The Gulf Stream has also affected exploration and trade. The westward-blowing African winds carried sailing ships to the Americas. The Gulf Stream then carried the same ships back to Europe quickly. Centuries ago, most ships followed that circular route. This resulted in the early colonization of South America and the Caribbean islands. Later, it helped influence the nature of trade to and from the Americas.

Answer Explanations

1 Ⓑ The professor mostly talks about the Gulf Stream, which is in the Atlantic Ocean.

2 Ⓑ The professor mainly talks about the size of the Gulf Stream and the path that it takes through the ocean.

D

Answers   1 Ⓐ   2 Ⓓ

| Script |

Listen to part of a lecture in a botany class.

W Professor: Tree grafting is a horticultural method in which a stem or bud from one tree is attached to the trunk of another one. This is most commonly done with fruit trees. Why do people do that? Well, there are several reasons . . . In some cases, they're attempting to create a new hybrid tree. They may do it to provide a stronger trunk for the buds or branches of a tree with a weak trunk. Grafting can also make trees more resistant to pests and diseases. What else . . . ? Let me see . . . Ah, another reason to do it is to influence the way a tree grows fruit. Tree grafting can influence the type of fruit, its size, the amount produced per tree, and how high above the ground it grows.

There are several methods to do tree grafts. But before I describe any of them, I need to teach you some vocabulary associated with it. In tree grafting, the stem or bud that is attached to a tree trunk is called the scion. That's spelled S-C-I-O-N. As for the tree trunk, it's referred to as the rootstock. Ah, yes . . . ? Question?

M Student: Yes, ma'am. Do the rootstock and scion have to be from the same species?

W: No, they don't. Now, uh, in most cases, they do come from the same tree species. So an apple tree scion is typically grafted onto an apple tree rootstock. However, that's not absolutely necessary. Many attempts at crossbreeding are made, so in those cases, the rootstock and scion are from different species. But just so you know, most tree grafting is done within the same species.

Fruit tree grafting is usually done with trees younger than five years as grafting with older trees tends to be more difficult. For the graft to take hold, the scion and rootstock must fuse together at the vascular level. This means that they join together. As a result, the tree's vascular system doesn't get blocked. This allows water and nutrients to flow freely between the rootstock and the scion. Most people also do grafting in late spring after the initial buds or stems grow on the scion.

There are several ways people graft fruit trees. One common method is known as budding. To engage in budding, only a bud—not a stem—is needed for the scion. A T-shaped cut is made in the back of the rootstock. The cut should be at least a meter above the ground. The rootstock shouldn't be too thin, or the graft won't take hold. The person should then peel back the bark and place the bud—uh, the scion—on the rootstock. After that, the bark should be pushed back and rubber grafting string used to bind it tightly. After about a month, the rubber string can be removed. If a branch begins to grow, then the graft is successful. Now, um, let me describe another method for you . . .

Answer Explanations

1 Ⓐ The professor mostly talks about grafting, which is how to attach a part of one tree to another.

2 Ⓓ The professor explains to the students the process of how to do budding.

Practice with Long Passages   p. 18

A

Answers	1 Ⓐ	2 Ⓒ	3 Ⓓ

| Script |

Listen to part of a conversation between a student and a Registrar's office employee.

W1 Registrar's Office Employee: Who's next in line . . . ? You can come over here, please . . . Ah, hello. How may I be of assistance today?

W2 Student: Good afternoon. Uh, I'm a senior and am going to be graduating next semester. Um, at least I think I'm going to be graduating. I was told that I need to come here to find out if I am going to have enough credits.

W1: Of course. We've been getting lots of students like you the past few days. Could you please give me your student ID card?

W2: Oh, yeah, sure. I've got it right, um . . . here. Here you are.

W1: All right . . . Let's see . . . Your name is Alicia Chung. Currently, you have a total of thirty-three credits . . . In order to graduate, you must have no fewer than thirty-six credits. So as long as you complete three more credits next semester, you'll graduate.

W2: Great. But, um, what about in my major? Have I taken enough classes to satisfy the requirements for it?

W1: I don't know. You'll have to speak with your academic advisor about that. That's something which I'm simply not qualified to answer.

W2: Ah, I understand. Thank you very much.

W1: You're welcome. Oh . . . Hold on a moment, please. I just noticed something on your record.

W2: You did? What's the matter?

W1: It's nothing too serious, but did you return a couple of books late to the library your junior year?

W2: Er . . . maybe. I guess.

W1: Okay, just so you know, unless you pay the fine you owe for them, you will not be permitted to graduate.

W2: Seriously? Um . . . how did a fine from the library get transferred to the Registrar's office?

W1: According to school policy, when a library fine hasn't been paid for more than one semester, it gets moved to the student's permanent record. You owe twenty-seven dollars in library fines. You can pay it any time before you graduate, but I recommend doing that as soon as possible. That way, uh, you won't forget about it.

W2: Good point. Hold on a moment while I get some money from my purse, please. I'm pretty sure I have enough cash on me right now.

Answer Explanations

1 Ⓐ The conversation is mostly about the student's academic record and whether or not she has enough credits to graduate.

2 Ⓒ The student asks, "How did a fine from the library

get transferred to the Registrar's office?" when she is told that she owes money. The employee then tells the student about the school's policy.

3 Ⓓ The student says, "Hold on a moment while I get some money from my purse, please. I'm pretty sure I have enough cash on me right now," so she will probably pay the employee the money that she owes.

Dictation

W1: Who's <u>next in line</u> . . . ? You can come over here, please . . . Ah, hello. How may I <u>be of assistance</u> today?

W2: Good afternoon. Uh, I'm a <u>senior</u> and am going to be <u>graduating</u> next semester. Um, at least I <u>think</u> I'm going to be graduating. I was told that I need to come here to <u>find out</u> if I am going to have <u>enough credits</u>.

W1: Of course. We've been getting lots of students like you the past few days. Could you please give me your <u>student ID card</u>?

W2: Oh, yeah, sure. I've got it right, um . . . here. <u>Here you are</u>.

B

Answers

1 Ⓒ   2 Fact: 1, 3   Not a Fact: 2, 4
3 Ⓑ   4 Ⓓ

| Script |

Listen to part of a lecture in a history class.

M Professor: Far in the northern part of Britain, visitors can see the remains of a defensive wall which once stretched across the land. This is Hadrian's Wall. The Romans built it to protect their lands in southern Britain from Celtic tribes living in the north in what's modern-day Scotland. The wall helped keep the Celts from moving south. It also served as a way for the Romans to control and tax trade moving between the northern and southern parts of Britain. In 122 A.D., Roman Emperor Hadrian visited Britain. It was then that the Romans began constructing the wall. It took six years to complete although the Romans made numerous additions and changes over the years.

The dimensions of Hadrian's Wall were nowhere near those of the Great Wall of China. Yet the wall was still impressive. Its length was just short of 118 kilometers. It ran in a general east-west direction. It started in the east near where the Tyne River meets the sea and went all the way to Solway Firth in the west. A firth, by the way, is a large inlet. The soldiers in the Roman legions who were stationed in Britain did most of the building. Highly skilled in engineering, they first dug a steep ditch in front of where the wall was going to be. Then, they built the

wall. It stood between four and five meters high and was around three meters in width. However, in some places, the wall is narrower than that.

W Student: What did they use to build the wall?

M: Mostly limestone. However, they also constructed earthen walls in some places due to a lack of stone. Those walls were replaced with stone taken from other regions later though. South of the wall was a road connecting the entire wall. Then, even further south was what the Romans called a *vallum*. Spell that V-A-L-L-U-M. That was a wide, flat-bottomed ditch with a high bank and mound on each side. It ran east-west the length of the wall. Historians debate the purpose of the *vallum*, but one hypothesis is that it signified the southern boundary of a military region in which nobody could enter without first obtaining permission.

Hadrian's Wall was manned by both Roman legions and local troops. The original idea was to build small forts capable of holding a few dozen soldiers in each one. The forts were to be placed at equal distances along the wall, and there would be smaller stone towers between them. The Romans soon decided that they wanted some larger forts along the wall, too. So they built fifteen . . . oh, no, sorry . . . fourteen bigger forts that could hold up to a thousand soldiers. Each fort had large gates that permitted cavalry to charge out to attack any advancing enemies.

Hadrian's Wall served Rome well until the legions finally left around 410 A.D. during the ongoing decline of the Roman Empire. What happened to the wall in the following years is still uncertain. Many archaeologists and historians believe some of the wall's forts served as homes for locals who rose to power. Several towns also arose in places near where forts had been built. Over the centuries, people took large numbers of the stones in the wall to use to construct their own buildings. However, despite that, the ruins of Hadrian's Wall are surprisingly intact in certain places. Well, uh, I should say that the wall itself is mainly intact. As for the buildings and forts, they're pretty much gone except for their foundation stones. A great deal of work is still going on at some sites. Archaeologists are endeavoring to put together clues about the lives of the people who built and manned Hadrian's Wall. If the opportunity to visit the wall ever arises, I highly recommend you check it out. It's a trip worth taking as you'll find it quite extraordinary.

Answer Explanations

1 Ⓒ The professor focuses on the major characteristics of Hadrian's Wall in his lecture.

2 Fact: 1, 3   Not a Fact: 2, 4
The professor says, "The Romans built it to protect their lands in southern Britain from Celtic tribes living in the north in what's modern-day Scotland. The wall helped keep the Celts from moving south." He also mentions,

"The soldiers in the Roman legions who were stationed in Britain did most of the building." However, it is not true that only Roman soldiers guarded it as the professor states, "Hadrian's Wall was manned by both Roman legions and local troops." And the professor adds, "So they built fifteen . . . oh, no, sorry . . . fourteen bigger forts that could hold up to a thousand soldiers."

3 Ⓑ About the *vallum*, the professor says, "Historians debate the purpose of the *vallum*, but one hypothesis is that it signified the southern boundary of a military region in which nobody could enter without first obtaining permission."

4 Ⓓ The professor tells the students, "If the opportunity to visit the wall ever arises, I highly recommend you check it out. It's a trip worth taking as you'll find it quite extraordinary."

Dictation

❶ The Romans built it to <u>protect</u> their lands in <u>southern</u> Britain from <u>Celtic</u> tribes living in the <u>north</u> in what's modern-day Scotland.

❷ The <u>dimensions</u> of Hadrian's Wall were <u>nowhere near</u> those of the Great Wall of China. <u>Yet</u> the wall was still <u>impressive</u>.

❸ Archaeologists are endeavoring to <u>put together clues</u> about the lives of the people who <u>built</u> and <u>manned</u> Hadrian's Wall.

iBT Practice Test
p. 22

Answers

PART 1

| 1 Ⓑ | 2 Ⓑ | 3 Ⓐ | 4 Ⓓ | 5 Ⓓ |

6 Fact: ②, ③   Not a Fact: ①, ④   7 ②, ③   8 Ⓓ

9 Ⓐ   10 Ⓐ

11 Glacial Action: ③, ④   Plate Tectonics: ①, ②

12 Ⓑ   13 Ⓐ   14 Ⓓ

PART 2

| 1 Ⓒ | 2 Ⓑ | 3 Ⓓ | 4 Ⓓ | 5 Ⓓ |

6 Ⓒ   7 Ⓐ   8 Ⓑ   9 Ⓒ

PART 1

Conversation [1–4]

| Script |

Listen to part of a conversation between a student and a professor.

M Student: Hello, Professor Peebles. Thank you for agreeing to meet with me on such short notice. I appreciate your willingness to do that.

W Professor: It's no problem at all, Mal. When you called me, it sounded like you had something important on your mind. So, um, I don't mind speaking with you since it's an urgent matter.

M: Thanks for saying that.

W: Now, uh, why don't you tell me what you want to discuss?

M: Sure thing. Um . . . as you know, I'm getting a double major in both history and mathematics. But I've been giving a considerable amount of thought to dropping history as one of my majors. I just don't . . . well, I don't think I can handle the workload at this time.

W: Remind me again how many classes you're taking this semester. I've got quite a few other students whom I advise, so I can't recall your course load.

M: I'm taking five classes this term. Two are history classes, one's in the Math Department, and the other two are electives.

W: All right . . . And of those classes, which would you say is the toughest? Uh, by that, I mean which one is taking up the greatest amount of your time?

M: It's definitely the history seminar with Professor Buchanan. To be honest, I didn't expect it to involve as much work as it does.

W: Well, seminars are research-intensive classes, and, unlike you, most students wait until their senior year to take them. So, yeah, I can see how that class would be taking up lots of your time.

M: You can say that again.

W: 🎧4 Are you doing anything else? For example, do you have a part-time job, or do you participate in any extracurricular activities?

M: **I don't have to work since I'm on a full academic scholarship.** But I am pretty heavily involved in other activities. I belong to, er, three clubs, and I also play various intramural sports.

W: I see. And how are your grades in your classes? You aren't failing anything, are you?

M: Oh, of course not. I believe I've got all A's so far, but I haven't received a couple of papers back that I submitted. So I don't know what my grades on them are.

W: You know, Mal, I don't see a need for you to drop one of your majors.

M: You don't? But . . . but all of this work is hard.

W: Sure, but we're almost done with the semester. After that, you'll only have three more semesters to go until you graduate. It would be a shame for you not to have a second major.

M: Then what do you think I should do about my workload?

W: Since you asked, I'd say that you ought to reduce the number of extracurricular activities you're doing. There's absolutely no need to play organized sports or to be in so many clubs. Sure, it might negatively affect your social life, but that isn't why you are attending college, is it?

M: Uh, yeah. I suppose you're right. Thanks for talking me through this, Professor.

W: It's my pleasure, Mal. I'm always happy to give advice to students who request it.

Answer Explanations

1 Gist-Content Question

Ⓑ The student tells the professor, "I don't think I can handle the workload at this time."

2 Understanding Attitude Question

Ⓑ First, the professor remarks, "When you called me, it sounded like you had something important on your mind. So, um, I don't mind speaking with you since it's an urgent matter." Next, all throughout the conversation, the professor listens closely, asks questions that show she is interested, and then provides the student with advice.

3 Detail Question

Ⓐ The professor advises the student, "Since you asked, I'd say that you ought to reduce the number of extracurricular activities you're doing. There's absolutely no need to play organized sports or to be in so many clubs."

4 Understanding Function Question

Ⓓ When a student is attending school on an academic scholarship, it can be inferred that the student gets good grades.

Lecture #1 [5-9]

| Script |

Listen to part of a lecture in an archaeology class.

M Professor: Before Europeans landed in the Americas, there were already large civilizations. I'm sure you're all aware of the Aztecs, Mayas, and Incas in Central and South America. There were also civilizations in what is now the United States. One of the largest was near the Mississippi River around where the city of St. Louis is located. Archaeologists tend to call the group that made this civilization the Mississippian people. The area itself is called the Cahokia site, but that's a name which does not relate to the people who built it. There was, however, a Cahokia tribe that lived in the region long after the civilization had vanished. So to avoid confusion, we shall call the site Cahokia and the builders the Mississippian people.

W Student: 🎧⁹ Is it possible that the Cahokia tribe descended from the Mississippian people?

M: It's possible. In fact, some archaeologists strongly argue in favor of that, Karen. **But the evidence for it is thin.** So let's just keep calling the founders the Mississippian people.

Most of the remains of this civilization have been lost to the ravages of time. However, there's still enough evidence that enables us to understand what their lives were like. Archaeologists believe the Mississippian people occupied the region from around 600 to 1400 A.D. It was an agricultural society which also depended on hunting, fishing, and trade for its survival. Estimates for its population vary between 10,000 and 40,000 people at its peak. Interestingly, it's their building skills that make the Mississippian people stand out among all of the native tribes of North America. You see, uh, they created a huge city complex whose dominant feature was large earthen mounds, many of which remain standing today.

Archaeologists have found evidence of about 120 mounds in the region. Around eighty are more or less intact. Many are grouped together to form a large complex. The highest mound rises thirty meters above the ground. It's called the Monk's Mound, and it's the centerpiece of the Cahokia site. It's almost 300 meters long and 250 meters wide, and it covers an area of about five and a half hectares. A large building once stood atop this great mound. The building might have been used for religious purposes. Oh, in case you're curious, Monk's Mound got its name because a group of monks once lived on it.

In front of Monk's Mound to the south lies a large open area called the Grand Plaza. Archaeologists believe it was used for ceremonies or various games. The Grand Plaza covers an area of twenty hectares. The Mississippian people leveled the entire area, so it's smooth and even. Around the plaza were many large homes, um, where the elite members of the tribe lived. This central region— Monk's Mound, the Grand Plaza, and the elites' homes— was surrounded by a wooded palisade. You know, a large fence. The rest of the Mississippian people—the non-elites—the common farmers and such, uh, lived outside the palisade. The palisade wasn't used to divide the elites from the commoners but was most likely used for defensive purposes.

The homes of the commoners were, as you would expect, smaller than those of the elites. These were mainly single-room homes with wooden walls and thatched roofs. Spread out among these homes were the rest of the mounds. Linking the entire area was a series of pathways and roads. Most of the complex has a mathematical precision to it. A great road the Mississippians built follows an exact east-west route. It's speculated that they had some knowledge of the movements of the sun, moon, and stars, which helped them lay out their complex.

The Mississippian people left no written records, but we can surmise a few things about their daily lives from the artifacts that have been recovered. The men hunted, fished, and worked on mound-building projects. The women wove mats, tended the crops, and made pottery. All of the people came together for various ceremonies. Exactly what happened at them is unknown. There is, however, evidence that some form of human sacrifice may have been involved.

W: How do they know that?

M: Well, archaeologists have found mass graves in the region showing that many people died violently at the same time.

Now, the decline of the Mississippian people is a mystery. The palisade suggests they had enemies. There's also evidence that the complex was rebuilt several times. There are several theories regarding this . . . War is one. Today, many archaeologists believe the Mississippians depleted their resources and had to leave. Other academics say there was a long drought. Whatever the case, sometime between 1350 and 1400, the last Mississippians left the site.

Okay, that's all I have time for today because I need to talk to you about your midterm exam. As you know, it's going to be next Monday. So let me go over a few things with you right now . . .

Answer Explanations

5 Gist-Content Question

Ⓓ The professor mostly talks about Cahokia, which was a place where the Mississippian people lived.

6 Detail Question

Fact: ②, ③ Not a Fact: ①, ④

The professor says, "It's called the Monk's Mound, and it's the centerpiece of the Cahokia site. It's almost 300 meters long and 250 meters wide, and it covers an area of about five and a half hectares." Then, he states, "The Grand Plaza covers an area of twenty hectares." He also mentions, "Estimates for its population vary between 10,000 and 40,000 people at its peak." However, commoners did not live next to the elites as he notes, "This central region—Monk's Mound, the Grand Plaza, and the elites' homes—was surrounded by a wooded palisade. You know, a large fence. The rest of the Mississippian people—the non-elites—the common farmers and such, uh, lived outside the palisade." And there were not fewer than 100 mounds near Cahokia as the professor says, "Archaeologists have found evidence of about 120 mounds in the region."

7 Detail Question

②, ③ The professor lectures, "Today, many archaeologists believe the Mississippians depleted their resources and had to leave. Other academics say there was a long drought."

8 Making Inferences Question

Ⓓ At the end of the lecture, the professor remarks, "Okay, that's all I have time for today because I need to talk to you about your midterm exam. As you know, it's going to be next Monday. So let me go over a few things with you right now."

9 Understanding Function Question

Ⓐ When the professor responds to the student's question by saying, "But the evidence for this is thin," he is giving his opinion on what he thinks.

Lecture #2 [10–14]

| Script |

Listen to part of a lecture in a geology class.

W Professor: Lakes are bodies of water surrounded by land. They can be found virtually everywhere in, uh, in all kinds of environments. That includes frozen polar areas and hot deserts. Lakes form almost anywhere there is a source of water that can fill them. They get water from many sources, such as, um, rainfall, melting snow and ice, and rivers, streams, and creeks. Lakes can be open or closed systems. 🎧14 An open lake is one where water flows in and out through streams and rivers. Can anyone tell me what a closed lake is? Peter, what do you think?

M Student: Um . . . **This is just a guess.** But I suppose it must be one where water enters the lake but, um, doesn't have any way of getting out.

W: Well, there actually is a way for it to get out. It's evaporation. But you're right in that there aren't any creeks, streams, or rivers removing water from the lake. Utah's Great Salt Lake is an example of a closed lake system.

But before delving too much into how lakes work, let's examine how they're formed. There are a number of manners in which they can be created. Most lakes are made when water fills an area of land that's deeper than the surrounding area. This depression is a land basin. Think of it as the sink in your kitchen or bathroom. Land basins usually form in three ways: glacial action, plate tectonics, and volcanic activity. Lakes are also created when large amounts of dirt and rock block a river. In some cases, they may form when a section of a river is cut off from the river's main part. Finally, animals and humans can make lakes by building artificial dams across flowing bodies of water. Let's look at each method individually now.

The vast majority of lakes in the Northern Hemisphere were created by glaciers. During the last ice age, uh, around 15,000 years ago, enormous sheets of ice moved south from the Arctic region. This ice carved out the land by digging it up and shaping it into what we see today. While the glaciers were moving, they carved thousands of land basins. When the ice began melting and retreating, the melting water filled in the basins. Glaciers also formed other lakes by pushing large amounts of dirt and rocks in front of them. When they stopped moving, the material was deposited. Sometimes it blocked valleys. When snowmelt and rain filled these valleys, lakes formed. Yes, Peter?

M: Can you give us an example of a lake made by glacial action?

W: Sure. There are many. Nearby Lake Jackson is one. In addition, the Great Lakes between Canada and the United States are the best-known examples.

All right, so what about plate tectonics? This refers to the notion that the Earth's crust is comprised of many pieces called plates. As the plates move and spread apart or buckle together, large cracks may appear in the land. If water fills in one of them, it forms a lake. The world's deepest lake, Lake Baikal in Russia, was formed this way.

Volcanoes can also create lakes when they erupt. At times, the top of a volcano may collapse on itself after an eruption. This forms a round depression called a caldera. Once the volcano becomes dormant, a lake may form if melted snow and rain fill the caldera. This is called a crater lake. The world's largest lake like this is Lake Toba in Indonesia. It was formed when a supervolcano erupted around 70,000 years ago. It's not exactly round, uh, being long and narrow instead. The reason is that the volcano which created it was very wide and massive and lacked the traditional round conical shape of most volcanoes.

Lakes also form when rivers change their paths. Rivers may meander across flat lands by moving in wide S-shaped patterns. The Mississippi River and some of its branches do that, so they have lots of wide bends. Over the course of time, a river may sometimes straighten out through the actions of silt and flooding. When that occurs, a wide bend may get cut off from the river's course. What's left is a long narrow lake that was once a river bend. We call this an oxbow lake. The name comes from the fact that the shape is similar to an oxbow, uh, a device used to hold oxen in a harness.

Last, artificial lakes can be created by animals and people. When beavers build large dams, they often create lakes behind them. These lakes may last a long time, or they may be temporary if the dams are somehow wrecked or abandoned by the beavers. People also build dams on rivers and streams. The water that gathers behind the dams forms large artificial lakes. The largest dam lake in the world is Lake Kariba on the Zambezi River in Africa. It's on the border between Zambia and Zimbabwe.

Answer Explanations

10 Gist-Content Question

Ⓐ During her lecture, the professor mainly talks about how lakes can be created.

11 Connecting Content Question

Glacial Action: ③, ④ Plate Tectonics: ①, ②

About glacial action, the professor says, "Glaciers also formed other lakes by pushing large amounts of dirt and rocks in front of them. When they stopped moving, the material was deposited. Sometimes it blocked valleys. When snowmelt and rain filled these valleys, lakes formed." She also notes, "The vast majority of lakes in the Northern Hemisphere were created by glaciers." As for plate tectonics, the professor comments, "So what about plate tectonics? This refers to the notion that the Earth's crust is comprised of many pieces called plates. As the plates move and spread apart or buckle together, large cracks may appear in the land. If water fills in one of them, it forms a lake. The world's deepest lake, Lake Baikal in Russia, was formed this way."

12 Understanding Organization Question

Ⓑ The professor comments, "Volcanoes can also create lakes when they erupt. At times, the top of a volcano may collapse on itself after an eruption. This forms a round depression called a caldera. Once the volcano becomes dormant, a lake may form if melted snow and rain fill the caldera. This is called a crater lake. The world's largest lake like this is Lake Toba in Indonesia."

13 Making Inferences Question

Ⓐ In stating the Lake Kariba is a dam lake, the professor is implying that it is an artificial lake.

14 Understanding Attitude Question

Ⓓ When the student states that he is making a guess, he means that he is not positive about his answer.

PART 2
Conversation [1–4]

| Script |

Listen to part of a conversation between a student and an information desk worker.

M Student: Excuse me. I'm here to attend the marketing expo. It's supposed to be held in the auditorium in Silas Hall right now, but nobody's there. In fact, there's nobody on the entire third floor. I'm pretty sure the date of the event is December 4, and that's today. Do you happen to know what's going on?

W Information Desk Worker: The expo has been moved to Walker Gymnasium.

M: Really? How come?

W: There was so much interest in it that the organizers needed to move the expo. 🎧4 The auditorium in this building just isn't big enough to hold everyone who wanted to attend.

M: Okay, I guess that makes sense. But how come there wasn't a sign?

W: **Are you sure there wasn't one there?**

M: Yes. I looked around the entire floor but didn't see anything. You would think that there would be a sign posted so that people like me would know where to go.

W: That's strange. There was one posted on the door to the auditorium about twenty minutes ago. I guess somebody must have taken it down.

M: Oh, well. It doesn't really matter. Thanks for your help. I guess I'll be on my way to the expo now.

W: Um, hold on a second. Have you registered yet?

M: Registered? I didn't know I was supposed to.

W: You know, the organizers haven't done a very good job this year. I've had several people coming here to ask about the location of the event since they didn't announce the change in locations. And the organizers didn't tell anyone about the need to register for the event either.

M: Gee, that's not good. How do I register?

W: If you have your student ID with you, I can do it for you in a couple of minutes. All I need to do is fill in a few items and then print a nametag for you to wear. And just so you know, there's no entry fee.

M: That's a relief. I was afraid you were going to tell me the organizers had decided to charge for entry. That would have been unfortunate.

W: Tell me about it. By the way, did you remember to bring some copies of your résumé? There will be many companies interviewing people today, and they'll also be collecting résumés. This is a great opportunity for you to make some contacts and maybe even to receive a job offer or two.

M: Yeah, I have several copies with me, and I even purchased this suit I'm wearing for the occasion. I hope a couple of recruiters ask me to sit down for an interview.

W: Good luck. I'm going to be attending the expo tomorrow, so I hope it goes well for me, too.

M: Tomorrow?

W: Yeah, when the location was changed, an extra day was added to the event. That's good news for me because I have to work here at the information booth all day long today. Fortunately, I don't have to work tomorrow, so I can try to get a job myself.

M: That's great. I'll probably go on both days then. So maybe I'll see you there tomorrow. Best of luck to you.

W: Thanks for saying that. Now, how about that ID card? Let's get you prepared for the expo.

Answer Explanations

1 **Gist-Content Question**

ⓒ The student indicates he does not know the location of the expo when commenting, "I'm here to attend the marketing expo. It's supposed to be held in the auditorium in Silas Hall right now, but nobody's there. In

fact, there's nobody on the entire third floor. I'm pretty sure the date of the event is December 4, and that's today. Do you happen to know what's going on?"

2 **Understanding Function Question**

Ⓑ The woman asks, "By the way, did you remember to bring some copies of your résumé? There will be many companies interviewing people today, and they'll also be collecting résumés. This is a great opportunity for you to make some contacts and maybe even to receive a job offer or two."

3 **Making Inferences Question**

Ⓓ At the end of the conversation, the woman says, "Now, how about that ID card? Let's get you prepared for the expo." So the student will probably give the woman his student identification card next.

4 **Understanding Attitude Question**

Ⓓ The student asks why there was not a sign about the expo. The woman asks, "Are you sure there wasn't one there?" It can therefore be inferred that she is surprised that the student did not see a sign.

Lecture [5-9]

| **Script** |

Listen to part of a lecture in a physiology class.

W Professor: One aspect of sleep that people still do not fully understand is the state between being asleep and being awake. We call the transition from one stage to the other hypnagogia. It is a combination of the Greek words for *sleep* and *guide*. It can be used to describe the state between being awake and being asleep as well as the reverse, uh, going from being asleep to being awake. However, it's more commonly used to refer to when we fall asleep than when we wake up. This period is like twilight and dawn, the periods when the sun isn't exactly up or down. It's brief and only lasts for a few minutes, but it's quite vivid.

As a person transitions from being asleep to being awake and vice versa, reality and imaginary images clash and form what some people describe as a surreal experience. To understand this better, numerous experiments have been conducted on people in sleep labs. This is mainly done by hooking up sensors to people's heads and studying their brainwave patterns as they fall asleep. These people are then interviewed immediately after waking up, so the memories of what they experienced are still fresh.

One key finding is that many people have unusual sensory experiences during the hypnagogic state. One common sensation is of falling and then suddenly jerking awake. People also frequently experience unusual sounds and images. Sounds may be words, phrases, music, or strange noises. They may be loud or quiet as well as clear or unclear. Images may include random ones, phosphenes, and what scientists call the Tetris Effect.

Phosphenes are like tiny specks or points of light that the brain can arrange into patterns like lines and geometric shapes. These shapes may or may not be colorful. The Tetris Effect is like the game Tetris. You know it, right? It's the game with falling blocks that you must put into various patterns. While in a hypnagogic state, people often do repetitive tasks from their daily lives. This could be something like operating a machine at work or learning the moves to a dance. It's believed that the Tetris Effect happens to people as a way to memorize new skills.

As to what causes these sensations, scientists believe it has to do with the clash of brainwaves. During a normal state of wakefulness, alpha waves are created. These induce a relaxed state in the brain. When a person is asleep, the brain is dominated by theta waves, which form during deep sleep. So what happens when a person transitions from being asleep to being awake is that the two types of brainwaves are present simultaneously for a few minutes. While there's no definite proof that this causes the imaginary sensory overload, it's a distinct possibility. Scientists have also noted that during the transition, the prefrontal cortex has a reduced amount of activity. The prefrontal cortex is the part of the brain that lets people make plans and decisions. It controls people's social behavior, too. So if it's in a reduced active mode, perhaps people are more open to the chaos of imaginary sensory experiences then.

M Student: I heard that some creative people actually want to have this type of experience.

W: You heard correctly. Salvador Dali enjoyed experiencing hypnagogia. Many of his works of art have a somewhat surreal look to them as well. Mary Shelley claimed she came up with the idea for her novel *Frankenstein* from an experience she had during a hypnagogic state.

But most people don't have such vivid experiences. In fact, not everyone even experiences hypnagogia. Only about a quarter to a third of people undergo it. Scientists have also found that younger people, and especially women, have more experiences than older people and men. Some people with sleep problems such as insomnia undergo it, too. So do people who frequently change their work schedules. This most likely happens because their sleep patterns get disrupted.

There has been some comparison of REM sleep with hypnagogia. Yes, there are some similarities, but there are also major differences. During both, the mind goes through many ideas, memories, and emotions and makes connections between them. People say that while in the dream world of REM sleep, they are more active and feel like they have some control in their dreams. For instance, they can choose to walk into a room and pick up an object. But in a hypnagogic state, they're more passive.

It's like they're observers and have no control. This can contribute to making imaginary experiences during hypnagogia frightening. 🎧9 Some people also experience sleep paralysis during hypnagogia. This is the feeling that you're awake and aware yet can't move or speak. **I've never experienced that, and, to be honest, I'm quite glad about that.**

Answer Explanations

5 Gist-Content Question

Ⓓ During most of her lecture, the professor talks about the effects that hypnagogia has on the human body.

6 Detail Question

Ⓒ The professor remarks, "When a person is asleep, the brain is dominated by theta waves, which form during deep sleep."

7 Understanding Organization Question

Ⓐ About Mary Shelley, the professor notes, "Mary Shelley claimed she came up with the idea for her novel *Frankenstein* from an experience she had during a hypnagogic state."

8 Connecting Content Question

Ⓑ The professor lectures, "There has been some comparison of REM sleep with hypnagogia. Yes, there are some similarities, but there are also major differences. During both, the mind goes through many ideas, memories, and emotions and makes connections between them. People say that while in the dream world of REM sleep, they are more active and feel like they have some control in their dreams. For instance, they can choose to walk into a room and pick up an object. But in a hypnagogic state, they're more passive. It's like they're observers and have no control."

9 Understanding Attitude Question

Ⓒ While the professor is talking about sleep paralysis during hypnagogia, she states, "I've never experienced that, and, to be honest, I'm quite glad about that." So she means that she does not want to experience sleep paralysis during hypnagogia.

Vocabulary Review
p. 32

Answers

A

1 boundary	2 definitive	3 hybrid
4 dozen	5 discharged	

B

1 a	2 b	3 a	4 b	5 b
6 a	7 b	8 a	9 b	10 b

Chapter 02 | Gist-Purpose

Practice with Short Passages   p. 36

A

| Script |

Listen to part of a conversation between a student and a student activities office employee.

M1 Student: Good afternoon. I'm Nathan Kent. I'm the president of the hiking club. I called about an hour ago. Are you Mr. Chapman?

M2 Student Activities Office Employee: That's correct. If I remember correctly, you wanted to know about transportation or something. You were a little vague on the phone though.

M1: Oh, sorry. Well, basically, it's like this. Everyone in the club wants to go hiking at Yellow Flower State Park in a couple of weeks. But not enough of us own cars to get there, and renting a bus is kind of expensive. So I was hoping you might be able to come up with a solution.

M2: Ah, I get it. You're an official club at the school?

M1: Yes, that's correct. But, um, we only receive a minimal amount of funding each semester.

M2: About how much would it cost to rent a bus? Did you find out?

M1: Yes, it would cost $500 for eight hours.

M2: All right. Since you're an official club, you can apply for a grant from the school. Here . . . You have to fill out this form as well as, uh . . . this one here. Then, you need to get the signatures of everyone who is planning to go on the trip. And you must submit everything no later than, um, this Thursday.

M1: If we do that, we can get the money?

M2: That's right. How does that sound?

M1: Incredible. Let me fill those forms out now.

Answer Explanations

1 Ⓐ The student asks about getting money for a trip that his club members want to go on, so he visits to ask about additional funding.

2 Ⓒ The employee provides the student with detailed instructions by explaining how to apply for funding.

B

| Script |

Listen to part of a conversation between a student and a professor.

M Student: Good morning, Professor Meyers. Would you happen to have a moment to speak with me?

W Professor: Of course, David. What's going on today?

M: I, uh, I've decided that I'm going to apply to law school, so I wonder if you'd be able to write a letter of recommendation for me.

W: Sure, I'd be more than happy to do that, but, uh . . . shouldn't this be something you ask your advisor or another professor? After all, you've only taken one of my classes, and that was, uh, a year ago, wasn't it?

M: Yes, ma'am, that's correct. Well, most of the law schools I'm applying to require three letters of recommendation. My advisor, Professor Sterns, wrote one letter while Professor Hampton in the Economics Department wrote another. I was planning to ask Professor Kennedy since I've taken several classes with him, but . . .

W: But what . . . ?

M: Well, he's out of the country for the next six weeks during winter break, and he never checks his e-mail. So, uh, I decided to ask you since I got an A in your class.

W: That's right. I recall that. So, um, what would you like for me to focus on in the letter I write?

M: Hmm . . . If you could mention that I worked hard, participated in class discussions, and did well on my papers and exams, I'd appreciate it.

W: All right. I can do that. By when do you need this?

M: Er . . . Three days from now. Sorry. Would that be possible? And I need four copies in signed and sealed envelopes.

W: Okay. Why don't you come back here tomorrow afternoon around, um, three? They should be ready by then.

Answer Explanations

1 Ⓒ The student comments, "I've decided that I'm going to apply to law school, so I wonder if you'd be able to write a letter of recommendation for me."

2 Ⓑ The professor asks the student, "So, um, what would you like for me to focus on in the letter I write?"

C

| Script |

Listen to part of a conversation between a student and a Math Department office secretary.

M Student: Hi. Um, do you happen to know if Professor Goodwin is around? He's supposed to be having office hours until noon, but, um, his door is locked, and he didn't answer when I knocked on it.

W Math Department Office Secretary: Ah, yes, Professor Goodwin is attending a meeting in the administration building. He wanted me to tell that to any students who came here asking to see him.

M: Er . . . So, uh, did he say when the meeting is going to be over?

W: Yes, he did. It's going to finish at noon. But after that, he's having lunch with the head of the department. And then he's got class at one.

M: I see. Well, um, I really need him to sign this paper. I have to drop his class, and today's the last day I can do that. When will he probably be back?

W: Hmm . . . He should be in his office around 2:30. Why don't you come back then?

M: I can't. I've got a class of my own at that time. Could I just leave this form here? And, uh, maybe you could ask him to sign it when he returns.

W: I'm terribly sorry, but according to school regulations, I can't do that. The administration insists that students give the form to the professor in person. That way, the professor and student can discuss the reason the student is dropping the class.

M: Oh, that makes sense. Okay, uh, I guess I'll just come here at 2:30 and be late for my class.

W: Sorry. I hope everything goes well for you.

Answer Explanations

1 Ⓐ The student says, "Um, do you happen to know if Professor Goodwin is around? He's supposed to be having office hours until noon, but, um, his door is locked, and he didn't answer when I knocked on it."

2 Ⓓ The student wants to know why the professor is not in his office having office hours, so the secretary describes the professor's schedule for the day.

D

| Script |

Listen to part of a lecture in an astronomy class.

M Professor: One of the biggest problems facing modern astronomers is light pollution. This is the glare from lights used for illumination at night. In every major city, thousands of lights burn all night long. They're mainly streetlights, but there are also lights from, uh, from buildings and parking lots. They cast a glow that shields the night sky from observation. In other words, we can't see through the glare of the lights. For astronomers, that's a big problem. Most telescopes rely on direct or reflected observation of light from the universe.

Fortunately, there are some solutions to the problem of light pollution. The easiest one is simply to avoid placing astronomical observatories near cities. Therefore, most of the world's large observatories are found in remote places, like, uh, mountaintops. The solitude and high altitudes provide clear skies for observing the stars. One example is the enormous observatory system in Hawaii on top of Mauna Kea. It has around a dozen telescopes and other scientific instruments at an elevation of more than 4,000 meters above sea level. But even in places like that, there are problems. Building large telescopes in isolated regions is expensive. The construction projects can also damage the local environment.

Another solution is to reduce light pollution. Some streetlights are shielded so that most of their light is reflected downward. It's also possible to put sensors on lights so that they only turn on when they detect motion. Such lights are often used for home and business security systems.

W Student: Don't most security lights already use that kind of technology?

M: Not really. Many shopping malls, factories, and warehouses keep security lights on all night. In some cases, such as parking lots, that's necessary and, um, understandable. But in places that get less human traffic, motion-detecting lights would serve better. And, yeah, it's expensive to install those lights, but they get used less over time. So they result in long-term savings on electric bills.

Something else people could do is use low-pressure sodium wavelength lights. They emit light in only a few wavelengths in the yellow color range. Such light allows a monochromic view of things without color. Basically, uh, you wouldn't see any colors except yellow. They can be used for streetlights for night driving but are unsuitable for indoor use. They're very energy efficient, so that's an advantage. They're used widely in Tucson, Arizona. That city has very strict laws against the emission of light at night. In Tucson, sodium streetlights have reduced light pollution so much that it's possible to observe the stars from the city itself. Hopefully, more cities will use these lights and therefore reduce light pollution in many places.

1 Ⓓ The professor explains about light pollution in order to show how it has a negative effect on astronomers.

2 Ⓒ The professor talks about how low-pressure sodium wavelength lights are used in Tucson and have been effective at eliminating a lot of light pollution there.

Practice with Long Passages   p. 40

A

| Answers | 1 Ⓒ | 2 Ⓓ | 3 Ⓒ |

| Script |

Listen to part of a conversation between a student and a professor.

W Student: Professor Burgess, do you have some time to speak with me about our paper?

M Professor: Paper? We don't have a paper due until the end of the semester.

W: Yes, that's the one I'm talking about. I was hoping to start working on it as soon as possible.

M: I guess you caught me by surprise since we're only in the third week of the semester. I don't believe that any student has ever asked me about doing a term paper until after the midterm.

W: Oh, yeah. I suppose I see why you were a bit confused by my request. In case you're curious, I've got a full load of classes this semester, and I also play on the varsity basketball team. So I'm basically trying to get as much work done as possible now before practice begins.

M: That's pretty smart. It's good to see that you're trying to be efficient with your studies. So tell me . . . What exactly do you want to know about the paper?

W: Well, I already know the requirements for the paper since you explained all of them on the syllabus. However, uh, I don't know what I should write about. Do you have any suggestions for topics?

M: Hmm . . . What aspect of ancient archaeology interests you the most? As you know, we're going to be studying archaeological digs from societies located all around the world.

W: I'd say that the archaeology of various Native American tribes is the most interesting to me. I've visited a few dig sites near my home and enjoy learning about them. We're going to cover them later in the semester, aren't we?

M: Yes, we are. If you're considering writing about them, then you ought to look at this book here.

W: Um . . . Can I borrow this?

M: Yeah, sure. Keep it in good condition, please, because that book isn't in print anymore. Read through it and see if any of the topics there pique your interest. Then, come back here, and we can talk some more to figure out a specific topic for you.

W: That's great, Professor Burgess. I really appreciate your help. When do you want me to come back?

M: That's mostly up to you and how fast you read through the book. But I've got office hours next week on Monday and Thursday afternoon, so one of those days might be ideal if you're looking to get started quickly.

Answer Explanations

1 Ⓒ The student asks the professor, "Professor Burgess, do you have some time to speak with me about our paper?"

2 Ⓓ The professor first comments, "I guess you caught me by surprise since we're only in the third week of the semester. I don't believe that any student has ever asked me about doing a term paper until after the midterm." Then, he remarks, "That's pretty smart. It's good to see that you're trying to be efficient with your studies." So he is clearly impressed by the student's hard work.

3 Ⓒ The professor tells the student, "If you're considering writing about them, then you ought to look at this book here."

Dictation

W: Professor Burgess, do you have some time to <u>speak with</u> me about our paper?

M: Paper? We don't have a paper <u>due</u> until the end of the <u>semester</u>.

W: Yes, that's the <u>one</u> I'm talking about. I was hoping to start <u>working on</u> it as soon as possible.

M: I guess you <u>caught</u> me by <u>surprise</u> since we're only in the <u>third</u> week of the semester. I <u>don't believe</u> that any student has ever asked me about doing a <u>term</u> paper until after the <u>midterm</u>.

W: Oh, yeah. I <u>suppose</u> I see why you were a bit confused by my <u>request</u>. In case you're curious, I've got a <u>full load</u> of classes this semester, and I also play on the <u>varsity</u> basketball team. So I'm basically trying to get <u>as</u> much work done <u>as possible</u> now before practice begins.

B

| Answers | 1 Ⓑ | 2 Ⓐ | 3 Ⓐ | 4 Ⓒ |

| Script |

Listen to part of a lecture in a zoology class.

W Professor: Okay, we've got enough time for one more

insect before we call it a day. I'd like to discuss the dragonfly, which is one of the most interesting insects I've studied. There are more than 5,000 species of them found around the world. Most have similar features. Look at page 198 in your books to see some pictures . . . Note that there are two pairs of large wings, which are transparent. Their colors differ from species to species, but most are very colorful, and many have practically a metallic sheen. The dragonfly's body is that of a normal insect. There are three parts: the head, the thorax, and the abdomen. Look at the detailed picture of the dragonfly's head in your books . . . See how large it is. Much of the head is taken up by the eyes. These large eyes give it remarkable vision in many directions. Notice as well the long abdomen that looks like a long tail. Interestingly, these insects were much larger in the past. We've found some fossils of dragonflies which were more than half a meter in length with very wide wingspans. Dragonflies, by the way, are among the oldest insects. The fossil record tells us they were here 300 million years ago.

Now, what about its life cycle . . . ? It begins with a female dragonfly laying eggs. Females lay their eggs on vegetation near a water source or directly in the water. About a week later, they hatch. If they aren't already in the water, they immediately crawl into it. Then, they go through the nymph stage. As they grow bigger, they shed their skin. Depending on the species, this can happen up to a dozen times. At this stage, the abdomen isn't fully extended, nor are the wings. Almost all dragonfly species spend the entire nymph stage in the water. At that time, they have gills, like fish, which let them breathe underwater. The length of time the dragonfly spends in this stage varies. Some species spend up to two years in the water. Eventually, they grow big enough to reach the adult stage. They crawl out of the water, and their bodies begin extending. The abdomen reaches its full length, and the wings emerge and spread out. Once they dry, the dragonfly is ready to fly.

M Student: What do they eat when they're in the water?

W: Almost anything they can catch. Dragonflies are carnivorous, so they eat meat. They have sharp teeth, which enable them to grasp and chew food. Their favorite food, both in and out of the water, is other insects. They especially love mosquitoes. A large adult dragonfly may consume dozens of mosquitoes in a single day. Dragonflies are capable of flying in a sort of stealth mode. Thus they can sneak up on unaware insects, uh, even ones that are flying. ∩4 Most dragonflies hunt insects in flight. They have evolved over time to do this. **They can fly in any direction, kind of like helicopters.** They can also make changes quickly, so they can move in different directions. Their large eyes also assist them in tracking and catching prey. They can fly long distances as well. In one case, a dragonfly was tracked flying over the Indian Ocean and back again, uh, a journey of nearly 18,000

kilometers.

Dragonflies have many enemies though. Birds and fish eat them both as adults and during the nymph stage. And if they don't get eaten, many have fairly short lives. Some live only a few weeks as adults. That's long enough for them to mate. Others may live as adults for two months. For many species, the average life span, from egg to nymph to adult, is around six months, but others live for shorter or much longer periods of time. Okay, that's all we have time for today.

Answer Explanations

1 Ⓑ The professor tells the students, "Look at page 198 in your books to see some pictures."

2 Ⓐ The professor is describing a part of the life cycle of the dragonfly when she explains its nymph stage.

3 Ⓐ At the end of the lecture, the professor remarks, "Okay, that's all we have time for today." So she will probably dismiss the class next.

4 Ⓒ In saying that dragonflies "can fly in any direction, kind of like helicopters," the professor is making a comparison.

Dictation

❶ I'd like to discuss the dragonfly, which is one of the most interesting insects I've studied.

❷ Almost all dragonfly species spend the entire nymph stage in the water.

❸ Dragonflies are capable of flying in a sort of stealth mode. Thus they can sneak up on unaware insects, uh, even ones that are flying.

iBT Practice Test
p. 44

Answers

PART 1

| 1 Ⓒ | 2 Ⓓ | 3 Ⓐ | 4 Ⓓ | 5 Ⓒ |
| 6 Ⓐ | 7 Ⓐ |

8 Edward Jenner: ⒈, ⒊, ⒋ Jonas Salk: ⒉ 9 Ⓓ

| 10 Ⓓ | 11 Ⓑ | 12 ⒈, ⒋ | 13 Ⓒ | 14 Ⓐ |

PART 2

| 1 Ⓐ | 2 Ⓐ | 3 Ⓒ | 4 Ⓐ | 5 Ⓐ |
| 6 Ⓒ | 7 Ⓓ | 8 Ⓑ | 9 Ⓑ |

PART 1

| Script |

Listen to part of a conversation between a student and a librarian.

W Student: Good evening, Mr. Jackson. Could you please assist me with a research project I'm doing?

M Librarian: Of course, Lee Ann. What are you working on this time?

W: I'm doing research for a paper in my medieval English literature class. Unfortunately, I'm having trouble finding several of the books and journal articles I need to write a decent paper.

M: Ah, yeah, we don't have too many books specifically on that topic. As for the journal articles, well, I need to see the titles. Could you show me exactly what you're looking for?

W: Sure. Here's the list of journal articles. The ones which I circled are unavailable. What do you think I should do to get a hold of them?

M: The easiest way would be to use interlibrary loan to get copies of the articles. I recognize the titles of these journals. We don't have any of them, but some other local universities do. You know, I suppose you could travel from school to school to get the articles if you don't want to use interlibrary loan.

W: No, I'd rather not do that. I'll just speak with Jackie and have her make the interlibrary loan requests for me. I guess I can wait a week or so for the articles to arrive.

M: Great. That's one problem out of the way. Now, uh, what about the books you need?

W: I've got the list of them, uh, right here. As you can see, I circled five books. And I need to get my hands on them rather urgently.

M: Oh, yeah? Why the rush for these but not the articles?

W: The articles will be somewhat useful to my research, but the books are absolutely critical.

M: Well, that rules out interlibrary loan since you are in a hurry.

W: What are my options?

M: You have a few. But the best one is to pay a visit to Seaside College to borrow these books from its library.

W: Um . . . what makes you think all of these books are at its library?

M: I worked there three years ago before I came here. One of the top scholars on medieval literature in the entire country teaches there, so the library has an incredible selection of works about that period. I'm positive that every one of those books on your list is available there.

W: Okay, that sounds promising. But how am I supposed

to check out books from that library? I'm not a student there.

M: You don't know about the agreement we have with Seaside College?

W: What agreement?

M: Er . . . I'll take that as a no. Anyway, City College and Seaside College let their students borrow books from each other's libraries. You need a special card to do that. Fortunately, I can help you get one.

W: That's awesome. Can I get the card right now? I'd love to go there first thing tomorrow morning and check out those books. That way, I can start doing the research for my paper.

M: Sure, it's a ten-minute process to make a card. Then after doing that, we can log on to Seaside's library system and confirm that the books are available.

Answer Explanations

1 Gist-Purpose Question

Ⓒ First, the student asks, "Could you please assist me with a research project I'm doing?" Then, she says, "I'm doing research for a paper in my medieval English literature class. Unfortunately, I'm having trouble finding several of the books and journal articles I need to write a decent paper."

2 Detail Question

Ⓓ The student comments, "I'll just speak with Jackie and have her make the interlibrary loan requests for me. I guess I can wait a week or so for the articles to arrive."

3 Understanding Function Question

Ⓐ About the library at Seaside College, the librarian remarks, "I worked there three years ago before I came here. One of the top scholars on medieval literature in the entire country teaches there, so the library has an incredible selection of works about that period. I'm positive that every one of those books on your list is available there."

4 Making Inferences Question

Ⓓ The student asks, "Can I get the card right now?" and the librarian agrees to do that for her.

Lecture #1 [5-9]

| Script |

Listen to part of a lecture in a physiology class.

M Professor: 🎧9 Has everyone submitted a final paper to me . . . ? Okay, great. I guess I got them all. **I'll be sure to go over these a lot faster than I did your previous reports.** Now, we're really busy today, so let's get started.

In the past, many diseases made people sick and killed large numbers of them each year. This began changing with the introduction of vaccines. A vaccine is a way to protect the body from a specific virus. It's given either by an injection or taken orally. The first vaccines were made in the late eighteenth century. By the mid-twentieth century, vaccines had eliminated or made less common such major illnesses as smallpox and polio. They had also protected people from a wide range of childhood illnesses. Some are mumps, chickenpox, whooping cough, diphtheria, and measles. Additionally, each year, millions of people get influenza shots to protect themselves from this common virus.

The basic manner in which vaccines work is that they make the body think it has a virus. This is usually done by introducing a mild or dormant form of the virus into the body. Doing this causes the body's immune system to fight the virus. It's sort of, um, sort of like a trick. The body thinks it's sick, but it really isn't because the injection is not an active or full-strength virus. But the body begins creating antibodies to fight the virus. Once a person's body has the antibodies needed to defeat the virus, there is a great chance that the individual won't get the virus in the future.

W Student: A great chance? Do you mean that vaccines are not entirely effective?

M: Unfortunately, there's no guarantee a vaccine will work. It does in most cases, but some people's bodies have trouble adapting to some vaccines. Sometimes the body doesn't produce the antibodies needed to protect it. This may happen when a person already has another medical problem. For instance, the bodies of people with diabetes often have difficulty accepting some vaccines. In other cases, people may lack the necessary cells to produce antibodies for certain viruses. An additional problem is that there's sometimes more than one strain of a virus. You may be aware that there are different types of flu vaccines. Each was created for a different type of the flu. And every year, there are some people who get vaccinated and then actually get the virus they were being vaccinated for or sometimes even die due to various complications after getting vaccinated. However, this is a small number, and many more people would die each year if we didn't have these vaccines.

Let me tell you about a couple of vaccines. I'll discuss smallpox first. It's a terrible disease that's caused by the smallpox virus. A person infected with smallpox suffers from a high fever, vomiting, and pus-filled sores that erupt all over the body. Sounds bad, huh? Well, it gets worse . . . Historically, the death rate for smallpox was over thirty percent. Survivors were often left with terrible scars while many were blinded. Smallpox killed millions of people well into the late twentieth century until vaccinations spread around the world. Credit for the modern smallpox vaccine goes to an English doctor named Edward Jenner. He made his vaccine in the late eighteenth century. This was one of the first vaccines ever made, and Jenner even

coined the word vaccine for his creation.

Jenner observed that dairy farm workers never got smallpox. He believed this happened because they contracted cowpox, a milder form of the disease, while working around cows. Somehow, he reasoned, having cowpox protected them from smallpox. In 1796, Jenner took some matter from a pus-filled lesion on a girl with cowpox. Then, he injected a young boy with the cowpox matter. About nine days later, he injected the boy with smallpox matter, but the boy didn't get the disease. His vaccine was a success. At that time, however, many people resisted the idea of being injected with one virus to protect them from another one. So Jenner had a hard time spreading awareness of his vaccine. It wasn't until much later, uh, in the 1900s, that the smallpox vaccine spread worldwide. The virus which once infected and killed millions yearly is believed to be totally eradicated today.

The man who developed the polio vaccine had much less trouble than Jenner regarding his creation. Polio is caused by a virus that attacks the nervous system and leaves many people paralyzed. Even worse, it often infects children. In the 1900s, many scientists were trying to make a vaccine for it. American researcher Jonas Salk accomplished this in 1952. After several years of testing it, his polio vaccine became widely available in 1955. The vaccine received worldwide attention in the media, which led to its acceptance. By the 1980s, the number of annual polio cases was down from millions to just a few hundred thousand. Presently, there are fewer than 100 cases worldwide each year.

Answer Explanations

5 Gist-Purpose Question

Ⓒ The professor explains some problems with vaccines to point out that they sometimes fail and may even hurt or kill people, so they are therefore not completely effective.

6 Making Inferences Question

Ⓐ In saying, "The virus which once infected and killed millions yearly is believed to be totally eradicated today," the professor implies that nobody has contracted smallpox in recent times.

7 Connecting Content Question

Ⓐ About smallpox, the professor says, "Survivors were often left with terrible scars while many were blinded." Regarding polio, the professor notes, "Polio is caused by a virus that attacks the nervous system and leaves many people paralyzed."

8 Detail Question

Edward Jenner: ☐1☐, ☐3☐, ☐4☐   Jonas Salk: ☐2☐

About Edward Jenner, the professor comments, "In 1796, Jenner took some matter from a pus-filled lesion on a girl with cowpox. Then, he injected a young boy with the cowpox matter. About nine days later, he injected the boy with smallpox matter, but the boy didn't get the disease." He also states, "He made his vaccine in the late eighteenth century. This was one of the first vaccines ever made, and Jenner even coined the word vaccine for his creation." As for Jonas Salk, the professor remarks, "American researcher Jonas Salk accomplished this in 1952. After several years of testing it, his polio vaccine became widely available in 1955. The vaccine received worldwide attention in the media, which led to its acceptance."

9 Understanding Attitude Question

Ⓓ In saying, "I'll be sure to go over these a lot faster than I did your previous reports," the professor implies that he took a long time to grade the first reports that the students turned in to him.

Lecture #2 [10–14]

| Script |

Listen to part of a lecture in a meteorology class.

W Professor: The last type of cloud formation I'd like to discuss is fog. You may not think of fog as a cloud, but it is. Fog often appears in mountainous regions, in low-lying areas, and on lakes, seas, and oceans. It can form in a variety of ways, but most of the time, uh, it's the interaction between warm and cold regions that produces fog. The type produced depends on a few factors. Among them are the terrain, the wind, the temperature, and, uh, some other conditions I'll mention. Uh, yes, Carl? I see your hand is up.

M Student: Yes, Professor Murdoch. I wonder if mist and fog are the same thing.

W: Not exactly. Each is made of water droplets suspended in the air. However, fog is thicker and reduces visibility to less than one kilometer. Mist, on the other hand, is thinner, so there is greater visibility in misty areas. Hmm . . . I guess I've just told you the first thing you need to understand about fog. That is, um, it's comprised of water droplets suspended in the air. These droplets saturate the air, so it's full of water. The moisture in the air condenses and forms droplets. Condensation usually occurs when the air is cooled to its dew point or when there's simply too much evaporated water vapor in the air. The dew point, in case you are wondering, is the temperature at which dew forms on grass. There also have to be enough dust or salt particles in the air for water to condense onto in order to form tiny droplets less than 0.1 millimeters in size. And there can't be strong winds. So . . . if all these conditions are present, fog will form. Let me recap . . . Water droplets form, and if they're lightweight and there's light wind, they'll remain suspended and form fog.

There's more than one kind of fog. First, there's radiation fog. It's more often called ground fog and is quite common. It forms after the ground traps heat during the day. Then, at night, the ground's surface begins to cool as the heat escapes from the ground. If the sky is clear, the ground cools faster, which causes the air next to it to cool. When the air above the ground reaches the dew point, water condensation starts. Then, light winds push the water droplets together and thicken them. So that's how radiation fog forms. 🎧14 It can create large fog banks up to thirty meters high at times. It usually dissipates during the day as the air becomes warmer and winds increase. **I'll explain how fog dissipation works in a moment, so hold your questions, please.**

Advection fog is another type of fog. It typically forms when warm, moist air passes over a cooler surface. This can happen on land but more frequently occurs over bodies of water when warm air flows over cold water. This is also called sea fog. When warm, moist air makes contact with the surface of cool water, condensation occurs, so fog forms. Over oceans and seas, water condenses on tiny pieces of salt in the air instead of dust like it does over land. Very often, advection fog forms along the coast and then moves further inland. Some places in the ocean, uh, where cold and warm waters meet, form very thick fog banks throughout the year. One such place is the Grand Banks off Newfoundland, Canada. That's where the warm Gulf Stream waters meet the cold waters of the Labrador Current.

A third type is evaporation fog. It forms over a body of water when cold air flows over warm water. The warm water evaporates, and, as it rises, it condenses in the cold air above and forms fog. This happens the most often over lakes and rivers. You might see it over a swimming pool if the water is heated, too.

Yet another type of fog is mountain fog. It's sometimes just low layers of clouds, but we call it fog when the clouds are close to the mountains. Other times, mountain fog forms when warm air rises up a mountain slope to higher elevations. There, it encounters colder temperatures. The water vapor reaches its dew point and condenses into droplets, thereby forming fog.

Now, let me discuss how fog dissipates. Uh, that is, how it disappears. During the day, the sun's heat causes warm, dry air to circulate upward from the ground. This makes the water droplets in fog evaporate. Fog banks normally evaporate from the edges inward. The reason is that the ground immediately under the fog doesn't get much warmth whereas the ground outside the fog bank's range heats up faster. The heated ground warms the air above it. It then rises and circulates, and it hits the edges of the fog bank. This causes the fog to begin evaporating. In addition, strong winds blowing can break up a fog bank and cause it to dissipate.

10 Gist-Content Question

Ⓓ Most of the lecture involves the professor discussing how various types of fog form.

11 Understanding Organization Question

Ⓑ The professor points out, "Advection fog is another type of fog. It typically forms when warm, moist air passes over a cooler surface. This can happen on land but more frequently occurs over bodies of water when warm air flows over cold water."

12 Detail Question

1, 4 The professor states, "This happens the most often over lakes and rivers."

13 Gist-Purpose Question

Ⓒ The professor says, "The heated ground warms the air above it. It then rises and circulates, and it hits the edges of the fog bank. This causes the fog to begin evaporating. In addition, strong winds blowing can break up a fog bank and cause it to dissipate."

14 Understanding Function Question

Ⓐ When the professor tells the students, "Hold your questions, please," she is telling them not to ask any questions yet.

PART 2

Conversation [1–4]

| Script |

Listen to part of a conversation between a student and a physical fitness advisor.

W Student: Excuse me. You're the school's physical fitness advisor, aren't you? I was informed by the lady in front that this is where you would be.

M Physical Fitness Advisor: Yes, that's correct. I'm Coach Atkins. What can I do for you today?

W: I heard that students here have to complete one Physical Education class before we can graduate. Is that correct? I had no idea about that, so I wonder if you could tell me about the requirement, please.

M: This is a new rule that only went into effect last year. You don't happen to be a junior or senior right now, do you? If you are, then you are exempt from the requirement and don't need to take the course.

W: I'm a sophomore.

M: Okay, it looks like you need to enroll in something then. When do you want to do it?

W: I'd rather do it next semester during spring. I'm probably going to be pretty busy during my junior and senior years, so I'm not particularly interested in taking a gym class during either of those years.

M: Not the active type, are you?

W: Well, I played volleyball when I was in high school, and I enjoy swimming as well, but I'm just not interested in taking a sports class.

M: Yeah, I've gotten that response from a lot of students, so you're not alone in how you think. And believe me, um, I'd much rather have motivated students taking classes than students who are annoyed at having to be at the gym.

W: So, uh, what are my options?

M: We actually have quite a few classes you can take. Let me think . . . Do you prefer indoor or outdoor activities?

W: I actually like outdoor activities more, but since it stays cold here until around April, I think I'd better do something indoors. I don't want to be running around in the cold and snow. That's a great way for me to get sick.

M: Okay. How about weightlifting?

W: Pass.

M: Are you interested in sports such as racquetball or squash? Those are high-energy activities, but I think you'd have fun doing them.

W: I've never played either, but I'll keep them in mind. What else is there?

M: There's a swimming class. We also offer classes in fencing, yoga, and tai chi.

W: All right, that doesn't sound too bad. It looks like I've got a few options to choose from. I thought I was just going to have to do cross country or weightlifting or something like that. How fast do the classes fill up? I mean, uh, am I going to have problems getting into the class that I want to take?

M: You don't have a thing to worry about. Most of the classes don't have limits on the number of students who can enroll in them. And those which do have limits typically only see them filled about halfway. I'm certain that you'll have no problems getting the class you want.

W: Coach, you've been a great help. Thank you so much for taking the time to talk to me. I guess I'll be seeing you sometime next semester.

Answer Explanations

1 Gist-Purpose Question

Ⓐ The student says, "I heard that students here have to complete one Physical Education class before we can graduate. Is that correct? I had no idea about that, so I wonder if you could tell me about the requirement, please."

2 Detail Question

Ⓐ The student comments, "I actually like outdoor activities more, but since it stays cold here until around April, I think I'd better do something indoors. I don't want to be running around in the cold and snow. That's a great way for me to get sick."

3 **Making Inferences Question**

Ⓒ When the physical fitness advisor asks the student if she is interested in taking a weightlifting class, she responds by stating, "Pass." It can therefore be inferred that she is uninterested in doing weightlifting.

4 **Understanding Function Question**

Ⓐ The student asks, "I mean, uh, am I going to have problems getting into the class that I want to take?" The physical fitness advisor then replies, "You don't have a thing to worry about. Most of the classes don't have limits on the number of students who can enroll in them. And those which do have limits typically only see them filled about halfway. I'm certain that you'll have no problems getting the class you want."

Lecture [5–9]

| Script |

Listen to part of a lecture in a history of technology class.

W Professor: After the telegraph and the telephone, the next big invention in the field of communications was the radio. Its development had three major stages. First included the discovery of the principles behind radio wave transmission and the early experiments in this field. Second was the invention of long-range wireless communication, mainly by the use of Morse Code and then of voice. Third was the utilization of mass radio broadcasting for entertainment and information purposes. Now, uh, before I begin, I'd like to make it clear that no single country or person can be declared the inventor of the radio. Different people working in various places all made contributions toward its creation.

Two of the most important of those people were James Maxwell and Heinrich Hertz. Maxwell was a Scottish scientist who proposed the idea of an electromagnetic spectrum in 1865. He placed the realms of electricity, magnetism, and light into one unified theory. From that theory came many modern-day technological advances. The other person I mentioned, Heinrich Hertz, was a German scientist. His experiments in the late 1880s proved that radio waves could be transmitted through the air. The name Hertz should be familiar to you. It's the unit we use to measure frequency. After these developments, many other scientists around the world began experimenting with what would eventually be called radio. Among them were Nikola Tesla and Guglielmo Marconi.

Tesla was born in Serbia but emigrated to the United States. He's more famous today for his role in developing electric systems, but he also had a hand in the wireless transmission of sounds. Unfortunately for Tesla, his experiments with wireless transmissions weren't as

successful as those of his rival, Marconi. The main problem for Tesla was that he started too late. By the time he began working on wireless transmissions, Marconi was far ahead of him. Marconi, just so you know, is almost always given credit for inventing the radio. During experiments in the 1890s, Marconi discovered how to increase the power and therefore the range of wireless transmissions. More experiments led to greater distances for transmissions. Eventually, he managed to send one across the entire Atlantic Ocean in 1901.

Now, there were some people who were skeptical of Marconi's claim to have done that. The main problem was that he transmitted during the daytime. Back then, it was well known that radio waves travel much farther and more clearly at night. However, over the next few years, Marconi proved his skeptics wrong as his wireless transmitters made great progress. One of the big steps was placing wireless transmitters on ships at sea. One dramatic usage of a transmitter came when the *Titanic* sank in April 1912. Before going under, the radio operator sent out a distress call that other ships picked up, which helped save many passengers' lives.

One big problem for the future of radio was that voice transmissions were difficult over long distances. The transmitters and receivers were bulky and expensive, too. During World War One, this frequently hindered military operations. While ships could carry wireless systems, doing so was more difficult for airplanes and troops on the group. So a great effort was made to reduce the size and weight of radio equipment while increasing its power during the war, which I believe was crucial to the popularity of radio. This helped pave the way for broadcast radio.

Following the war, people wanted their own radios at home. From this desire grew broadcast radio. Initially, many home radios were bulky and looked like cabinets. But they quickly became smaller and could fit anywhere inside a home. They were receive-only devices. By the end of the 1920s, roughly sixty percent of American homes had a radio. The initial problem was, well, there wasn't anything to listen to. However, the void was quickly filled. The first commercial radio broadcast was done by a station in Pittsburgh, Pennsylvania, in 1920. Soon, other stations started broadcasting music, news, weather, and sports. The idea of broadcast radio spread around the world, and many famous companies were born then. This included the BBC in England in 1922. With the growth of radio, the governments of many countries stepped in to control who could broadcast and what could be broadcast. One way that governments were able to control radio was through a licensing system. Basically, a radio station had to apply and receive a radio broadcast license from the government before it could go on the air.

By the 1930s, radio was like television is today. Everyone had one, and everyone listened to it. Entertainment shows, especially ones following the soap opera format familiar to TV viewers today, became very popular. Live sports broadcasts allowed people to follow their favorite teams without leaving home. Eventually, broadcast radio would suffer from the invention and development of television in the 1940s. But it hasn't disappeared yet and is still popular with people today.

Answer Explanations

5 Detail Question

(A) The professor says, "The other person I mentioned, Heinrich Hertz, was a German scientist. His experiments in the late 1880s proved that radio waves could be transmitted through the air."

6 Connecting Content Question

(C) First, the professor tells the class, "Now, uh, before I begin, I'd like to make it clear that no single country or person can be declared the inventor of the radio." Then, the professor states, "Marconi, just so you know, is almost always given credit for inventing the radio." Because of her first comment, the professor implies that Guglielmo Marconi should not be considered the real inventor of the radio.

7 Understanding Function Question

(D) The professor notes, "Following the war, people wanted their own radios at home. From this desire grew broadcast radio. Initially, many home radios were bulky and looked like cabinets. But they quickly became smaller and could fit anywhere inside a home. They were receive-only devices. By the end of the 1920s, roughly sixty percent of American homes had a radio."

8 Gist-Purpose Question

(B) The professor comments, "With the growth of radio, the governments of many countries stepped in to control who could broadcast and what could be broadcast. One way that governments were able to control radio was through a licensing system. Basically, a radio station had to apply and receive a radio broadcast license from the government before it could go on the air."

9 Understanding Organization Question

(B) During her talk on the development of the radio, the professor describes the important events in chronological order.

Answers

A
1 Efficient   2 trap
3 participated   4 requirements   5 emitting

B

1 b	2 b	3 a	4 a	5 a
6 b	7 b	8 a	9 b	10 a

Practice with Short Passages   p. 58

A

Answers   1 Ⓐ, Ⓓ   2 Ⓒ

| Script |

Listen to part of a conversation between a student and a student services office employee.

M Student: Hello. Are you the person I should speak with regarding parking?

W Student Services Office Employee: That's right. Do you need to purchase a parking sticker for your vehicle?

M: Er, I'm not sure. You see, um, I already have one, but it's for the parking lot which is located behind Vernon Hall.

W: Ah, you're a freshman, right?

M: That's correct. But there's something of a problem. Um . . . it's nearly impossible to find a place to park there any time after five o'clock. I have a part-time job off campus, so I typically don't get back here until after ten. By that time, the parking lot is full, so I have to park on the streets.

W: That's not good. Have you gotten ticketed?

M: Three times in the past ten days. So, uh, basically, I need to get a parking sticker that will permit me to park in some of the other lots. Is that possible for first-year students?

W: Yes, you can upgrade, but it's going to cost you.

M: How much?

W: There are two types of stickers you can buy. One will let you park in two other lots. The other will give you access to every single lot on campus. The first costs an extra $150 for the semester while the second one requires an extra $300.

M: Ouch. That's really going to hurt my pocketbook. But I guess it's less expensive than paying a bunch of fines to the city. I'll take the cheaper option, please.

Answer Explanations

1 Ⓐ, Ⓓ First, the student says, "I typically don't get back here until after ten. By that time, the parking lot is full, so I have to park on the streets." Then, after the employee asks, "Have you gotten ticketed?" the student responds, "Three times in the past ten days."

2 Ⓒ The employee tells the student about "two types of stickers" he can buy. In response, the student comments, "I'll take the cheaper option, please."

B

Answers   1 Fact: 1, 2, 3   Not a Fact: 4   2 Ⓓ

| Script |

Listen to part of a lecture in a psychology class.

W Professor: Memory is the ability to recall events which have already occurred. It's also the ability to recall information. We know from our experiences that memory isn't always perfect. As a matter of fact, we often get details about past events wrong. A part of the reason for this failure is the inability of the brain to store and recall every detail in our lives. This is especially true about unimportant details. Here's an example . . . I bet most of you can't even remember what you wore yesterday. Am I right . . . ? As for me, I have no idea what I wore.

Another problem with memory recall is that much of it's based on emotions. Memories of important events in our lives are easier to recall because of the emotions triggered by these events. For instance, the day you get married and the day a family member you're close to dies are two days you'll likely remember for the rest of your life. One is a positive event while the other is negative in nature. You remember each of them more easily than everyday events because of the powerful emotions you experience. We can also recall positive events and remember details about them more easily than negative ones.

The main reason we can remember emotional events has to do with encoding. This is the process through which the brain records events. The more emotional we are, the more we narrowly focus our attention on details. Basically, uh, we can cancel out other stimuli not related to the details of the event. This enables us to remember the details but not all the information surrounding the event. Let me give you an example that comes from a study done on victims of crime. Many criminals use weapons such as guns. When questioned later, most victims could recall the weapons better than the people holding them, uh, the attackers. What happened was that their emotions were focused on the weapon and the potential harm it could cause. Their brains prioritized the weapons as the more important factors and therefore encoded them better than any images of their attackers.

M Student: Does that mean eyewitness testimonies in some criminal cases are flawed?

W: It's most certainly possible. Since there are so many emotions unleashed, remembering all of the details can be difficult for people. There's also another factor involved in memory retrieval. It's called mood congruence. Testing on memory recall shows that the types of memories we can recall depend on our current moods. If we're happy, we can more easily recall happy memories. Likewise, we can remember the details of sad events better when we're sad. As for crime victims, it's hard for people to recall terrifying events since it's difficult to get them in the same emotional situation. That's one reason the police try to question victims so soon after incidents happen.

Answer Explanations

1 Fact: ①, ②, ③   Not a Fact: ④

The professor states, "The more emotional we are, the more we narrowly focus our attention on details." She also notes, "A part of the reason for this failure is the inability of the brain to store and recall every detail in our lives. This is especially true about unimportant details." And she comments, "Another problem with memory recall is that much of it's based on emotions. Memories of important events in our lives are easier to recall because of the emotions triggered by these events. For instance, the day you get married and the day a family member you're close to dies are two days you'll likely remember for the rest of your life. One is a positive event while the other is negative in nature. You remember each of them more easily than everyday events because of the powerful emotions you experience." However, it is not true that people recall happy events well when they are sad. In fact, the professor says the opposite, "If we're happy, we can more easily recall happy memories. Likewise, we can remember the details of sad events better when we're sad."

2 ⒟ The professor says, "The main reason we can remember emotional events has to do with encoding. This is the process through which the brain records events."

C

Answers   1 Fact: ②, ③, ④   Not a Fact: ①   2 ⒝

| Script |

Listen to part of a lecture in a physics class.

M Professor: The Earth has a large magnetic field which is created in its core. The magnetic field surrounds the planet but is not a perfect circle. It's shaped more like a, uh, a tadpole—you know, a baby frog—with its head facing toward the sun and its tail extending in the opposite direction. This distorted shape is due to solar winds hitting the magnetic field and subsequently being deflected by it. The magnetic field acts as a barrier by keeping the Earth safe from these dangerous solar winds. It protects the ozone layer, which the solar winds would strip away if they hit it. Were there no ozone layer, dangerous ultraviolet light waves from the sun would strike the planet and cause great harm. It's safe to say that

without the magnetic field, life on the Earth would most likely cease to exist.

Let me give you an example of what the magnetic field is like. Hmm . . . Picture a bar magnet, uh, like the ones we used in last week's experiment. Imagine the bar magnet in the middle of the Earth with each end extended. These ends are the magnetic poles. They don't exactly line up with the geographic North and South poles though. Instead, they are inclined about eleven degrees away from the geographic poles. The magnetic poles move slightly each year, so over time, they shift positions. For the past century or so, the north magnetic pole was located in Canada's far north. Now, it's shifting and moving toward the geographic North Pole. Oh, interestingly, the north and south magnetic poles flip positions sometimes, so the south magnetic pole becomes the north magnetic pole and vice versa. This happens irregularly. The last time was around 800,000 years ago.

W Student: Seriously? How can we know something like that happened so long ago?

M: Good question. We know this by studying rocks, particularly basalt rocks. Basalt is a volcanic rock. As lava cools, it sometimes forms basalt rocks. In these rocks, the direction of the magnetic field is permanently recorded as it cools. So by using dating methods on basalt rocks, we can tell when the poles were reversed.

Another good question is this: What makes the magnetic field? The most accepted theory today is the dynamo theory. Basically, it claims that the rotations of the Earth and the core generate an electric field that, in turn, creates a magnetic field. Let me explain . . . We know from our previous studies that an electric field can generate a magnetic field. Deep in the planet is the core, which is mostly comprised of nickel and iron. There's a solid inner core and a liquid outer core. Both are extremely hot and create convection waves as the heat moves. While the Earth rotates, it causes the liquid metal to move. All this movement of molten metal creates an electric field, and a magnetic field is thusly created, too.

Answer Explanations

1 Fact: ②, ③, ④   Not a Fact: ①

The professor says, "The magnetic poles move slightly each year, so over time, they shift positions. For the past century or so, the north magnetic pole was located in Canada's far north. Now, it's shifting and moving toward the geographic North Pole." He also notes, "The magnetic field acts as a barrier by keeping the Earth safe from these dangerous solar winds. It protects the ozone layer, which the solar winds would strip away if they hit it." Finally, he remarks, "These ends are the magnetic poles. They don't exactly line up with the geographic North and South poles though. Instead, they are inclined about eleven degrees away from the geographic poles." However, the magnetic field is not shaped like a perfect circle as the professor comments, "The magnetic field surrounds the planet but is not a perfect circle. It's more like a, uh, a tadpole—you know, a baby frog—with its head facing toward the sun and its tail extending in the opposite direction."

2 Ⓑ The professor remarks, "The most accepted theory today is the dynamo theory. Basically, it claims that the rotations of the Earth and the core generate an electric field that, in turn, creates a magnetic field."

D

| Answers | 1 Ⓐ, Ⓒ | 2 Ⓒ |

| Script |

Listen to part of a lecture in an art history class.

W Professor: Today, we're going to discuss Minimalism. Let me tell you a bit about it, and then we'll analyze some Minimalist works. Minimalism developed in the mid-twentieth century and had its peak in the 1960s and 1970s. Minimalist art, as the name suggests, is simplistic, and works in the style have been pared down to the basics. There's nothing elaborate about Minimalism. Minimalist paintings and sculptures even utilize basic materials and primary colors. Also common is the usage of straight lines and simple geometric shapes.

The overall theme of Minimalist art is that it should have no theme. Sound strange? Okay, then let me explain a bit more. Minimalist artists wanted to create art that had no hidden meanings, no elaborate composition, no symbolism, and no emotion. Furthermore, they made no effort to say anything about life, mankind, or society. Essentially, Minimalist art is exactly what you see with nothing added or hidden underneath. Another aspect of it is the attempt to blur the lines between painting and sculpture. Minimalists believed there was no difference between the two art forms. They tried to prove that belief by using simple materials, colors, and shapes in both the paintings and sculptures they created.

Since this might be a bit confusing, let me show you some examples while I talk about the history of the movement. Art historians say that Minimalism developed in the 1950s in the United States as a reaction to Abstract Expressionism. Artists in that movement tried to express their emotions through art. But some artists believed doing that was too personal and also a bit pretentious. One of the first artists to break away from Abstract Expressionism was American artist Frank Stella. He's often considered the first Minimalist. Here are some of his works . . . note the basic black and white colors . . . and some with more colorful oranges . . . and yellows . . . See the geometric forms . . . the repeating patterns . . . and the overall lack of any theme or message.

M Student: Um . . . none of that looks like art at all. I bet I could paint some of those.

W: Well, what is art and what isn't art is often left up to the viewer to decide, Jim. And you know, actually, I think the Minimalists would appreciate your comment.

M: What? Why do you say that?

W: It's simple. They didn't want their art to look like what people would normally call art. To illustrate my point, let's look at some of the works of American Donald Judd, who was both a painter and sculptor. Observe the simple square shapes in his sculptures . . . There are basic forms . . . with nothing fancy . . . This one here . . . looks almost like a group of bookshelves. I'd say that Judd achieved what the Minimalists wanted: to remove the idea that art was something special with hidden meanings.

Answer Explanations

1 Ⓐ, Ⓒ About Minimalist art, the professor tells the students, "Minimalist artists wanted to create art that had no hidden meanings, no elaborate composition, no symbolism, and no emotion." She also states, "Minimalist paintings and sculptures even utilize basic materials and primary colors."

2 Ⓒ The professor remarks, "To illustrate my point, let's look at some of the works of American Donald Judd, who was both a painter and sculptor."

Practice with Long Passages   p. 62

A

| Answers | 1 Ⓐ | 2 Ⓑ | 3 Ⓐ |

| Script |

Listen to part of a conversation between a student and a professor.

M1 Student: Before I leave, there's one last thing I'd like to speak to you about, sir.

M2 Professor: What is it?

M1: Have you heard about the economics conference that's going to be held in St. Louis this coming weekend?

M2: I think I remember hearing Professor Kenwood talk about it when we were having lunch together one day. But since I'm a chemist, I don't have much interest in it. Why do you ask?

M1: Well, I'm going to be attending that conference. I submitted a paper there, and it was accepted, so I'm going to be presenting it. Actually, I'll be going there with Professor Kenwood and a couple of other people from the department.

M2: That's great news. Congratulations. But, um, why are you bringing this up?

M1: Ah, yeah. The reason is that the conference lasts from Friday to Sunday. We're going to be driving there this Thursday night and returning on Monday evening. So, uh, I'm going to miss two of our classes. Is that going to be a problem?

M2: Well, as you know, your attendance—or lack of attendance—won't affect your grade at all. However . . .

M1: Yes?

M2: You need to be sure to acquire the notes from the classes you miss from someone you trust. Those two lessons are going to be rather important for your upcoming midterm.

M1: 🎧3 I, uh, I don't actually know anyone in the class. Is there a student you could recommend that I speak with to borrow notes from?

M2: **Hmm . . . I'll talk to David Greenwood since he is one of the top students in the class.** Just be sure to remind me when you return.

M1: I really appreciate that. Oh, and what about assignments? Are there going to be any assignments that I have to submit?

M2: No, there won't, but I will be speaking about the term paper in Friday morning's class. However, you can get the information you need about that on the class webpage. It should be posted over the weekend.

M1: That sounds good to me. Thanks for all your help, Professor.

M2: It's my pleasure. And good luck with your presentation. The conference should be a great learning experience for you, so be sure to attend as many talks as you can while you're there.

M1: Yes, I'm really looking forward to going there.

Answer Explanations

1 Ⓐ Professor Kenwood is in the Economics Department. And the professor states, "I think I remember hearing Professor Kenwood talk about it when we were having lunch together one day. But since I'm a chemist, I don't have much interest in it." So it can be inferred that the two professors are in different departments.

2 Ⓑ The student notes, "I submitted a paper there, and it was accepted, so I'm going to be presenting it."

3 Ⓐ The student asks if the professor can recommend a student from whom he can borrow the class notes. When the professor responds, "I'll talk to David Greenwood," he is agreeing to the student's request.

Dictation

M2: You need to <u>be sure to</u> acquire the notes from the classes you miss from someone you <u>trust</u>. Those two lessons are going to be <u>rather important</u> for your

upcoming midterm.

M1: I, uh, I don't <u>actually know</u> anyone in the class. Is there a student you <u>could recommend</u> that I speak with to <u>borrow notes from</u>?

M2: Hmm . . . I'll talk to David Greenwood since he is one of the <u>top students</u> in the class. Just be sure to <u>remind me</u> when you return.

M1: I really <u>appreciate</u> that.

B

Answers

1 Ⓒ 2 Ⓓ
3 Fact: ③, ④ Not a Fact: ①, ② 4 Ⓑ

| Script |

Listen to part of a lecture in a geology class.

M Professor: A tsunami is an ocean wave larger than normal that can strike coastlines and cause a great amount of damage. It's sometimes called a tidal wave or seismic sea wave. There are three primary causes of tsunamis as well as, uh, several lesser ones. The main causes are the following: earthquakes, volcanoes, and landslides. When one of these things happens underwater or close to the ocean, the sudden movement of land disturbs the water. This, in turn, creates waves. These waves may be small at first, but they grow larger as they spread. How do they spread . . . ? Well, what happens if you throw a rock into a pond with calm water?

W Student: I know. Ripples or waves form in all directions from where the rock hits the water.

M: Precisely. And that's exactly what happens in the case of tsunamis. Some tsunamis can travel thousands of kilometers across entire oceans. Do you remember the huge earthquake in December 2004? It happened near Indonesia and launched tsunamis in various directions. More than 200,000 people were killed when the waves made it to various shores. Waves caused by the earthquake even managed to hit places in Africa. Yes, Julie?

W: I know that the word tsunami comes from the Japanese language, but what does it mean in English?

M: It means harbor wave. The first part, *tsu*, means harbor while the second part, uh, *nami*, means wave. And yes, you're correct. It is Japanese. The Japanese have been dealing with tsunamis their entire history, so it should come as no surprise that they have a word for them.

Now, uh, let's look in depth at tsunamis. Undersea earthquakes cause them more than anything else. If an earthquake's epicenter is close to a coastline and not too deep underground, it can create a tsunami. Big tsunamis only happen due to earthquakes that rank seven or higher on the Richter Scale. So what happens . . . ? Well, the sudden movement of earth associated with earthquakes releases energy into the water. This energy disturbs the water and causes waves to build up. These waves may be long but aren't high at first. However, they move extremely fast. Some have been recorded moving more than 900 kilometers per hour. Imagine that. Reaching coastal areas, tsunamis slow down in shallow water. But the shallow water makes them grow higher, thereby allowing them to travel far inland. It's estimated that some tsunamis are more than thirty meters high when they strike land. And oftentimes, a series of waves hit the same area.

The other two primary causes of tsunamis happen in a similar manner. Underwater volcanoes and landslides underwater can both disturb the earth and release energy. However, they are rarer than earthquakes. There have also been tsunamis caused by massive volcanic eruptions above the ocean's surface. In 1883, the volcano Krakatoa in Indonesia erupted. It caused tsunamis which killed approximately 35,000 people on nearby islands. Other less frequent causes of tsunamis include landslides into lakes or narrow inlets, the breaking off into the ocean of large chunks of ice from glaciers, the detonating of atomic weapons underwater, and meteorites striking the ocean.

Nowadays, fortunately, there are warning systems in place that let people know a tsunami is coming. Seismic recorders around the world know when and where there are underwater disturbances. There are also numerous buoys anchored deep underwater that can detect approaching tsunamis. Using that information, emergency broadcasts and warning sirens can let people know of impending danger. Still, it's not enough if people don't respond quickly and get to higher ground. For example, in 2011, a tsunami in Japan caused by a powerful earthquake killed nearly 16,000 people despite numerous efforts to warn them of the approaching danger.

Answer Explanations

1 Ⓒ The professor asks a question and lets a student answer it, and he also answers a question that the student asks. It can therefore be inferred that he encourages the students to participate in class.

2 Ⓓ The professor lectures, "Now, uh, let's look in depth at tsunamis. Undersea earthquakes cause them more than anything else."

3 Fact: ③, ④ Not a Fact: ①, ②
The professor says, "Some tsunamis can travel thousands of kilometers across entire oceans," and mentions, "Other less frequent causes of tsunamis include landslides into lakes or narrow inlets, the breaking off into the ocean of large chunks of ice from glaciers, the detonating of atomic weapons underwater, and meteorites striking the ocean." However, tsunamis do

not become faster when they reach shallow water as the professor notes, "Reaching coastal areas, tsunamis slow down in shallow water." And tsunamis do not move in a single direction after forming as the professor states that they move in all directions.

4 Ⓑ The professor remarks, "There have also been tsunamis caused by massive volcanic eruptions above the ocean's surface. In 1883, the volcano Krakatoa in Indonesia erupted. It caused tsunamis which killed approximately 35,000 people on nearby islands."

Dictation

❶ A tsunami is an ocean wave larger than normal that can strike coastlines and cause a great amount of damage.

❷ There have also been tsunamis caused by massive volcanic eruptions above the ocean's surface.

❸ For example, in 2011, a tsunami in Japan caused by a powerful earthquake killed nearly 16,000 people despite numerous efforts to warn them of the approaching danger.

iBT Practice Test   p. 66

Answers

PART 1

1 Ⓒ	2 Ⓑ	3 Ⓑ	4 ②, ④	5 Ⓑ
6 Ⓐ	7 ③, ④	8 Ⓒ	9 Ⓑ	10 Ⓐ
11 Ⓒ	12 Ⓑ	13 Fact: ①, ②, ④ Not a Fact: ③		
14 Ⓓ				

PART 2

| 1 Ⓓ | 2 Ⓐ | 3 ①, ③ | 4 Ⓑ | 5 Ⓒ |
| 6 Ⓐ | 7 Ⓓ | 8 Ⓒ | 9 Ⓑ | |

PART 1

Conversation [1–4]

| Script |

Listen to part of a conversation between a student and a professor.

W Student: Thank you for explaining how to do the assignment, sir. I totally understand everything now.

M Professor: That's great news, Maria. I hope you can improve your grade in the class now that you know how to do the work.

W: So do I. Now, uh, if you've got a couple more minutes to spare, I'd like to speak with you about one more thing.

M: Well, I suppose so. But I don't have much time because there are two other students waiting outside my office. And my office hours are scheduled to end in ten minutes. So I'd like to make sure they get to speak with me as well.

W: Of course. This shouldn't take too long.

M: All right, then go ahead, please.

W: Thank you. Um, basically, I'm wondering what you think I ought to do this coming summer.

M: What are your options?

W: There are three I can think of. The first is for me to focus on my academics and take summer school during both summer sessions. And the second is for me to get a job both to earn some money and to get some experience.

M: And the third one?

W: I could apply for an internship and work at a company this summer. Oh, I suppose a fourth one would be to do, um, a combination of summer school and part-time work or an internship. But that might be a bit exhausting for me.

M: Okay, so you've essentially got three possibilities to choose from. Are there any important factors that will help determine your ultimate selection?

W: Er . . . what exactly do you mean?

M: For instance, are you in danger of not graduating on time? If that is the case, then you should make summer school your top priority. Or is money an issue? Are you going to be able to pay for the increase in tuition that will happen next fall? If doing that will be difficult, then you should focus on money. That's what I mean.

W: Ah, I see. No, I'm on schedule to graduate on time, and my grades are good, too. As for summer school, I'm considering it because there are some classes being offered then that I'd like to take. And I won't have time to enroll in them during the regular year.

M: And money?

W: My family can afford to pay the tuition here.

M: Okay, then what are you planning to do after you graduate? Will you attend graduate school or get a job?

W: Hmm . . . I haven't decided yet, but I'm leaning toward getting a job in the finance sector. I might want to go to grad school at a later time, but I don't think I'll do that right after I finish my undergraduate work.

M: In that case, I would suggest doing two things. First, apply for an internship or two. Doing one can get you some valuable experience in the field you'd like to work in after graduating. Next, apply for regular jobs in case you don't get accepted for an internship. They are, after all, highly competitive.

W: That makes sense. Thanks, sir. I think I'll do exactly what you said.

1 Gist-Content Question

ⓒ Almost the entire conversation is about what the student should do for the summer.

2 Gist-Purpose Question

ⓑ The professor asks, "Okay, then what are you planning to do after you graduate? Will you attend graduate school or get a job?"

3 Understanding Attitude Question

ⓑ The professor tells the student, "First, apply for an internship or two. Doing one can get you some valuable experience in the field you'd like to work in after graduating."

4 Detail Question

2, 4 The professor recommends, "First, apply for an internship or two. Doing one can get you some valuable experience in the field you'd like to work in after graduating. Next, apply for regular jobs in case you don't get accepted for an internship."

Lecture #1 [5-9]

| Script |

Listen to part of a lecture in an archaeology class.

W Professor: Since ancient times, people have used glass. One of the first glasslike substances people used was stone obsidian, which is created by volcanoes. Prehistoric people used obsidian for spear points and employed it as a cutting tool. As for the first glass people made themselves, it was manufactured either in Egypt or Mesopotamia. There are arguments favoring both sides, but there's a stronger case for glass having been invented in Egypt.

It was long thought that the Mesopotamians had invented glass though. The reason is that archaeologists found samples of glass at Mesopotamian sites that dated from before 3500 B.C. Yet recent research suggests that these glass items weren't from that time but instead came from a later time in history. The new theory many archaeologists subscribe to is that the Mesopotamians traded for glass with the Egyptians. There's plenty of evidence showing that the Egyptians were making glass by 3500 B.C. Their glass came in many colors, including yellow, green, orange, and blue. The colors were the result of impurities in the materials used to make the glass. The Egyptians made glass into large chunks, which were easy to transport. Numerous small pieces of colored glass have also been found at many sites around the Mediterranean Sea and in Mesopotamia. Egypt had a long history of trading throughout the ancient world, so we can conclude that the glass found at the oldest of these sites was most likely Egyptian in origin.

M Student: How did the Egyptians manage to discover the

secret of making glass?

W: It's highly likely that it happened by accident. Glass requires silica, which is found in sand. Soda ash, which is made by burning plant matter, and a lot of heat are needed, too. Uh, by the way, soda ash is known as sodium carbonate. If you've studied chemistry, you should be familiar with it. So, um, based upon the ingredients, I can imagine three possible scenarios . . . People making fires on sand discovered that the sand underneath had transformed into a hardened rocklike substance after the fire cooled. Or maybe glass was a byproduct of metalworking and was produced by accident in the same way. A third scenario is that when making a product called faience . . . that's F-A-I-E-N-C-E . . . um, while making faience, a kind of ceramic, the Egyptians accidentally made glass. In all three cases, heat, sand, and soda ash would have combined to form glass.

The first glass items made were beads. They were sometimes whole glass objects and sometimes glass wrapped around small rounded stones. By 1500 B.C., the Egyptians had learned to use various methods to make glass into different shapes. One method is called drawing. It involves taking molten glass on a metal stick and twisting and turning it to make the desired shape before the glass cools. While hot, glass is soft and can be drawn to great lengths. It can be wound around an inner mold many times, so when it cools, a glass vessel has been created. Sand and water were made into a hardened paste to create these inner molds. Sand easily forms molds that can just as easily be broken and discarded. The mold was also sometimes dipped directly into molten glass to make a vessel since the glass stuck to the mold. The Egyptians later learned to make more elaborate molds into which they poured molten glass in a process known as casting.

Despite being skilled at making glass, Egyptian technology lagged far behind what can be done today. For one, they never discovered glassblowing. The Phoenicians did that. Since glass was popular, it was inevitable that the secret of how to make it would spread around the Mediterranean world. When the Phoenicians learned it, they began experimenting and discovered glassblowing in the first century B.C. This is done by blowing air through a hollow metal tube that has a glob of molten glass at the end. The air forces the glass to expand and to form a rounded shape. Today, it's the most common method used to make glass vessels. At that time, Phoenicia belonged to Rome. The news of this new method spread quickly, so glassblowing became common throughout the Roman Empire. In fact, glass became so easy to make that its price fell throughout the empire. It was actually cheaper and more common than pottery for a while.

At that time, Egypt also belonged to Rome. Egyptian glass masters found a way to make clear glass around 100 A.D. They did this by adding manganese oxide to the glass mixture. It wasn't as clear as modern-day glass is, but it was still pretty transparent. This led to glass windows appearing in many parts of the Roman Empire. Now, I'd like to show you a video of some glassmaking techniques. This should give you a better idea of how it was made. Could someone get the lights, please?

Answer Explanations

5 Detail Question

Ⓑ The professor says, "It was long thought that the Mesopotamians had invented glass though. The reason is that archaeologists found samples of glass at Mesopotamian sites that dated from before 3500 B.C. Yet recent research suggests that these glass items weren't from that time but instead came from a later time in history."

6 Understanding Organization Question

Ⓐ According to the professor, soda ash is one of the ingredients that is needed to make glass.

7 Detail Question

3, 4 The professor tells the students, "By 1500 B.C., the Egyptians had learned to use various methods to make glass into different shapes. One method is called drawing. It involves taking molten glass on a metal stick and twisting and turning it to make the desired shape before the glass cools." Then, she says, "The Egyptians later learned to make more elaborate molds into which they poured molten glass in a process known as casting."

8 Connecting Content Question

Ⓒ The professor discusses how the Egyptians used drawing and casting to make glass and then talks about how the Phoenicians discovered glassblowing.

9 Making Inferences Question

Ⓑ At the end of the lecture, the professor states, "Now, I'd like to show you a video of some glassmaking techniques. This should give you a better idea of how it was made. Could someone get the lights, please?"

Lecture #2 [10-14]

| Script |

Listen to part of a lecture in an economics class.

W1 Professor: There's another theory, however, which states that economic activity comes in periodic waves. Essentially, there are periods of good economic times that are followed by bad periods. This notion was first proposed by Russian economist Nikolai Kondratiev in 1925. He believed that economies go through a cycle starting with expansion, then leading to stagnation, and finally winding up in a recession or depression. Kondratiev based his theory on the international capitalism that took place in the 1800s. He proposed that the cycles ran in sixty-year periods, uh, give or take a few years. Today, these cycles are sometimes called K-waves.

To best illustrate K-waves, imagine each one as being a year. During spring, there's new production and good economic times as most people have jobs. Prices and interest rates are initially stable. There's also some technological innovation which helps improve the economy. But there's also slightly increasing inflation. In the summer phase, the cycle reaches its peak, and people think the good times will never end. Historically, this phase has seen major wars, which lead to economic trouble. People worry because of rising prices, shortages of goods, and increasing debt. In the autumn phase, the economy reaches a plateau as it stagnates. Prices fall, and interest rates decline, so there's more consumer spending. But there's also more debt as people borrow money to buy things they cannot afford. Finally, a recession or depression hits in the winter phase. Prices fall further, there's more unemployment, profits reach lows, and stock markets decline. Yet there's hope since low inflation and low interest rates will soon kick-start a new spring phase of economic good times.

W2 Student: I've never heard anything like this. How accurate is the theory?

W1: I'd say that it's quite accurate. However, you should be aware that there is some criticism of it, which I'll get into later. But let's look at the last 200 years of history in North America and Europe to demonstrate how precise these K-waves are. Please look at the sixth page of the handout package I gave you at the beginning of class. Look at the diagram there . . . Notice on the far left is the latter part of the eighteenth century. That roughly marks the development of steam engines and the booming of the textile industry. Basically, um, it was the start of the Industrial Revolution. That's also the start of the first historically recognizable K-wave. During the summer peak were the Napoleonic Wars. Then, there was a plateau of around twenty years after the wars ended in 1815. This was followed by a sharp decline for a few years. Then, in the 1840s, the development of railways and trains, uh, spurred on by the making of strong steel, led to a new technological revolution. This was the spring of the second wave. It lasted for a couple of decades until the wars of the mid-1800s. I'm referring to the American Civil War and the wars of unification in Germany and Italy. This wave plateaued in the 1870s. Around that time, most of Europe and the United States had extensive railway systems with room for no more. Then, a new downturn began.

🎧14 The third wave began at the end of the 1800s with the development of electric systems and electric goods, innovations in chemistry, and the mass-produced internal combustion engine. Next, World War I happened and was followed by a plateau in the 1920s. Then, of course, came the Great Depression in the 1930s and the hardship and devastation of World War II in the 1940s.

That was a really long winter. Then, in the 1950s and 1960s, the fourth wave came. There were advances in airplane designs, new steps in computer technology, and an increase in mass-produced consumer goods such as televisions. Again, there was a major war, uh, in Vietnam this time, in the 1960s. It was followed by a plateau in the 1970s and a minor depression in the early 1980s. Then, after this fourth wave, the fifth wave began. It's the one we're living in. It started in the late 1980s. First came major innovations in computers so that most people could afford one. Then came the Internet, cell phones, and social media networks.

M: What part of the fifth wave are we in now?

W: I'd say we're in the plateau, uh, the autumn phase. But some people would argue this point. There were major wars in Afghanistan and Iraq, so the summer phase is over. Now, we're coasting along with little room for growth. Computer and cell phone markets are saturated, and the next technological innovations haven't appeared yet. Other economists argue that we're at the end of the fifth wave and that the economic problems of 2008 were the onset of the depression in the wave. Others, of course, dispute the existence of K-waves entirely. Let's dig a bit into why they disbelieve Kondratiev's theory.

Answer Explanations

10 Gist-Content Question

Ⓐ The lecture is about a theory on economic cycles known as K-waves.

11 Understanding Organization Question

Ⓒ The professor makes an extensive comparison when talking about how the K-wave cycle works. She compares how K-waves work with the passing of the seasons in a year.

12 Understanding Attitude Question

Ⓑ About the K-wave theory, the professor remarks, "I'd say that it's quite accurate."

13 Detail Question

Fact: ①, ②, ④   Not a Fact: ③
The professor says, "He proposed that the cycles ran in sixty-year periods, uh, give or take a few years." She also mentions, "In the summer phase, the cycle reaches its peak, and people think the good times will never end. But historically, this phase has seen major wars, which lead to economic trouble." And she adds that there have been five waves since the 1800s. However, it is not true that K-waves can be used to show economic activity in ancient times as the professor notes, "Kondratiev based his theory on the international capitalism that took place in the 1800s."

14 Understanding Function Question

Ⓓ When the professor says, "That was a really long

winter," she is stating that the last part of the K-wave cycle lasted a very long time.

PART 2

Conversation [1–4]

| Script |

Listen to part of a conversation between a student and a professor.

M Student: Good afternoon, Professor Coleman. I'm here for our 2:30 appointment. Thanks for agreeing to see me on such short notice.

W Professor: It's no problem, Chris. You appeared to be rather, uh, worried in the email you wrote. Is everything all right?

M: Oh, yes. I don't have any problems at school or with my family.

W: That's good to know.

M: So, uh, the reason I need to talk to you is that I could use some advice. Remember that I told you about my plans to take a couple of classes here this summer?

W: 🎧4 Yes. You mentioned you wanted to take two classes . . . I believe one of them will be a class in the Psychology Department while the other will be, hmm . . . a class in the Chemistry Department? Is that right?

M: **You've got an outstanding memory, Professor.** So, uh, yeah, I registered to take two classes this summer. But, well, I received an email last night, and it looks like my plans might change. I was just awarded an internship at Mercy Hospital. So, um . . . I'm not sure what to do.

W: Do the internship. Mercy Hospital is one of the most prestigious medical centers in the entire country. You'll have the opportunity to work alongside some of the finest doctors anywhere. This shouldn't even be something you need to think much about.

M: Well, here's the thing . . . The internship is for an entire year, and it's unpaid. I'm going to be working really long hours there, and I'm not sure how it's going to affect my grades. What if, uh . . . what if my grades suffer while I'm doing this internship? I might not get accepted to any medical schools when I start applying this coming fall.

W: I see your point. But do you know what? Medical schools will understand if your grades fall a bit. They're going to notice you did an internship at Mercy Hospital and realize the situation. Plus, whenever I write letters of recommendation for you, I'll be sure to point that fact out to them. Oh, there's one more thing . . .

M: Yes?

W: I've had two other students do internships at Mercy Hospital. Both had outstanding grades—just like you— and both saw their overall GPAs decline slightly after they started their internships. But that didn't stop them from

getting accepted to some top medical schools. Each is currently a doctor and is doing quite well.

M: Wow, I had no idea. Thanks. Oh, uh, one more question . . . As I mentioned, I won't receive any compensation for the internship.

W: Is that a problem?

M: Money is tight in my family. And the situation won't get better since I can't do my part-time job if I do the internship.

W: Try explaining the situation to your parents. I'm sure they'll understand. This is really a life-changing opportunity, Chris, and it's something you shouldn't turn down.

M: Okay, you've convinced me. I'll talk to my parents and let them know what you said.

W: Great. Let me know if you need anything else. Oh, and don't forget to cancel your summer classes. If you do that by the end of the day, you'll receive a full refund.

M: Oh . . . That's wonderful news. I'd better head over to the Registrar's office now.

W: Sounds good. Thanks for stopping by, Chris.

Answer Explanations

1 Gist-Content Question

Ⓓ In the conversation, the speakers are mostly discussing the student's plans for the coming months.

2 Understanding Attitude Question

Ⓐ The professor shows that she believes Mercy Hospital has excellent doctors working at it when she tells the student, "Mercy Hospital is one of the most prestigious medical centers in the entire country. You'll have the opportunity to work alongside some of the finest doctors anywhere."

3 Detail Question

1, 3 The student says, "The internship is for an entire year, and it's unpaid. I'm going to be working really long hours there, and I'm not sure how it's going to affect my grades." He also adds, "Money is tight in my family. And the situation won't get better since I can't do my part-time job if I do the internship."

4 Understanding Function Question

Ⓑ The professor tells the student that she believes he is planning to take classes in the Psychology and Chemistry departments this summer. The student then responds, "You've got an outstanding memory, Professor." It can therefore be inferred from the student's response that he intends to take a Psychology class.

| Script |

Listen to part of a lecture in an art history class.

W Professor: Another common painting method is finger-painting. Now, uh, I know what most of you are thinking. You're thinking that finger-painting is for children. And, um, you're right . . . partially. But finger-painting can be done by anyone. In fact, in some countries, such as China, it's considered a form of high art. So let me tell you about finger-painting in three basic parts: what its history is, how it's done, and why it's used to teach children to paint.

Evidence of hands and fingers being used to make art dates back to prehistoric times. Look at this picture of cave art from France . . . It's at least 30,000 years old. You can see the outlines of many hands. Note that most of them are the artist's left hand. Basically, the left hand was placed on the stone wall. The artist would hold a tube in his right hand and blow paint through the tube. The paint then made an outline of the hand. Well, that's what we think happened. We're not totally sure. So it wasn't like modern finger-painting, but it was a start.

Even more similar is what are called finger flutings. Look at these images from a different French cave. Here . . . and here . . . and how about this one . . . ? Ancient people would rub their hands along the soft clay on cave walls. Sometimes they would make images in the clay by using their fingers. Later, the clay hardened, and the images were preserved. Many of these finger flutings are so small that they must have been made by children.

Now, let's move on to China, where finger-painting became an art form more than 300 years ago. The Chinese credit Gao Qipei in the Qing Dynasty as the father of Chinese finger-painting. This was around the late seventeenth and early eighteenth centuries. He was a civil servant who painted as a hobby. He began by painting with brushes but later switched to finger-painting. Gao Qipei claimed that the idea came to him in a dream. He was noted for growing his fingernails very long to improve his painting style. Here are some of his works on the screen . . . You can see that most of them were done in simple black ink . . . with long lines . . . often made with fingernails. Gao Qipei had many followers, and he taught them his methods. Today, finger-painting is a revered art form in China.

M Student: Did the Chinese spread this method around the world?

W: As far as I know, they did not. Back when Gao Qipei lived, China was a closed-off society. The methods of finger-painting used today actually evolved mainly for children in school settings. There's a strong claim for the origins of this in Italy in 1926. An American teacher at a school in Rome—uh, her name was Ruth Shaw—gets credit for popularizing finger-painting for children. The story goes that one day, a student cut his finger in class. She put some iodine on it to help his cut get better. The boy then went to the bathroom and used the iodine on his finger to paint all over the walls. Shaw got mad at him, but when the other students saw what he had done, they wanted to try it, too. So, uh, this story may or may not be true. But whatever the case, Shaw began teaching her class to paint by using their fingers.

Shaw also taught other teachers what to do. She did some research and created a paint that was safe for children to use. It was nontoxic and could be easily washed off the hands. Shaw later started a business to produce finger paint. Her ideas spread far and wide and made finger-painting quite popular.

Okay, so what about some finger-painting techniques . . . ? The basic idea is to use the fingers to apply paint to a surface. This surface could be canvas, paper, glass, tile, or anything else which paint can be applied to. Sometimes the entire hand and even the forearms are used in finger-painting. There is also the splash method, where the painter picks up some paint with several fingers and then either drips the paint on the surface or splashes it by throwing the paint. As I'm sure you have figured out, finger-painting can be messy but also fun.

There are several reasons why finger-painting is a good way to teach children to paint. First, it's easier for them to use their fingers than to hold a brush. It also involves a sensory experience with bright colors. Children learn about colors and how to mix them. Finger-painting additionally helps children develop motor skills in their fingers and hands. It requires hand-eye coordination, too, and involves the senses, particularly sight, touch, and smell. Finally, finger-painting is an exciting way for children to learn about art.

Answer Explanations

5 **Gist-Content Question**

Ⓒ The professor mainly discuses how finger-painting has been practiced over time during her lecture.

6 **Detail Question**

Ⓐ About finger flutings, the professor says, "Ancient people would rub their hands along the soft clay on cave walls. Sometimes they would make images in the clay by using their fingers. Later, the clay hardened, and the images were preserved."

7 **Understanding Organization Question**

Ⓓ In discussing Gao Qipei, the professor focuses on describing his role in promoting finger-painting in China.

8 **Detail Question**

Ⓒ The professor remarks, "But whatever the case, Shaw began teaching her class to paint by using their fingers. Shaw also taught other teachers what to do. She did some research and created a paint that was safe for children to use. It was nontoxic and could be easily washed off the hands. Shaw later started a business to produce finger paint. Her ideas spread far and wide and made finger-painting quite popular."

9 Understanding Attitude Question

Ⓑ About finger-painting, the professor notes, "There are several reasons why finger-painting is a good way to teach children to paint."

| Vocabulary Review

Answers

A

1 submit	**2** periodic	**3** determine
4 vice versa	**5** byproduct	

B

1 a	**2** a	**3** b	**4** b	**5** b
6 a	**7** b	**8** b	**9** a	**10** a

Chapter 04 | Making Inferences

Practice with Short Passages

p. 80

A

Answers   1 ⓒ   2 Ⓐ

| Script |

Listen to part of a conversation between a student and a study abroad office employee.

M1 Study Abroad Office Employee: Welcome to the study abroad office. Is there anything in particular you're looking for today?

M2 Student: Hi. Uh, yeah . . . Next year is going to be my junior year, and I'm giving some serious thought to spending a semester abroad.

M1: Just one semester? You don't want to stay away for the entire year?

M2: Oh, I'd love to do a year abroad, but I'm a civil engineering major, so I'd probably fall behind my classmates if I spent two semesters in another country.

M1: Not necessarily. There happen to be quite a few universities in both Europe and Japan that have strong engineering programs.

M2: Hmm . . . That sounds appealing, um, but are the classes taught in English? I'm afraid that my foreign language skills are a bit, um, lacking.

M1: I totally understand. Most of the programs do offer classes in English. Where are you thinking of going?

M2: I've got my heart set on either Germany or Italy. Are there any schools in those countries that would fit my major?

M1: I believe so. Here, uh, read through this brochure . . . and this one . . . Both of them are for schools in Germany. And if you don't mind waiting a bit, I'll dig up a couple of brochures from schools in Italy.

M2: Excellent. I'll just take a seat over here then. Thanks.

Answer Explanations

1 ⓒ The student asks, "Are the classes taught in English? I'm afraid that my foreign language skills are a bit, um, lacking." So it can be inferred that he cannot speak German well.

2 Ⓐ The employee tells the student, "Here, uh, read through this brochure . . . and this one . . . Both of them are for schools in Germany. And if you don't mind waiting a bit, I'll dig up a couple of brochures from schools in Italy." So the student will probably look at the brochures while he waits.

B

Answers   1 Ⓐ   2 ⓒ

| Script |

Listen to part of a lecture in an archaeology class.

M Professor: Look at this picture . . . It's a passage grave. Remains of this type of grave have been found in Ireland, England, Scotland, and various places in Western Europe. A passage grave consists of a long passage ending in a burial chamber. The passage and chamber are both built of stone, which has a dirt roof. This produces a large mound with a single entrance leading to the long passage. Oftentimes, the burial chamber is laid out in the form of a cross.

W Student: Were the builders Christians?

M: No. Most passage graves were built long before Christianity was a religion. Some of the oldest are approximately 5,000 years old. The reason why the builders used cross shapes for their burial chambers is unknown. But there's obviously a religious purpose for the graves, um, as is the case with most ancient burial chambers.

Many passage graves were elaborate structures built with precision and care. Some were aligned so that sunlight on the winter solstice shone through the passage and into the burial chamber. The winter solstice, for your information, is in late December and is the shortest day of the year. In some ancient cultures, it marked the beginning of a new year. It's likely that for a brief time on the winter solstice, people would gather and watch the sunlight enter the passage grave.

One well-known example of this kind of grave is the Newgrange passage grave in Ireland. Here's a picture of it on the screen . . . Archaeologists estimate it was built around 3200 B.C. This makes it older than Stonehenge and the Great Pyramid of Giza. It's large, being eighty-five meters in diameter and thirteen meters high. It's surrounded by ninety-seven large stones . . . Many of the stones contain engravings of ancient symbols. Here is one . . . and another . . . and another . . . The passage to the burial chamber is nineteen meters in length. The chamber inside, uh, here . . . is in the shape of a cross. One other special thing about Newgrange is the roof of the passage chamber. There is a special structure above the passage entrance called a roof box . . . It allows light to enter the passage on the winter solstice. Another example of a large passage grave aligned like that is the one located at Maeshowe in the Orkney Islands in Scotland. I've got a picture of it . . . ah, yes, right here . . .

Chapter 04   **33**

The effort it required to build passage graves shows that Neolithic people were highly organized and skilled builders. Large groups of people must have spent years constructing some of these graves. As for who was buried in them, that's difficult to determine. Many passage graves were lost and buried under large amounts of earth and vegetation until being discovered in recent centuries. When they were opened, archaeologists found bones and other items. But in others, they found nothing but carvings on the inner stone walls. Now, uh, I've got a few pictures of the treasures that have been found in a few passage graves . . .

Answer Explanations

1 Ⓐ The professor lectures, "Some were aligned so that sunlight on the winter solstice shone through the passage and into the burial chamber. The winter solstice, for your information, is in late December and is the shortest day of the year. In some ancient cultures, it marked the beginning of a new year. It's likely that for a brief time on the winter solstice, people would gather and watch the sunlight enter the passage grave." Since the graves were often aligned to let sunlight in one day of the year, it can be inferred that the solstice was an important day in some ancient societies.

2 Ⓒ At the end of the lecture, the professor states, "Now, uh, I've got a few pictures of the treasures that have been found in a few passage graves."

C

Answers 1 Ⓒ 2 Ⓓ

| Script |

Listen to part of a lecture in an environmental science class.

W Professor: Okay, let's move on to another common coastal feature. I'm referring to mudflats. These are wide areas comprised mostly of mud but which are sometimes mixed with sand. They typically form where a river meets the ocean, causing a sandbar to form across the mouth of the river. The sandbar protects the area behind it from the ocean's waves. If the river flows slowly, then lots of silt carried by the river gets deposited behind the sandbar. This results in large mudflats forming over time. During periods of high tide, the ocean water covers the sandbar and mudflats, but both are exposed during low tide. Some dramatic examples of wide mudflats are found in regions with the highest tides in the world. Two such places are the many rivers along the Bay of Fundy in eastern Canada and the area around the city of Incheon in South Korea.

Mudflats are vital ecosystems because they are home to a wide variety of plant and animal life. Lots of biological matter from dead plants and animals gets trapped in mudflats. It comes, uh, from the rivers flowing to them

and from the daily tidal wash. Numerous shellfish, including clams, mussels, and crabs, make their homes in mudflats. Mudflats also attract huge flocks of migratory birds looking for easy meals in the mud. Each spring and fall, birds flying north and south use mudflats as way stations. These are crucial links in birds' annual migratory patterns.

M Student: Do any plants grow on mudflats? It doesn't seem like they would.

W: You're correct, Tom. There really aren't many. That's due to the high salt content from the ocean water brought in by the rising tide every day. Of course, there are some plants on mudflats, but they only grow in places where the mud is high enough so that it's not covered by ocean water at high tide. These higher areas are like, um, small islands that rise above the mudflats.

In addition, along the edges of mudflats, we can often find salt marshes. These are places that have built up steadily over a long time so that large parts of them are above the daily tide levels. In salt marshes, a great amount of vegetation grows. But keep in mind that the water the plants depend on has a high salt content. So what grows in them are plants that have adapted to live in brackish water. The plants' roots may grow in salty water, but their stems and leaves are above the water line. These roots actually help stabilize the areas they grow in and prevent them from eroding. As such, salt marshes serve as intermediate zones between mudflats and higher, drier ground. Let's take a short break, and then we'll continue talking about them ten minutes from now.

Answer Explanations

1 Ⓒ The professor says, "If the river flows slowly, then lots of silt carried by the river gets deposited behind the sandbar. This results in large mudflats forming over time." Then, she says, "Some dramatic examples of wide mudflats are found in regions with the highest tides in the world. Two such places are the many rivers along the Bay of Fundy in eastern Canada and the area around the city of Incheon in South Korea." So it can be inferred that the rivers flowing to the Bay of Fundy move slowly.

2 Ⓓ The professor comments, "Let's take a short break, and then we'll continue talking about them ten minutes from now."

D

Answers 1 Ⓒ 2 Ⓒ

| Script |

Listen to part of a lecture in an economics class.

M Professor: The longest railway in the world is the Trans-Siberian Railway. It links the far eastern part of Russia with the western region. The railway is 9,288 kilometers long and crosses ten time zones. It passes through eighty-seven cities and crosses sixteen large rivers. It's not just one railway line though. Uh, it's a series of connected lines with branches extending into Mongolia and China. The western terminus is in Moscow while it ends in Vladivostok in the east. The journey takes seven days of continuous riding or lasts longer if the passenger decides to stop somewhere.

The construction of the railway started in 1891 and wasn't completed until 1916. The main reason for its construction was to provide a link between eastern and western Russia. At that time, there were few roads connecting the east and west. Those which did exist were poorly made, and many were unusable during periods of heavy snow and the spring thaws.

In the early 1890s, it appeared that there would be war in the east as China and Japan were both becoming regional powers. The only possible way to move Russian soldiers and supplies such a vast distance was by train. Tsar Alexander III therefore ordered the construction of a continuous railway line. Work began in May 1891. The main line was completed by 1903, but many of the stations, bridges, tunnels, and spur lines were of a temporary nature. The entire railway wasn't fully done until 1916.

W Student: It must have cost a fortune to build.

M: 🎧2 You're right, but we aren't exactly sure how much. Most economists estimate the Trans-Siberian Railway cost between seven hundred million and one billion U.S. dollars in 1916 money. No matter what the cost, it was an enormous drain on the Russian economy at the time. **Despite that . . . the railway has more than made up for the cost of construction since then.** You could, in fact, say that it has saved Russia in more ways than one. First, it allowed for massive amounts of grain and other food products to be shipped easily from farmland in the east to cities in the west. It also enabled millions of Russians to move east to settle in towns that grew up along the railway's route. This expanded the Russian economic base by giving the country greater access to the timber, mineral, and oil resources of Siberia.

A third benefit was its strategic use in wartime. Were it not for the Trans-Siberian Railway, Russia most likely would have been overrun by the Germans in World War II. The railway allowed the Russians easily to ship soldiers and supplies from the east to the west. And it also transported people and supplies from the west to the east to avoid the invading German armies. Today, the railway provides a strong link to most parts of the world's biggest country. This has strengthened both Russia's economic and strategic positions.

Answer Explanations

1 Ⓒ The professor notes, "The construction of the railway started in 1891 and wasn't completed until 1916. The

main reason for its construction was to provide a link between eastern and western Russia. At that time, there were few roads connecting the east and west. Those which did exist were poorly made, and many were unusable during periods of heavy snow and the spring thaws." The professor therefore implies that traveling to the eastern part of Russia was hard in the 1800s.

2 Ⓒ When the professor states that "the railway has more than made up for the cost of construction since then," she is implying that the railway has benefitted Russia financially in various ways.

Practice with Long Passages   p. 84

A

Answers   1 Ⓑ   2 Ⓓ   3 Ⓒ

| Script |

Listen to part of a conversation between a student and a professor.

W Student: Professor Taylor, how are you doing? Do you have a few minutes to speak with me before our class begins?

M Professor: Hi, Melanie. Yeah, as long as you don't need too much of my time because I need to discuss something with the head of my department before I go to the classroom.

W: Oh, sure. This shouldn't take too long. This is about the biology project I'm doing. I know we are supposed to submit the weekly update on how the project is going in class today. But, uh, I'm afraid I don't have anything prepared for today.

M: And why is that?

W: My partner and I are having trouble getting into the lab to do the experiments we want to conduct.

M: Um . . . can you be a bit more specific, please? What exactly is keeping you from getting into the lab?

W: It's a couple of things. First, both Kevin and I have full schedules and work part time, so there are a limited number of times we can meet. Second, on those occasions where we have time to get together, well . . . um, the lab is being used by a class, so we can't gain access.

M: I see.

W: So . . . what are we supposed to do? 🎧3 Is there any way we can change lab partners? Uh, I mean, Kevin and I get along great. But maybe it would be better if we had partners with schedules that fit each of ours.

M: **Well, that would have been a good idea two or three weeks ago.** But the other groups have already been doing good work on their projects. So I don't see how I can ask any of them to give up their work for you two.

W: Is there anything else we can do?

M: There's really only one thing I can think of . . . You're going to have to do work on the project individually.

W: How so?

M: It's simple. You need to do all of the work for the project, and your partner needs to do the same thing. That way, you can visit the lab during your free time and when it's available, and so can Kevin.

W: But . . . but . . . that's going to be a lot of extra work since we'll be working alone.

M: True, but you were the one who chose your partner. You should have checked on your schedules before you made that decision.

W: Yes, I see your point. Okay, I'll let him know what you've decided. Thanks, sir.

Answer Explanations

1 Ⓑ The student states, "My partner and I are having trouble getting into the lab to do the experiments we want to conduct."

2 Ⓓ The professor remarks, "True, but you were the one who chose your partner. You should have checked on your schedules before you made that decision." He says this with regard to the student's problem of getting into the lab. So he is implying that the student made a poor choice for her partner.

3 Ⓒ The professor rejects the student's suggestion when he answers, "Well, that would have been a good idea two or three weeks ago." He means that she could have changed partners earlier, but she cannot do that now.

Dictation

W: So . . . what <u>are</u> we <u>supposed to</u> do? Is there <u>any way</u> we can change lab partners? Uh, I mean, Kevin and I <u>get along great</u>. But maybe it would be better if we had partners with schedules <u>that fit</u> each of ours.

M: Well, that <u>would have been</u> a good idea two or three weeks ago. But the other groups <u>have already been doing</u> good work on their projects. So I don't <u>see how</u> I can ask any of them to <u>give up</u> their work for you two.

W: Is there <u>anything else</u> we can do?

M: There's really only one thing I can <u>think of</u> . . . You're going to have to do work on the project <u>individually</u>.

B

Answers   1 Ⓑ   2 Ⓑ   3 Ⓐ   4 Ⓓ

| Script |

Listen to part of a lecture in a geology class.

M Professor: Another way the Earth's landscape can be changed is through the movement of glaciers. Countless changes were made by glaciers during the last ice age, but there are still glaciers actively rearranging the landscape today. They do this through a combination of pressure and time. Remember that glaciers are moving rivers of ice that weigh massive amounts. As they push forward or backward, they can alter the landscape all around them.

Most glaciers move slowly, um, traveling short distances each year. Some, of course, may move many meters each day, but most of them move less than a meter per day. When glaciers melt and start moving backward, their retreats can alter the landscape. What's left behind after this happens is land that looks completely different than it used to. Some common land formations caused by the movement of glaciers are valleys, fjords, cirques, arêtes, and horns. ᐄ4 Many of the valleys in northern parts of the Northern Hemisphere were created by glaciers during the last ice age.

W Student: Professor Raven, if it's all right with you, I have a question.

M: **By all means, be my guest.**

W: Thanks. How can we tell which valleys were made by glaciers and which ones were made by something else, such as, um, river erosion? Is it possible to tell the difference?

M: It sure is. You can tell by the shape of the valley. Valleys made by glaciers are usually U-shaped and have rounded floors and steep, nearly vertical sides. This conforms to the shape of most glaciers. Valleys eroded by rivers are more V-shaped though. They have narrower bottoms and gentler slopes. Fjords are a great example of glacial action. Fjords are steep-sided inlets near the sea. To make them, glaciers cut through mountains near water and opened passages to the sea. These, in turn, flooded the new valleys as the glaciers retreated. Fjords are common sights in Scandinavia in Europe and parts of northern Canada.

Many mountains show evidence of being acted upon by glaciers as well. Cirques are dish-shaped indentions on mountainsides and were created by glacial erosion. These formations are hollows with steep uphill faces and look like, uh, dishes lying on their sides. Here, look . . . This picture on the screen is a cirque on the Matterhorn in Switzerland. Another formation is called an arête. Arêtes are steep, jagged ridges formed when two glaciers passed close to each other yet never met. The glaciers cut away the land on both sides, leaving a steep ridge of rock. A third mountain feature caused by glaciers is a horn.

Horns are high, narrow peaks of jagged rock that look like animal horns, uh, hence the name. Several glaciers moving around a mountain produce this feature by eroding the entire rock except for its central part.

When glaciers retreat, more formations result. When glaciers stop moving, there are large deposits of earth and rock around them. This material was ground up beneath the glaciers and pushed forward and to their sides. Sometimes a glacier's melting water washes the earth and rock away. Other times, it doesn't. Instead, long, narrow ridges of soil and rock called moraines are left behind. If you ever see a moraine, you should know that you've found the farthest forward advance of a glacier.

Drumlins are yet another formation left behind by glaciers. Glaciers create these narrow, teardrop-shaped hills beneath them while moving forward. Upon retreating, drumlins are left behind. An interesting feature of drumlins is that they have high, steep front faces and longer, lower sections in the rear which taper to a narrow shape, uh, almost like a tail. The direction the tail points in is the direction the glacier that made the drumlin was moving. In some places near the Great Lakes, formations of hundreds of drumlins can be seen from the air. Here, uh, let me show you . . .

Answer Explanations

1 Ⓑ During the entire lecture, the professor focuses on the land formations that are created by glaciers.

2 Ⓑ The professor states, "Arêtes are steep, jagged ridges formed when two glaciers passed close to each other yet never met. The glaciers cut away the land on both sides, leaving a steep ridge of rock."

3 Ⓐ The professor says, "In some places near the Great Lakes, formations of hundreds of drumlins can be seen from the air. Here, uh, let me show you." So she will most likely show a picture to the students.

4 Ⓓ When the student requests permission to ask a question, the professor responds, "By all means, be my guest." In saying that, he is indicating that the student has his permission to ask her question.

Dictation

❶ Remember that glaciers are moving rivers of ice that weigh massive amounts.

❷ Valleys made by glaciers are usually U-shaped and have rounded floors and steep, nearly vertical sides.

❸ Sometimes a glacier's melting water washes the earth and rock away. Other times, it doesn't.

Answers

PART 1

1 Ⓑ	2 Ⓒ	3 Fact: ①, ③ Not a Fact: ②, ④	
4 Ⓓ	5 Ⓓ	6 Ⓓ	7 Ⓐ	8 Ⓒ
9 Cavity Nest: ① Cup Nest: ③, ④ Suspended Nest: ②			
10 Ⓒ	11 Ⓑ	12 Ⓑ	13 ②, ④	14 Ⓐ

PART 2

1 Ⓒ	2 Ⓓ	3 Ⓐ	4 Ⓒ	5 Ⓓ
6 Ⓐ	7 Ⓒ	8 Ⓓ	9 Ⓒ	

PART 1

Conversation [1–4]

| Script |

Listen to part of a conversation between a student and a chemistry laboratory instructor.

M Student: Ms. Starling, could I speak with you about my lab report, please?

W Chemistry Laboratory Instructor: Sure. Um, could you tell me your name, please? We've only had one lab so far, so I don't know every student's name yet.

M: Ah, yeah, of course. My name is Larry Fulton. I, uh, I got a sixty-two on the lab report you handed back at the start of the lab. Er . . . I kind of thought I had done much better than that, so I wonder if you can tell me what I did wrong.

W: May I see your lab report, please?

M: Yes . . . Here you are.

W: Thanks. Just a minute . . . Ah, yeah, I remember this one. Um . . . Larry, I was actually pretty generous with your grade. Your methodology was completely wrong. And you didn't write the lab report the way it was supposed to be written.

M: I didn't?

W: Have you ever taken a lab course here?

M: No. In fact, um, I'm just a freshman, so this is my first semester here.

W: You're a freshman? How did you get into this class? It's supposed to be for sophomores or students who have at least taken Chemistry 104.

M: Oh . . . I wasn't aware of that. I just read the course description, and it seemed like this would be an interesting course to take.

W: I see. Well, your advisor should have stopped you from taking this class. You need to complete a lower-level class before you attempt this one.

M: So, er, what do you think I should do?

W: If I were you, I'd drop this class immediately. There's no way you're going to be able to do a sufficient job in this class. The highest grade you can expect to get is a C. And that will only happen if you're really lucky.

M: Um . . . but I'm planning to major in Chemistry, so I need to take at least one class in the department this semester, right?

W: Yes. What you should do is register for Professor Glassman's class. It's an introductory chemistry class with a lab. You'll learn about the basics of chemistry, and you'll also get to conduct lab experiments.

M: All right.

W: The best part is that the labs are typically small. They are around, oh, twenty to twenty-five students, so you'll get plenty of individual training in the labs. It's not like this class, where, as you can see, we've got fifty students in the lab.

M: Okay. That sounds good, but isn't it too late to drop a class and to sign up for another one?

W: Actually, freshmen can drop classes on the last day of the semester. As for adding a new one, the date for that is tomorrow. I know there's room in the class though since I just spoke with Professor Glassman about it this morning.

M: Do I need to get his approval to take the class?

W: Yes. Tell you what . . . Let me clean up the lab right now. That should take about five or ten minutes. Then, I'll take you to his office and introduce you to him. He can tell you about the class and help you register for it if you want.

M: Wow, thanks. I really appreciate your help.

Answer Explanations

1 Gist-Content Question

Ⓑ The speakers mostly talk about which class the student needs to be enrolled in.

2 Making Inferences Question

Ⓒ The laboratory instructor comments, "Larry, I was actually pretty generous with your grade. Your methodology was completely wrong. And you didn't write the lab report the way it was supposed to be written." She therefore implies that the student should have gotten a lower grade on the report.

3 Detail Question

Fact: ①, ③ Not a Fact: ②, ④
The laboratory instructor mentions, "You'll also get to conduct lab experiments," and, "I know there's room in the class though since I just spoke with Professor Glassman about it this morning." However, she remarks, "They are around, oh, twenty to twenty-five students," so there are not more than fifty students in the class. And she says nothing about the professor encouraging the

students to ask questions during his lectures.

4 Detail Question

Ⓓ The laboratory instructor says, "Then, I'll take you to his office and introduce you to him."

Lecture #1 [5-9]

| Script |

Listen to part of a lecture in a zoology class.

W Professor: As I'm sure everyone's aware, most birds lay their eggs and hatch them in nests. The main purpose of a bird's nest is to provide a secure place to lay eggs, hatch them, and then raise the young until they're capable of living on their own. Of course, you've all seen the common circular nests made of twigs and grass and which are found in trees. But these are not the only types of nests which birds live in. There are, for instance, nests built into the sides of cliffs and nests located on ledges of cliffs and in crevices in cliffs themselves. Other nests are built very close to the ground while some are made in cavities of trees. Some birds build their nests in bushes and shrubs, and some have adapted to modern life by making nests in buildings and other manmade structures. Finally, some birds, such as penguins and auks, don't build any nests at all. They merely lay their eggs on the ground or on a cliff ledge.

M Student: It sounds like there are lots of nests. How many types are there?

W: There are a wide variety of them, but there are seven main types. They are the following: the scrape nest, the ground nest, the burrow nest, the cavity nest, the platform nest, the cup nest, and the suspended nest. Let's look at them in turn . . .

The scrape nest is merely a depression dug into the ground and sometimes lined with leaves or stones. It's a common type of nest for shorebirds such as seagulls and terns. Ostriches, pheasants, and quail also build them. The eggs of these birds are on the ground, so they're highly exposed to predators. To counter that, most birds which make scrape nests have eggs colored to blend in with the ground or the material used to line their nests.

Other types of nests built on or close to the ground are lumped together in a group and called ground nests. One common type is a cup-shaped nest with steep sides made of grass and twigs. Sometimes it has a dome on the top to help hide the eggs from predators.

Next is, uh, the burrow nest. Swallows, kingfishers, and many species of owls build burrow nests. To make one, a bird digs a deep hole in the ground or in the dirt of a cliff face. A burrow nest usually has a long tunnel and then a wider chamber, where the bird lays its eggs. Some birds use burrows that were built and subsequently abandoned by other animals. Like, uh, some birds use abandoned prairie dog, rabbit, and rodent burrows. One advantage of this type of nest is that the eggs are well protected. The young hatchlings are also safe and can be kept warm deep inside the burrow. However, if a predator finds the burrow and digs its way in, there's no way for the hatchlings to escape.

Cavity nests have advantages and disadvantages similar to those of burrow nests. Most cavity-nesting birds use natural cavities instead of making their own nests. One exception is the woodpecker, which constructs its own cavity. Passerines, woodpeckers, owls, and parrots are common cavity nest dwellers or builders. Often, uh, when woodpeckers abandon their cavity nests, other cavity-nesting birds move in.

The platform nest is another unusual one. This type of nest is very flat. A bird may make it on the ground, in a tree, or in shallow water. It's a large nest built by large birds, such as the osprey. Some water birds even make floating platform nests.

A more common type is the cup nest. It's the type most often seen in trees, but it can also be found on the ground and in or on buildings. As its name suggests, it's cup shaped with steep sides or, um, sometimes shallow sides. Cup nests with shallow sides are occasionally called saucer nests or plate nests. A cup nest is usually made of grass and twigs and, uh, on occasion, mud. Some are placed where tree branches can support them from the bottom or by the rims of the cup. Other cup nests are attached to the sides of trees or buildings by mud or sometimes the bird's saliva, which forms a kind of glue. Many small birds, like swifts, swallows, and hummingbirds, make cup nests. Their main advantage is that their steep sides keep eggs warm and hide them from predators.

The final type is the suspended nest. Basically, uh, a bird builds a nest so that it's hanging down from a support structure such as a tree. The nest droops down from a tree branch and often has the shape of a pendant or sphere. A small hole in the nest allows access in and out. Orioles, weavers, and vireos all build suspended nests. Inside, the mostly enclosed structures keep eggs warm and hidden from predators.

Answer Explanations

5 Gist-Content Question

Ⓓ The entire lecture is about the different kinds of nests that birds build.

6 Making Inferences Question

Ⓓ The professor remarks, "Ostriches, pheasants, and quail also build them. The eggs of these birds are on the ground, so they're highly exposed to predators. To counter that, most birds which make scrape nests have eggs colored to blend in with the ground or the material used to line their nests." It can therefore be inferred that ostriches, pheasants, and quail lay eggs which are the same color as their nests.

7 Understanding Attitude Question

Ⓐ The professor tells the students, "One advantage of this type of nest is that the eggs are well protected."

8 Detail Question

Ⓒ The professor notes, "Some water birds even make floating platform nests."

9 Connecting Content Question

Cavity Nest: ① Cup Nest: ③, ④ Suspended Nest: ② About the cavity nest, the professor says, "Passerines, woodpeckers, owls, and parrots are common cavity nest dwellers or builders." Regarding the cup nest, the professor notes, "A cup nest is usually made of grass and twigs and, uh, on occasion, mud. Some are placed where tree branches can support them from the bottom or by the rims of the cup. Other cup nests are attached to the sides of trees or buildings by mud or sometimes the bird's saliva, which forms a kind of glue." She also mentions, "Cup nests with shallow sides are occasionally called saucer nests or plate nests." As for the suspended nest, the professor comments, "A small hole in the nest allows access in and out."

Lecture #2 [10-14]

| Script |

Listen to part of a lecture in a history class.

M Professor: Until the late 1800s, Japan was an agricultural society with little industrial production. Yet within a few short decades, it rose to become a global power that defeated China and Russia militarily. By the 1930s, Japan was on its way to wider conquests in China and throughout the Pacific Ocean. How this came about is one of the more fascinating lessons of modern history. Basically, uh, the Japanese abruptly threw away hundreds of years of tradition and embraced change. It wasn't easy, and there was resistance. But in the end, Japan became a great power with one of the world's top economies today.

It started when Japan opened its doors to international trade. For centuries, Japan was a closed society, and few foreigners were allowed to visit. Since the early 1600s, a series of strong leaders, called shoguns, from the Tokugawa family had ruled Japan. There was an emperor, but he had little to do with actually ruling the country. Most of the people were peasant farmers ruled by local lords. Then, changes started taking place in 1853. Prior to that, foreign powers had tried to entice Japan to open its ports. They wanted both to trade with the Japanese and to be able to resupply their ships in Japanese ports. Yet the shoguns had constantly rejected their requests. Finally, the Americans decided to show the Japanese what real power was. In 1853, Commodore Matthew Perry led a naval force of four warships into Tokyo Harbor. The Japanese were awed by the large ships with powerful cannons. Keep in mind that actions such as these, called gunboat diplomacy, were common at that time. Under the threat of violence, the Japanese agreed to open two ports to American ships for them to take on supplies. Once that happened, other foreign powers rushed in. By 1860, several nations were trading in Japan.

W Student: Why didn't the Japanese resist? I mean, uh, it sounds obvious that they didn't want to have anything to do with other countries.

M: They didn't resist because they would have lost. The fact of the matter is that Japan was so backward that it hardly had any modern tools of war. Its fighting forces still depended on swords, spears, and bows and arrows. There were few guns in Japan because the samurai class of warriors and leaders rejected them. But suddenly, um, there was a great outcry about foreigners on Japanese land. Blame was placed on the shoguns for not handling the matter better. In late 1867, the last shogun stepped down, clearing the way for the emperor to take power. In January 1868, Emperor Mutsuhito took control of the government. He chose the name Meiji, which means "enlightened rule," for his period of rule. His reign, which lasted the next forty-five years, would be called the Meiji Era. The events that led to the return of the emperor to power are known as the Meiji Restoration.

The emperor was aware that Japan had been humiliated by the foreign powers due to its weakness. His government immediately set about reforming Japan by learning everything it could from those countries. Japan sent ambassadors to foreign nations, had students enroll in foreign universities, and made engineers travel abroad to learn about industrial practices. The Japanese basically copied everything they could or hired foreign experts to teach them how to do things. Soon, Japan had modern roads, railways, electric power, telegraph and telephone systems, and a growing industrial base.

W: How quickly did Japan modernize?

M: Pretty fast. For example, the first railway in the country, um, from Tokyo to Yokohama, was completed in 1872. By 1914, the country had more than 11,000 kilometers of railways. By that time, it also had increasing coal production, growing steel and shipbuilding industries, and thousands of other small industries. The emperor oversaw the introduction of other reforms to ensure that his work couldn't be undone. He created a constitution and parliament based on Western models, called for universal education for children, and built a modern navy and army. The Japanese constitution and army were based on Germany's, the navy on Britain's, and the education system on the United States'.

Not everyone was happy with these changes. The samurai class was particularly displeased since much of its power was based on the old ways. During the first month of the Meiji Restoration, the samurai started a rebellion. A civil war lasting eighteen months promptly began. The imperial army finally defeated the rebels in June 1869.

Attempts to control the former ruling class and samurai by taking away their rights led to more open rebellion in 1877. After nine months of civil war, the imperial army again defeated the samurai rebels. Not all of the samurai rebelled though. 🎧14 Many embraced the changes, and the emperor rewarded them with high places in his regime. They became leaders in different areas of government, industry, education, and the army and navy. By the 1890s, Japan was ready to show the world how powerful it was. **As we're about to see, its chosen path was war.**

Answer Explanations

10 Making Inferences Question

Ⓒ The professor says, "There was an emperor, but he had little to do with actually ruling the country."

11 Understanding Organization Question

Ⓑ The professor tells the students, "In 1853, Commodore Matthew Perry led a naval force of four warships into Tokyo Harbor. The Japanese were awed by the large ships with powerful cannons. Keep in mind that actions such as these, called gunboat diplomacy, were common at that time. Under the threat of violence, the Japanese agreed to open two ports to American ships for them to take on supplies."

12 Understanding Function Question

Ⓑ The professor talks about the events of the Meiji Era to let the students know how Japan was able to modernize so quickly.

13 Detail Question

②, ④ The professor lectures, "The emperor oversaw the introduction of other reforms to ensure that his work couldn't be undone. He created a constitution and parliament based on Western models, called for universal education for children, and built a modern navy and army."

14 Understanding Attitude Question

Ⓐ In stating, "As we're about to see, its chosen path was war," the professor implies that he is going to continue lecturing to the class.

PART 2

Conversation [1–4]

| Script |

Listen to part of a conversation between a student and an art museum curator.

M Student: Ms. Bird, I finished the proposal for this spring's student art exhibition. I was heading to your office to give it to you.

W Art Museum Curator: Thanks, Adam. I don't have time to

read it now, so would you mind giving me the highlights? I've got a few minutes before I head off to lunch with some faculty members.

M: Sure. First, I thought a lot about charging admission to this year's exhibition, and I feel we should do that on a conditional basis.

W: Conditional? What do you mean?

M: I don't believe any students, faculty, or staff members here at the school should be charged entry. According to last year's numbers, people associated with the school comprised more than seventy percent of all attendees. If we charge them to enter, we might see attendance decline significantly.

W: Yes, that makes sense. And most students would argue that their student activities fees should cover admission to events like that.

M: I argued that exact point in my proposal.

W: Great. I'm glad we agree.

M: Me, too. Now, uh, I indicated that some people should pay admission. In my opinion, we should charge a small fee of, uh two or three dollars, to anyone not associated with the school. I don't think too many people will mind paying a small amount of money. We can hang up a sign noting that all proceeds will go to the museum or to benefitting students.

W: That makes sense. We might not make much money, but every dollar counts during this time of university budget cuts. I approve. What else do you have for me?

M: Okay, this is a bit more controversial . . .

W: Yeah? What?

M: ⌂4 I suggest that we allow students to sell their paintings at the exhibition.

W: You want to put price tags on the paintings? **I don't think that's appropriate.**

M: No, no, nothing like that. What I mean is that if someone approaches you or another museum employee and inquires about buying a painting, the student who made it should be permitted to negotiate a price.

W: Why do you say that?

M: Many of us in the Art Department aspire to become professional artists. I've made tons of paintings, but I have yet to sell even one. Honestly, it would be a huge confidence builder if I were able to sell something. And, uh, to be frank, some of us could use the money.

W: You probably wouldn't make much.

M: I don't care if somebody buys one of my paintings for twenty dollars. In addition to putting some money in my pocket, it would indicate that someone likes my work enough to pay for it. That would mean a great deal to me. Several other students whose work will be exhibited have spoken to me about that, and they also hope you approve.

W: Hmm . . . Okay, I see your point. But this is something I can't approve by myself. I'll have to arrange a meeting and talk to someone in the university administration about it. When I attend the meeting, you'll go with me and make your argument. So have your talking points ready. Okay?

M: I'll be prepared. Just let me know when the meeting is.

Answer Explanations

1 Gist-Content Question
Ⓒ The speakers are mostly talking about some preparations for an upcoming art exhibition.

2 Detail Question
Ⓓ The student states, "In my opinion, we should charge a small fee of, uh two or three dollars, to anyone not associated with the school."

3 Making Inferences Question
Ⓐ The woman remarks, "We might not make much money, but every dollar counts during this time of university budget cuts." She therefore implies that the university has less money to spend these days due to budget cuts.

4 Understanding Function Question
Ⓒ When the student says, "I suggest that we allow students to sell their paintings at the exhibition," the woman responds by commenting, "I don't think that's appropriate." Her response is therefore meant to reject the student's suggestion.

Lecture [5–9]

| Script |

Listen to part of a lecture in a sociology class.

M Professor: Fast food is typically defined as food which can be bought cheaply and served quickly, thereby making it very convenient. Typical modern fast-food items include hamburgers, hotdogs, French fries, pizza, fried chicken, fish and chips, and sandwiches. We often think of fast food as a modern invention, but it actually has deep roots in history. Only in the last hundred years, however, have fast-food restaurants become part of the food-service scene.

In the past, people frequently purchased food from street vendors. In ancient Rome, most multistory apartments lacked cooking facilities, so people would buy bread, wine, and meals from street vendors. In addition, noodles purchased at street stalls have been a staple of Chinese society for centuries. In England, fish and chips sold at takeaway stalls became popular in the late 1800s. In the United States, numerous food stalls offered hotdogs, hamburgers, sandwiches, and fried chicken for sale. They could be found at festivals, fairs, and amusement parks such as Coney Island in New York.

In the early twentieth century, the automat became popular in big cities. This was a place that had rows of machines which were like modern vending machines. However, they sold premade meals. People could buy items like, uh, like sandwiches, soups, salads, and some desserts. They could look inside a small window to see the food they wanted. Then, they inserted some coins, took out their food, and either ate it at nearby tables or took it to their workplaces or homes. The first large automat opened in New York City in 1902.

W Student: The automat sounds kind of like a combination of a fast-food restaurant and a cafeteria.

M: There are many who call the automat the beginning of the fast-food industry. But other historians argue that the distinction goes to White Castle. The first White Castle restaurant opened in Wichita, Kansas, in 1921. It had the hallmarks of modern fast-food restaurants. Nevertheless, it was similar to the automat. Most of the food was precooked, so service was quick. People could take the food out or eat it at the restaurant. There was no table service, and diners didn't have to leave a tip. The main difference between White Castle and the automat was the kind of food diners could order. While the automat had many items for sale, White Castle served a small number of them, and it made the hamburger the main meal. Eventually, automats went out of business while fast-food restaurants thrived. So I think we can see which model was more popular.

Now, uh, many people believe that fast-food restaurants spread rapidly around the world. But that's far from the truth. In fact, eating at fast-food restaurants didn't become popular for a few decades after their introduction. Many people actually looked down on the idea. Going to a restaurant was considered a big event for most families. They dressed up, sat at a nice table, ordered from an extensive menu, and had a waiter or waitress serve them. In order to change people's perception of fast-food restaurants, White Castle made its restaurants attractive. They were painted white and looked pristine. Their interiors were clean, and diners could see the cooks making the food.

Soon afterward, the notion of franchising developed. People interested in running a fast-food restaurant would be trained and helped by a parent company such as White Castle. Then, they would open their own establishment and run it. Franchising helped the fast-food industry develop and also let each company have a set of standards practiced at all of its restaurants.

Gradually, the idea of fast food as a meal option grew in the United States and around the world. This was aided by the booming auto industry and the lack of time in many people's busy lives. For people who were always on the go, fast food became convenient for them. By the 1950s, having a car was the norm for most families.

Owning a car meant they could drive to a fast-food restaurant, get their food, drive home, and eat it before it got cold. There were also many drive-in restaurants. A&W was one. People parked their cars, they ordered from a speaker or from a waitress on roller skates, and their meals were brought to their cars. Drive-through service soon followed. People could order their food, pick it up, and pay for it without having to leave their cars.

It was around the 1950s that many famous fast-food places started. Among them were McDonald's, Burger King, and KFC. McDonald's first used the idea of fast-food assembly lines, which most other fast-food establishments quickly copied. Today, fast-food restaurants serve billions of meals each year. There are some drawbacks to fast food though. The primary one concerns the healthiness of the food. Let's take a ten-minute break, and when we come back, I'll talk about some negative effects.

Answer Explanations

5 Gist-Content Question

Ⓓ During the entire lecture, the professor mainly discusses the development of fast food from the past to the present.

6 Detail Question

Ⓐ About the automat, the professor remarks, "In the early twentieth century, the automat became popular in big cities. This was a place that had rows of machines which were like modern vending machines. However, they sold premade meals. People could buy items like, uh, like sandwiches, soups, salads, and some desserts. They could look inside a small window to see the food they wanted. Then, they inserted some coins, took out their food, and either ate it at nearby tables or took it to their workplaces or homes."

7 Understanding Organization Question

Ⓒ While discussing White Castle, the professor focuses mostly on describing its contributions to the fast-food industry.

8 Detail Question

Ⓓ The professor lectures, "Gradually, the idea of fast food as a meal option grew in the United States and around the world. This was aided by the booming auto industry and the lack of time in many people's busy lives. For people who were always on the go, fast food became convenient for them. By the 1950s, having a car was the norm for most families. Owning a car meant they could drive to a fast-food restaurant, get their food, drive home, and eat it before it got cold."

9 Making Inferences Question

Ⓒ At the end of the lecture, the professor states, "Let's take a ten-minute break, and when we come back, I'll talk about some negative effects."

Answers

A

1 steep
2 aligned
3 sophomore
4 proceeds
5 appealing

B

| 1 b | 2 a | 3 b | 4 b | 5 a |
| 6 b | 7 a | 8 a | 9 b | 10 b |

Practice with Short Passages
p. 102

A

| Answers | 1 ⒟ | 2 ⒝ |

| Script |

Listen to part of a conversation between a student and a professor.

W1 Student: Professor Steele, I have a question for you concerning our class.

W2 Professor: Sure. What do you want to know about?

W1: ∩² It concerns the textbook. I wonder how important the book is to the class and if you think I should buy it or not.

W2: **You don't already have it?** You can't possibly be serious, can you? I mean, uh, this is fourth week of class. How are you doing your reading assignments?

W1: Oh, uh, I haven't actually done them yet. I'm basically just making sure I take good notes in class. I figure that I can review them before the test.

W2: But, uh, not everything that's going to be on your tests is covered in class. You are supposed to do the reading in the textbook to get more information. So, uh, why don't you have the book yet?

W1: Well, I went to the bookstore, but it was sold out. And then I went to the library to get a copy of the book, but both copies were checked out. So I didn't know what to do.

W2: You know, there are several used bookstores within walking distance of the campus. I'm sure you could find it there. And I know for a fact that it's available to order online. You could probably get it used and pay a fairly low price if you did that.

W1: Oh, uh . . . I never even thought of those options. I'll visit a website and order it today.

W2: Good. And please make sure you get the books for all your classes. They are important, and you won't do well in your classes without them.

Answer Explanations

1 ⒟ In talking about the textbook, the professor remarks, "You know, there are several used bookstores within walking distance of the campus. I'm sure you could find it there."

2 ⒝ The professor expresses her surprise in asking the student the question. In this case, the professor's tone of voice can help show that she is surprised.

B

| Answers | 1 Ⓐ | 2 Ⓒ |

| Script |

Listen to part of a conversation between a student and a student housing office employee.

M Student Housing Office Employee: Hello. You've been waiting for your turn for quite a while. ∩¹ Thanks for your patience.

W Student: It's all right. I guess you must be busy like this all the time.

M: **Pretty much.** So what can I help you with today?

W: Um, I was told by the resident assistant in my dorm that I need to speak with someone in this office. My name is Samantha Jenkins. You know, uh, I'm not sure what this is about.

M: All right, let me look you up on the computer . . . Ah, here you are. You currently live in room 409 of Marconi Hall?

W: Yes, that's correct.

M: Okay, apparently, somebody noticed that you have too many possessions in your room. You have a couple of sofas and some other furniture in addition to the furniture that the room comes with. Is that right?

W: Er, yes. Is there a problem with that?

M: Actually, yes, there is. ∩² You see, uh, if you have too much furniture in your room, it's considered a fire hazard. So you need to remove some of the items at once.

W: A fire hazard? **That's a joke, isn't it?**

M: I'm afraid not. If you don't remove at least one of the sofas by the end of the day, you'll be forced to leave your room. I'm really sorry that I can't give you more time. But I have to follow the rules.

W: Well, this puts me in something of a bind. Hmm . . . I guess I can remove one of the sofas, but I'm not sure where I can put it. I'll have to figure something out.

Answer Explanations

1 Ⓐ When the man responds, "Pretty much," he is acknowledging that the student is correct when she says that he must be busy all the time.

2 Ⓒ When the student asks, "That's a joke, isn't it?" she is expressing her disbelief at the man's comment that she needs to remove some furniture from her room.

C

| Script |

Listen to part of a lecture in a zoology class.

W Professor: There are many reasons that zoologists count wildlife populations. A major one is to understand what species and how many of each species live in a certain area. A second important reason is to understand the range of a species' habitat and to learn how many animals of that species the habitat can support. A third reason is to understand in which seasons various species reside in certain areas. Coupled with the last reason is the need to understand wildlife migration patterns.

Unfortunately, counting animals in the wild is hard. Zoologists can't simply stand near a pride of lions and start counting. That's, uh, that's a great way to get eaten. After all, wild animals are dangerous, and getting close to them isn't always easy. Nor is doing so advisable. Another problem is that animals frequently travel in huge herds and are constantly moving, so it's impossible to count individual members. A third problem is that many animals hide, so it's difficult to determine how many are in a location. A final problem is that many species are active only at night. As a result, counting nocturnal animals is problematic.

Nevertheless, zoologists can make good estimates of animal populations. We do this in three main ways. They are called total counts, sample counts, and index counts. A total count is an attempt to count the exact number of animals in a small area. Total counts are primarily used for fenced-in areas such as wildlife parks since biologists know that animals can't leave or enter those places. A sample count is done by counting the total number of animals in a small area and then using the sample numbers to guess the total number in a larger area. 🎧2 This method makes two assumptions. First, sample counting assumes that all the animals in the sample area are seen and counted. Second, it assumes that the animals are evenly spread out in the larger area. **Obviously, this method is less than perfect.** The third way, uh, index counts, is a more indirect method. It employs statistics over a long period to make count estimates. One index count method is the hunting index. For example, if the number of hunters who successfully shoot a deer each season remains constant, then the deer population is presumed to be stable. But if some hunters fail to shoot any deer for several years, the population is considered to be declining.

M Student: Um, but how do zoologists physically count the animals? What do they do?

W: There are three primary methods. Scientists can walk through an area if it's not considered dangerous. Or they may use vehicles to drive through an area to provide them with mobility and safety. In other situations, they use airplanes to make low-level flights over a wide area. Airplanes let them cover more ground and see more animals. Of course, they're expensive, and it can be difficult to observe animals while flying above areas with lots of foliage.

Answer Explanations

1 Ⓐ The professor describes an indirect counting method when talking about the hunting index.

2 Ⓒ In stating, "Obviously, this method is less than perfect," the professor is letting the students know that there are flaws in the sample counting method.

D

| Script |

Listen to part of a lecture in an architecture class.

M Professor: 🎧1 Can anyone tell me what this castle looks like . . . ? **I see a lot of hands going up.** How about you in the front row?

W1 Student: That looks like the castle at Disney World.

M: Correct. This is Neuschwanstein Castle in Bavaria, Germany. It was the inspiration for Walt Disney for the castle he had built at Disney World. Neuschwanstein Castle was constructed by King Ludwig the Second of Bavaria between 1869 and 1886. Ludwig wanted the castle to be a personal home, so it wasn't a military structure like castles traditionally were. He paid for most of the cost of building it from his own pockets but had to borrow money as well.

Ludwig chose a high hill for the castle. Construction began in 1869 with the removal of the ruins of two older castles on the site. Ludwig had often visited those ruins as a boy and had fallen in love with the place. Look at the pictures here . . . Isn't the view spectacular . . . ? You can understand why he loved the place so much . . .

Now, let's look at the exterior . . . Much of the castle is built of concrete and brick . . . but there's a limestone covering which gives it its white sheen. There's also plenty of sandstone and marble on the outer layers. It's rather elongated and narrow due to the dimensions of the hill. The castle was built in sections. After the first part was completed, Ludwig moved into it. 🎧2 As for the style of the exterior, it's often described as a combination of several, including Romanesque Revival, Gothic, and Byzantine.

W2 Student: I'm sorry, sir, but what is Romanesque Revival?

M: Ah, right. **We haven't covered that yet.** It was a nineteenth-century style similar to the Romanesque style of the eleventh and twelfth centuries. Both styles are noted for their use of round-shaped arches for windows. We'll cover it more in next week's class.

Now, onto the castle's interior. It was never completed during Ludwig's lifetime. There were plans for a few hundred rooms, but only a dozen or so were finished before Ludwig died. He had intended for the rooms to have a style that expressed his love of Germanic history and the operas of Richard Wagner. But Ludwig's ambitions caused him to go into debt. The main reason was that he kept changing his mind about the castle's design. By 1886, he owed fourteen million marks, a tremendous sum at the time. He requested a loan from the Bavarian government but was rejected. The government tried to have him declared mentally unfit and removed from power, but Ludwig resisted. Then, on June 13, 1886, he drowned in a nearby lake. Some suggested that he was murdered.

Anyway, after Ludwig's death, his family opened the castle to paying visitors. This let them pay off all the debt. Now, let me show you some of the rooms that were completed. I think you'll be impressed.

Answer Explanations

1 Ⓐ When the professor says, "I see lots of hands going up," he is implying that many students know the answer to the question he asked.

2 Ⓒ When the professor says, "We haven't covered that yet," it can be inferred that he is going to discuss Romanesque Revival at a later time. The key word in the sentence is "yet."

Practice with Long Passages   p. 106

A

Answers	1 Ⓒ	2 Ⓑ	3 Ⓒ

| Script |

Listen to part of a conversation between a student and the dean of students.

W Dean of Students: Please come in and have a seat, Mr. Harper. I'm Jodie Schuler, the dean of students here. It's a pleasure to meet you.

M Student: It's a pleasure to meet you as well, Dean Schuler.

W: So . . . you're here because you're one of the three finalists for the Jason Walker Scholarship, which is awarded on an annual basis. This is one of the most prestigious scholarships at the school. It goes only to students who have outstanding grades, participate in extracurricular activities, and do volunteer work in the community.

M: Yes, ma'am. It's a real honor simply to be nominated for the award.

W: You are correct about that. ∩3 Now, as for the award itself, it not only covers your tuition and room and board for an entire year, but it also provides you with a monthly stipend of $1,500. That's done so that the winner can devote himself, uh, or herself, to academics and not have to work part time during the semester.

M: **That's one of the most appealing aspects to me.** I'd love to be able to focus solely on my schoolwork and not have to worry about making money.

W: All right. Well, let me ask you the question I asked the other two candidates . . .

M: Yes?

W: Why should we select you and not the other nominees?

M: Oh, good question. Well, I believe my academic record speaks for itself. I've also been deeply involved in both school life and the local community.

W: Yes, but so have the others.

M: I realize that. However, I think my family circumstances should be considered, too. Since I was ten, it has just been my father, my two younger sisters, and me. I've helped my dad raise my sisters, and I've assisted my family financially by working since I was eleven.

W: Are you still doing that now?

M: Yes, ma'am. I send home more than half of the money I earn each month to help out my little sisters, both of whom are attending high school.

W: Is there anything else you believe should be a factor when we determine to whom to award this scholarship?

M: Yes, there's something else I'd like to mention. In fact, I didn't write about it in my application essay, but I'd like to discuss it with you now if you don't mind.

Answer Explanations

1 Ⓒ The entire conversation is an interview that the dean is conducting with the student regarding a scholarship the student hopes to receive.

2 Ⓑ The student tells the dean, "I send home more than half of the money I earn each month to help out my little sisters, both of whom are attending high school."

3 Ⓒ When the student points out that the monthly stipend is "one of the most appealing aspects" to him, he is stating why he is interested in winning the scholarship.

Dictation

W: <u>Why should we</u> select you and not the other nominees?

M: Oh, good question. Well, I believe my academic record <u>speaks for itself</u>. I've also been deeply <u>involved</u> in both school life and the local community.

W: Yes, but so have the others.

M: I realize that. However, I think my family circumstances should be considered, too. Since I was ten, it has just been my father, my two younger sisters, and me. I've helped my dad raise my sisters, and I've assisted my family financially by working since I was eleven.

W: Are you still doing that now?

M: Yes, ma'am. I send home more than half of the money I earn each month to help out my little sisters, both of whom are attending high school.

B

Answers

1 Coniferous Trees: ②, ③, ④ Deciduous Trees: ①
2 ⓒ   3 ⓓ   4 Ⓐ

| Script |

Listen to part of a lecture in an environmental science class.

W Professor: Some of the world's greatest forests are the taiga forests that stretch across most of Northern Europe, Russia, Alaska, and Canada. Oh, uh, in case you don't know, another name for a taiga forest is a boreal forest. Taken together, the North American and Eurasian taiga biomes comprise the largest forested region in the world. It represents nearly thirty percent of the world's total forest covering. The taiga is home to plants and animals that must be hardy because conditions there are so harsh. Winter is long and frigid with temperatures often averaging far below zero degrees Celsius. Summer is short, warm, and wet with plenty of rain and temperatures seldom rising above twenty degrees Celsius. Spring and autumn are so short in these northern latitudes that it's often hard to identify when they begin and end.

Unlike other biomes, such as, um, oceans and tropical forests, there is little diversity of species in the taiga. The main plant species there is the coniferous tree. The most common types are spruces, pines, and firs. In the more southern parts, however, some mixed coniferous and deciduous forests can be found. Common deciduous trees include oaks, willows, birches, and alders. Yet in most of the taiga, the soil is too thin and acidic to support large deciduous forests. Just to remind you, deciduous trees lose their leaves in fall while coniferous trees don't.

Coniferous trees, however, thrive in such conditions. They have several advantages over deciduous trees in the taiga. First off, they have long, thin, waxy needles rather than broad leaves. The waxy coating allows them to retain water better. The coating also protects them from freezing cold, so they never fall off. Any amount of sunlight at any time of the year allows the needles instantly to begin the process of photosynthesis, too. The dark colors of the trees additionally help them absorb heat from the sun.

Finally, coniferous trees in the taiga grow close together in vast forests. This closeness provides protection from the harsh winds which blow in winter. 🎧4 So you can see that they're tough enough to survive that far north.

M Student: Wouldn't the fact that the trees grow so close to one another make them vulnerable to forest fires?

W: **It's a logical assumption to make, so you're thinking the right way, but that's not what happens in reality.** The reason is that conifers growing in the taiga have adapted and established defenses against forest fires. They have thick bark, so the inner vital parts of the trees can survive fires. The outer branches and needles may burn off, yet the trees can still survive. And you may be surprised to learn that fires can be good for forests. They clear away underbrush, allowing new growth. And burning the tops of trees allows sunlight to reach lower down in the forest, which stimulates new tree growth.

Okay, um, how about the animals living in the taiga . . . ? Most of them are mammals, birds, and fish. Few reptiles or amphibians live there because they're cold blooded, so they can't survive the freezing winters. Among the largest mammals in the taiga are elk, deer, moose, reindeer, and caribou. Predators such as the lynx, fox, wolverine, bear, bobcat, and wolf live there as well. Smaller mammals include rabbits, squirrels, and voles. All of these mammals have thick fur and bodies well adapted to the cold. Some of the prey animals also change their fur color, which helps them hide from predators. The snowshoe hare, for instance, is dark brown in summer but has white hair in winter.

Birds are the most common other type of animal in the taiga. They usually flock there in huge numbers in summertime. One reason is that there are many bogs and swamps in the taiga. These watery areas breed plenty of insects, which the birds feed on. But when it starts getting cold again, most of the birds fly south to warmer lands.

Answer Explanations

1 Coniferous Trees: ②, ③, ④ Deciduous Trees: ①
   About coniferous trees, the professor says, "Any amount of sunlight at any time of the year allows the needles instantly to begin the process of photosynthesis, too." She also remarks that the acidic soil is good for them. Finally, she notes, "The reason is that conifers growing in the taiga have adapted and established defenses against forest fires. They have thick bark, so the inner vital parts of the trees can survive fires." As for deciduous trees, the professor mentions, "In the more southern parts, however, some mixed coniferous and deciduous forests can be found."

2 ⓒ The professor states, "All of these mammals have thick fur and bodies well adapted to the cold."

3 ⓓ The professor comments, "They usually flock there in huge numbers in summertime. One reason is that there

are many bogs and swamps in the taiga. These watery areas breed plenty of insects, which the birds feed on."

4 (A) When the professor responds, "It's a logical assumption to make, so you're thinking the right way, but that's not what happens in reality," she is giving praise to the student for his use of logic even though he got the answer wrong.

Dictation

❶ Oh, uh, <u>in case you don't know</u>, another name for a taiga forest is a boreal forest.

❷ It's a <u>logical</u> assumption to make, so you're thinking the <u>right way</u>, but that's not what happens <u>in reality</u>.

❸ They usually flock there in huge numbers in summertime. <u>One reason is that</u> there are many bogs and swamps in the taiga.

iBT Practice Test   p. 110

Answers

PART 1

1 (B)   2 (C)   3 (D)   4 (C)   5 (D)

6 (B)   7 (A)   8 (B)   9 (B)   10 (C)

11 (A)   12 Fact: [1], [2]   Not a Fact: [3], [4]

13 (A)   14 (B)

PART 2

1 (B)   2 (B)   3 [2], [4]   4 (C)   5 (B)

6 (D)   7 (B)   8 (C)   9 (C)

PART 1

Conversation [1–4]

| Script |

Listen to part of a conversation between a student and a language center employee.

M Student: Good afternoon, ma'am. I wonder if you're hiring any student employees for the summer.

W Language Center Employee: Hi. Yes, we sometimes require part-time workers. What kind of job are you looking for?

M: I was hoping to be employed here as a language tutor. One of my friends worked here a year ago. Her name is Karen Washington. She told me there are often students who pay to get tutored in foreign languages during the summer session. So, uh, I thought I'd see if you're hiring.

W: Ah, sure, I remember Karen. She was one of our best French language tutors until she graduated. How's she doing?

M: She's doing great. She's currently attending graduate school in Paris.

W: Good for her. And, yes, Karen was right about what she told you. We do hire students as tutors.

M: Excellent. How do I apply for a job?

W: Hold on a moment. I have to tell you a few things about the positions first.

M: Oh, all right. What do I need to know?

W: To begin with, these are not regular positions like, uh, say, working at the library or something. So our workers don't get assigned regular shifts.

M: How do they work then?

W: Basically, our language tutors get work if a student wants to learn the language they are proficient in. If there are a couple of students interested in learning a language, a tutor might only get three or four hours of work a week. On the other hand, if you happen to know a language that's in high demand, it's possible that you could work up to fifteen or twenty hours a week.

M: I see. So, uh, this isn't something that I should do as my primary job, right?

W: Exactly. If you're hoping for steady employment, you ought to find a regular job somewhere else. Then, you can apply here to supplement your income by working a few extra hours a week. Out of curiosity, what language are you hoping to work as a tutor in?

M: Italian. I lived there for five years and speak it fluently. 🎧4 I'm also getting a minor in Italian Literature. I figure that if I tutor students in it, I can help maintain my speaking and writing skills. It's a pretty popular language, so I imagine there's a good amount of interest in it.

W: **Not as much as there is for French or Spanish.** We'll probably get, um, three or four students asking for tutoring in it during the summer session. At least, that's how many we've gotten the past couple of years.

M: Ah, that's not too many. Do you have another Italian tutor on the staff?

W: Not anymore. He's about to graduate, so he stopped working here. So, um, assuming you can pass a fluency test, you would be our only Italian tutor.

M: A test? Sure, I can do that. Would you like me to take it now? I have plenty of time for that.

W: Oh, I don't conduct the tests myself. I need to make the arrangements with one of the professors in the Italian Language Department to give it to you. It will be a combination of reading, writing, speaking, and listening. When are you available to be tested?

M: Anytime in the afternoon next week is fine with me.

1 Gist-Content Question

Ⓑ Most of the conversation is about a job that the student wants to have at the language center during the summer.

2 Detail Question

Ⓒ The student comments, "One of my friends worked here a year ago. Her name is Karen Washington. She told me there are often students who pay to get tutored in foreign languages during the summer session."

3 Understanding Function Question

Ⓓ About the test the student needs to take, the employee remarks, "Oh, I don't conduct the tests myself. I need to make the arrangements with one of the professors in the Italian Language Department to give it to you."

4 Understanding Function Question

Ⓒ The student states that there are probably many students who want to learn Italian, and the woman responds, "Not as much as there is for French and Spanish." In saying that, she responds negatively to the student's statement.

Lecture #1 [5-9]

| Script |

Listen to part of a lecture in a history class.

M Professor: After the United States purchased the Louisiana Territory from France in 1803, the size of the country practically doubled overnight. President Thomas Jefferson naturally wanted to know about the land, so he commissioned an expedition to explore it. It lasted from 1804 to 1806 and is known as the Lewis and Clark Expedition. Two army officers, Meriwether Lewis and William Clark, led the group, which mostly consisted of soldiers. Their primary objectives were to map the western lands, to observe the animals and plants there, to make contact with the native tribes and to establish good relations with them, to find a water route between the eastern and western parts of the continent, and to establish the sovereignty of the United States in the region.

How did they do this . . . ? Well, first, they went to St. Louis, which is located alongside the Mississippi River, to establish a base camp. Lewis and Clark planned to use riverboats to row up the Missouri River. That would take them into the northwestern region of the Louisiana Territory. You can see the route they took if you look at the map on page, um, page forty-seven in your texts. Go ahead and check it out . . . They left St. Louis on May 14, 1804, and didn't return until September 1806. The expedition seemed to be blessed with good fortune. During the entire journey, they lost but a single man, who suffered a ruptured appendix. Along the way, they met several native tribes, who were, uh, for the most part, friendly. 🎧9 The natives helped the expedition survive and reach its goals by providing guides, supplies, and many horses on one occasion. Most of the help was provided when the members of the expedition traded various items they were carrying.

W Student: How did they communicate with the natives?

M: **Badly on occasion.** The native tribes in the upper Missouri River region spoke a variety of dialects. But, again, luck was with them. They often ran into white men, um, trappers, hunters, and traders, who knew the natives well and could speak their languages. They also met a native woman named Sacajawea, who helped them tremendously. I'm sure that most of you are familiar with her name as she's one of the most famous women in early American history.

When winter set in, the expedition hadn't reached the upper Missouri yet, so they built a fort they called Fort Mandan to wait for the cold months to pass. They resumed their journey in early April 1805. It was then that they discovered there was no direct water route to the Pacific Ocean. So, uh, they failed in that objective but not through any fault of their own. The problem was that the mountain ranges in the west divide the western United States into two major watersheds. One leads to the Pacific Ocean while the other goes toward the Mississippi River and the Gulf of Mexico. The dividing line between the two is the Continental Divide.

Fortunately for the expedition, they managed to acquire horses from a native tribe to carry them over the mountains. Eventually, they found the Columbia River and followed it to the Pacific Ocean, which they reached on November 20, 1805. Once again, they built a fort for the winter. Trading with the natives provided them with enough food to survive. In spring, they departed back east and made it to St. Louis in September 1806.

W: So was their mission a success or a failure?

M: Mostly a success. Now, they didn't find a water route to the Pacific because there was none. But they did find an overland route there. As for their other goals . . . Well, let's see . . . They made contact with dozens of native tribes and established friendly relations with most of them. Lewis and Clark mapped the region as they traveled and examined numerous species of plant and animal life. They drew 140 maps in total. The expedition discovered more than 100 species of animals and close to 200 species of plants. They also discovered the Yellowstone region and its wondrous geysers and spectacular sights.

Furthermore, they established American sovereignty over the land. To do that, they carried medals to give to the natives. They were called Indian Peace Medals and were frequently used to establish contact between Americans and the natives. Lewis and Clark carried ones with a picture of President Jefferson on one side and two outstretched hands shaking each other in a symbol of friendship. Remember that the expedition was very well armed. Even though they were a small group, the men were soldiers and carried plenty of firepower. They were able to awe the natives with it. Finally, the group constructed two forts, which helped them establish American control over the land. So to answer your question, I'd say that while not every objective was reached, the mission was a tremendous success and helped open the west to the millions of people who would eventually settle there in the next few decades.

Answer Explanations

5 Gist-Content Question

Ⓓ During his lecture, the professor focuses on how the Lewis and Clark Expedition managed to attain most of its objectives.

6 Understanding Function Question

Ⓑ The professor says, "You can see the route they took if you look at the map on page, um, page forty-seven in your texts. Go ahead and check it out."

7 Understanding Organization Question

Ⓐ The professor lectures, "It was then that they discovered there was no direct water route to the Pacific Ocean. So, uh, they failed in that objective but not through any fault of their own. The problem was that the mountain ranges in the west divide the western United States into two major watersheds. One leads to the Pacific Ocean while the other goes toward the Mississippi River and the Gulf of Mexico. The dividing line between the two is the Continental Divide."

8 Understanding Attitude Question

Ⓑ The professor says, "The expedition seemed to be blessed with good fortune," and, "But, again, luck was with them," which shows how he felt that the expedition was lucky at times.

9 Understanding Function Question

Ⓑ In stating, "Badly on occasion," the professor implies that the expedition members had trouble talking to the natives they met on their trip.

Lecture #2 [10–14]

| Script |

Listen to part of a lecture in a geology class.

W Professor: To understand why we have volcanoes and earthquakes, an understanding of the theory of plate tectonics is necessary. We studied that a couple of weeks ago, but let me review it really quickly just in case some of you forgot. According to the theory, the Earth's crust is comprised of a series of connecting plates. These plates rest on top of the mantle. The mantle, as you will recall, is not a solid piece but is instead a moving semi-liquid.

This causes the plates making up the crust to move. While doing that, they grind against one another and pull apart. These actions cause earthquakes and volcanoes. And the place where the majority of them occur is the Ring of Fire in the Pacific Ocean.

Now, um, it's called a ring, but it's more like an incomplete circle or a horseshoe. The Ring of Fire stretches for about 40,000 kilometers. It begins in southern Chile in South America. From there, it heads north through Central and North America and goes across Alaska to Siberia in Asia. Then, it goes down through Japan and Indonesia before ending around New Zealand. 🎧14 This path sees the majority of the world's earthquakes and volcanic activity.

M Student: **Pardon the interruption, but what do you mean when you say majority?**

W: Well, approximately 450 volcanoes exist along the ring. That's seventy-five percent of all the volcanoes in the world that have erupted in human history. On top of that, around ninety percent of all earthquakes occur there. As you can imagine, the Ring of Fire is an appropriate name for the area.

The largest part of the Ring of Fire follows the boundaries of the enormous Pacific Plate. Near the region of Central and South America are two smaller plates. The Cocos Plate is by Central America while the Nazca Plate is next to the west coast of South America. The movements of these three plates have created islands, mountain chains, and deep ocean trenches. The Andes Mountains, for instance, rose because the Pacific Plate is slowly sliding under the South American Plate. Now, um, these plates not only push together but also pull apart. When that happens underwater, it's called a seafloor spread. This action allows hot magma to bubble up from below. In one place, um, where the Cocos and Nazca plates are spreading apart from the Pacific Plate, a gigantic series of underwater volcanoes has formed. It's called the East Pacific Rise and extends from southern California almost all the way to Antarctica.

Most above-water volcanoes are located in the western Pacific region. Some famous ones are Japan's Mount Fuji, Krakatoa in Indonesia, and Mount Ruapehu in New Zealand. There are fewer volcanoes on the eastern edge of the Ring of Fire. There are a few notable exceptions though. This includes Mount St. Helens in Washington, USA, which last erupted in 1980.

Another underwater feature is that the deepest parts of the world's oceans are in the Ring of Fire. Where the plates are sliding under one another, they form deep regions known as trenches. Some are found along the Central and South American coasts. A long one extends along the southern boundary of Alaska's Aleutian Islands. Several deep trenches lie to the east of Japan. The deepest of all is the Marianas Trench, which is east of Guam. It's almost 11,000 meters deep. To imagine how deep that is, imagine Mount Everest, the world's highest mountain. If it sat in the Marianas Trench, its peak would still be 2,000 meters beneath the surface.

As for earthquakes, they occur all along the Ring of Fire. Most happen along well-known fault lines, which are places where plates rub against other ones. When plates on fault lines suddenly move, they release tremendous amounts of energy. The San Andreas Fault in California, USA, is one famous fault. Major earthquakes often happen in New Zealand, Indonesia, Japan, Alaska, and Chile.

Millions of people live in the region covered by the Ring of Fire. Their lives are in constant danger due to all the tectonic activity. Enormous sums of money have been spent preparing for earthquakes and volcanoes. Let's use Japan to illustrate this point. It has some of the best earthquake warning systems. And Japanese building laws require buildings to be able to withstand earthquakes. Yet it still suffers when they hit. In 1995, an earthquake hit the city of Kobe and killed more than 6,000 people. The powerful earthquake in 2011 unleashed a tsunami that killed more than 15,000 people. I suppose that if Japan were less prepared, more people would have died. But it's still unfortunate that so many lives were lost due to these natural disasters. And it's highly likely that even more will die when huge earthquakes hit and powerful volcanoes erupt. Let me tell you about some powerful volcanic eruptions that happened in the Ring of Fire now to let you know how deadly they can be . . .

Answer Explanations

10 Gist-Purpose Question

ⓒ The professor comments, "To understand why we have volcanoes and earthquakes, an understanding of the theory of plate tectonics is necessary."

11 Understanding Organization Question

ⓐ The professor remarks, "The movements of these three plates have created islands, mountain chains, and deep ocean trenches. The Andes Mountains, for instance, rose because the Pacific Plate is slowly sliding under the South American Plate."

12 Detail Question

Fact: ①, ② Not a Fact: ③, ④
About the Ring of Fire, the professor says, "The movements of these three plates have created islands, mountain chains, and deep ocean trenches," and, "Most above-water volcanoes are located in the western Pacific region." However, the professor also states, "Well, approximately 450 volcanoes exist along the ring. That's seventy-five percent of all the volcanoes in the world that have erupted in human history." And she adds, "The largest part of the Ring of Fire follows the boundaries of the enormous Pacific Plate. Near the region of Central and South America are two smaller plates."

13 Detail Question

ⓐ The professor tells the students, "And Japanese building laws require buildings to be able to withstand earthquakes."

14 Understanding Function Question

ⓑ When the student states, "What do you mean when you say majority?" he is requesting that the professor be more specific about a comment that she just made.

PART 2
Conversation [1–4]

| Script |

Listen to part of a conversation between a student and a professor.

W Student: Professor Watkins, I've been thinking about the model bridge I have to create for your class, but I'm having some problems with it.

M Professor: What's the matter, Angie?

W: I was planning to create a suspension bridge, but I don't believe that's going to be possible.

M: Why not?

W: To be honest, it's going to take a serious investment of time, and I don't have much of that available this semester. I'm on the school's basketball team, and because we're doing really well this year, Coach Williamson is having us practice more than usual. She is convinced that we have a chance to go far in the playoffs this year.

M: Okay, I guess that's a legitimate excuse. Practice time is a matter out of your control unless you quit the team, and I don't want to see that happen.

W: Me neither. I'm on an athletic scholarship here. If I quit the team, I'd almost certainly have to drop out of school.

M: I understand. So . . . what type of model bridge are you thinking of building?

W: I thought a covered bridge would be nice. I'm from rural New England, and we've got them all over the place there. I've never really given them much thought from a design standpoint though. So I think this could be quite an educational experience.

M: Sure, I like the sound of that. But tell me . . . What do you know about covered bridges?

W: Not too much. However, I did some research last night and learned that most of them are truss bridges.

M: Do you know what that means?

W: Not exactly.

M: Okay . . . Look at this picture of a truss bridge here. What do you notice?

W: What stands out to me is that all of the supports are shaped like right triangles. Do they help make the bridge stronger?

M: That's a good guess. It's also a correct one. The trusses help distribute the weight of the entire bridge. That does a couple of things. First, it lets engineers design rather long bridges, so they can be built over wide rivers. Second, truss bridges can carry heavy loads, so they're able to support a great deal of weight.

W: That sounds cool. Okay, then why are so many bridges covered? I've never been able to figure that out. How does the cover help strengthen a bridge?

M: It doesn't. It serves another purpose. Let me see if you can figure it out . . . What are the covered bridges where you live made of?

W: Wood . . . Oh, I see. Wood rots, doesn't it?

M: Precisely. The purpose of a cover on a covered bridge is to ensure that the bridge itself lasts for a long time. When a wooden bridge doesn't have a cover and is exposed to the elements—you know, rain, wind, and snow—the wood it's made of weakens and needs to be completely replaced after around twenty years. However, if the bridge and the trusses are covered, like the bridges you're familiar with, then the structure can last much longer. A lot of the wood in covered bridges doesn't need to be replaced for a century or even longer. That's why so many of them look old. They, uh, they actually are old.

W: That's fascinating, sir. Thanks so much for your assistance. I'm definitely going to do my project on covered truss bridges now.

Answer Explanations

1 Gist-Purpose Question

Ⓑ The student mentions that she needs assistance with an assignment when she states, "Professor Watkins, I've been thinking about the model bridge I have to create for your class, but I'm having some problems with it."

2 Understanding Attitude Question

Ⓑ The professor shows that he understands why the student does not have much time because of the basketball team when he tells the student, "Okay, I guess that's a legitimate excuse. Practice time is a matter out of your control unless you quit the team, and I don't want to see that happen."

3 Detail Question

②, ④ About trusses, the professor remarks, "The trusses help distribute the weight of the entire bridge. That does a couple of things. First, it lets engineers design rather long bridges, so they can be built over wide rivers. Second, truss bridges can carry heavy loads, so they're able to support a great deal of weight."

4 Understanding Function Question

Ⓒ The student asks, "Okay, then why are so many bridges covered? I've never been able to figure that out. How does the cover help strengthen a bridge?" The

professor then responds by asking the student his own question. He says, "It doesn't. It serves another purpose. Let me see if you can figure it out . . . What are the covered bridges where you live made of?" He does that in order to have the student answer her own question, which she does.

Lecture [5-9]

| Script |

Listen to part of a lecture in a biology class.

W Professor: Yet another sense that animals share with humans is vision. Virtually every animal has some sort of vision receptors which allow it to see the world around it. In particular, vision permits animals to recognize objects and to assess them. For an animal, objects are viewed in a variety of ways. For example, they may be seen as food sources, as possible mates, as danger, such as, uh, predators, or perhaps as places to build homes or to hide from danger.

The advantage of sight for both animals and humans is that it's a sense which operates at a distance. Unlike touch, taste, and smell, animals don't have to get close to an object because they can see it from afar. They can therefore safely assess the nature of an object without getting too close to potential danger. So we can say that for animals, vision may have been an evolutionary step allowing them to survive.

Let's examine what animals' vision receptors are like . . . Some animals are only capable of distinguishing between light and dark. This is vision at its most basic form. Most animals, however, have highly sophisticated visual systems similar to what humans have. They have a similar eye structure with a round eyeball, a lens, a retina, and cones to distinguish colors. They have optic nerves which carry signals from the eye to the brain, which then interprets those signals. Some animals have only two eyes while others, like various insects, have multiple eyes. Animals typically have either binocular or monocular vision. An animal with its eyes on the sides of its head, which many birds have, has monocular vision. These animals can see well to the sides but not so well to the front. Other animals, especially mammals, have two eyes at the front of their heads. This gives them binocular vision, so they can see well in front of them but not as well to the sides.

M Student: Can animals see colors like humans?

W: It depends on the animal. Some can see the entire visual spectrum while others have limited color vision. Dogs and cats see color only in a few spectrums, so they can't see every color. But some animals have even better color sight than we do. You have to remember, um, that sight is the brain's interpretation of wavelengths of light as they enter the eye. Humans perceive light between 400 and 700 nanometers, which is mainly from the reds to the blues on the color spectrum. Many animals can see outside this range. Bees, for instance, can see in the ultraviolet range of light. They use this ability to see flowers and to know where the nectar in them is.

Here's something that I find interesting . . . Another aspect of animal vision is the use of camouflage. Many prey animals hide thanks to the color of their skin or fur being similar to that of their environment. You know, there are brown deer in forests and white rabbits in the Arctic. Other animals have color patterns that are designed to confuse predators. These patterns can blur the edges of the animals' bodies. We know that one way both people and animals pick out objects by sight is by noticing the edges of these objects. They make the objects stand out. But if the edges are blurred, they become more difficult to see. According to one theory, this is an effect of zebras' stripes. When many zebras are grazing together, their stripes form patterns that blur the outlines of individual zebras. So when lions or cheetahs stalk zebras, their focus is disrupted. They try to attack one zebra but get confused if the zebras are massed together. That's why they often pick out a lone zebra—one that is slower and has been left behind. The reason is that it's easier for them to see an animal all by itself.

One problem we biologists have in studying animal sight and how they perceive objects is knowing exactly what's going on in their eyes and brains. Experiments have shown that most animals react to visual stimuli in a certain way. Scientists have proved that animals can see and understand what an object is and can pick out that same object when it's placed with different ones. They can also recognize the same object in a variety of light levels, in different colors, and in different placements. This suggests that they build memories of these objects. However, sometimes animals cannot tell the difference between two different objects that belong to similar categories. Here's an example . . . Experiments done with monkeys showed they could recognize objects that were very different from one another. They could easily distinguish between pictures of flowers, human faces, fruits, birds, and other animals. But when shown pictures of two different flowers, they had trouble differentiating them.

Answer Explanations

5 Gist-Content Question

Ⓑ The professor mainly focuses on discussing various aspects of animal vision in her lecture.

6 Detail Question

Ⓓ The professor lectures, "An animal with its eyes on the sides of its head, which many birds have, has monocular vision. These animals can see well to the sides but not so well to the front."

7 Understanding Function Question

Ⓑ A student asks the professor if animals can see colors like humans. So to respond to his question, she discusses color vision in animals.

8 Understanding Organization Question

Ⓒ The professor mentions zebras to point out how their stripes affect predators' vision by writing, "Other animals have color patterns that are designed to confuse predators. These patterns can blur the edges of the animals' bodies. We know that one way both people and animals pick out objects by sight is by noticing the edges of these objects. They make the objects stand out. But if the edges are blurred, they become more difficult to see. According to one theory, this is an effect of zebras' stripes. When many zebras are grazing together, their stripes form patterns that blur the outlines of individual zebras. So when lions or cheetahs stalk zebras, their focus is disrupted. They try to attack one zebra but get confused if the zebras are massed together. That's why they often pick out a lone zebra—one that is slower and has been left behind. The reason is that it's easier for them to see an animal all by itself."

9 Making Inferences Question

Ⓒ The professor states, "Experiments done with monkeys showed they could recognize objects that were very different from one another. They could easily distinguish between pictures of flowers, human faces, fruits, birds, and other animals. But when shown pictures of two different flowers, they had trouble differentiating them." She therefore implies that monkeys cannot tell the difference between two objects of the same type.

Vocabulary Review   p. 120

Answers

A
1 distinguish   2 extracurricular
3 assumption   4 notable
5 checked out

B
1 a   2 b   3 a   4 b   5 b
6 b   7 b   8 a   9 b   10 a

Practice with Short Passages
p. 124

A

Answers   1 ⓓ   2 ⓐ

| Script |

Listen to part of a conversation between a student and a professor.

W1 Student: Good morning, Professor Radcliffe. Um, since you're all alone in your office, I'd like to ask a quick question if you don't mind.

W2 Professor: That's not a problem at all. Please go ahead and ask whatever is on your mind.

W1: Are you going to be teaching Art History 206 next fall? I remember you taught it in the fall semester, but another professor, um . . . Professor Tauber, I think . . . taught it this spring. And nobody's name is listed on that information sheet I got from the office. So, uh, I have no clue who's going to be teaching it.

W2: Sorry about the confusion. When that got printed, a decision about the professor hadn't been made yet.

W1: Oh . . . So when will we find out?

W2: 🎧² Actually, I was informed this morning that I'll be teaching the class. Are you going to sign up for it?

W1: **You bet.** I've been looking forward to taking another class with you for a while.

W2: I'm pleased to hear that, Stephanie. But you'd better hurry up and register.

W1: Huh? Why do you say that?

W2: The class size is being limited. Normally, fifty students are permitted to enroll in the class. Next fall, however, that number is going to change due to some budget cuts here. So the class limit is going to decrease to thirty.

W1: Wow, that's a huge drop-off. Is the class popular?

W2: It's popular enough. And I can guarantee that it will be full, so you'd better sign up soon. If you do that, you'll be sure to get a seat in the class.

Answer Explanations

1   ⓓ The student mentions that Professor Tauber taught the class she wants to take. But she asks the professor if he will be teaching the class and then indicates she will sign up for it. So it can be inferred that she prefers Professor Radcliffe to Professor Tauber.

2   ⓐ When the student says, "You bet," she means that she intends to sign up for the professor's class.

B

Answers   1 ⓑ   2 ⓐ

| Script |

Listen to part of a conversation between a student and an admissions office employee.

M Admissions Office Employee: Thank you very much for accepting our offer of being a tour guide here, Marla.

W Student: And thanks a lot for giving me the job, Mr. Reeves. I'm looking forward to starting giving tours to visitors on campus tomorrow.

M: Actually, you won't be doing that immediately.

W: I won't? But I thought that was the reason you're hiring me.

M: 🎧² Well, before you can give tours of the campus, you need to learn about every building on campus. For example, um . . . can you tell me what departments are located in Asbury Hall?

W: **Uh . . . Yeah, I guess I see your point now that you mention it.** So what do you want me to do tomorrow?

M: You're going to be working from one to four. During that time, there will be three tours of the campus, each of which will last an hour. I want you to go on all three tours. Listen to everything the guides say. And pay close attention to the questions the visitors ask. Oh, and don't say anything yourself. You'll be there merely as an observer.

W: Okay, great. Oh, and I have a question for you if you don't mind.

M: Sure. What is it?

W: How can I learn more about the campus? I'd really like to learn more so that I can do the best I can.

M: I'm glad you asked. Here, uh, take this. It contains nearly everything you need to know about the school. And just so you know . . . before we let you lead your own tour, you'll have to pass a comprehensive exam on the information here.

Answer Explanations

1   ⓑ The student asks, "How can I learn more about the campus? I'd really like to learn more so that I can do the best I can," so she is interested in learning her job as well as possible.

2   ⓐ When the man asks the student a question about the campus, she answers, "Yeah, I guess I see your point now that you mention it." In saying that, it can be inferred that she does not know the answer since she failed to try

to respond to the question with an answer.

C

| Script |

Listen to part of a lecture in an environmental science class.

M Professor: One important feature of the world's polar areas is the layer of underground permafrost. This is a layer of frozen ground with a temperature of zero degrees Celsius or lower that lasts for at least two years. Permafrost is below the level of the surface because the surface itself freezes and thaws with the changing of the seasons. The area of ground that's above the permafrost is called the active layer because it freezes and thaws each year.

W Student: 🎧² How thick are those two layers? Does their thickness vary from place to place? Hmm . . . I suppose that it must.

M: **You thought that out rather well, Sue.** You're correct in that the active layer and permafrost vary in thickness. As a general rule, um, the active layer is around thirty to 100 centimeters thick. As for the permafrost, it has been measured to an average depth of fifty meters in many places. And if you go to some parts of the Arctic, the permafrost is more than 650 meters thick. Imagine that. The general rule is that the farther north toward the North Pole or south toward the South Pole that you go, the colder it gets. Therefore, the permafrost becomes thicker as well.

Permafrost is classified as either continuous or discontinuous. Continuous permafrost is a layer of ground frozen over a continuous wide region. Discontinuous permafrost has patches of permafrost and non-permafrost ground mixed together. This occurs because the temperature underground varies from place to place due to several factors. One is shade from mountains, which causes lower temperatures in the shaded areas. Where there's more shade, there's more permafrost. However, a nearby sunnier area may have no permafrost at all. Another factor is temperature changes from year to year. They can cause continuous permafrost regions to become discontinuous and vice versa.

Most of the world's permafrost can be found in the Polar Regions. In some places, it has lasted for thousands of years. About one quarter of the northern regions have permafrost. It's mostly found in Alaska, Canada, Greenland, Russia, and Scandinavia. In the Southern Hemisphere, the areas with large amounts of permafrost are in Antarctica and the mountainous regions of South America. Oh, there's also permafrost in high alpine regions such as the Rocky Mountains and the Alps.

Interestingly, a major concern about permafrost is its potential to thaw a great amount at once. Some experts predict that if temperatures in the Arctic rise a few degrees, then lots of permafrost will melt. This could change the landscape. The melting would cause erosion and landslides. There's also lots of organic matter frozen in the ground. If large areas of permafrost thaw, this matter will decay and release methane gas into the atmosphere. This would be an alarming event because it could make the temperature rise even more. That would result in more thawing, which could have global implications.

Answer Explanations

1 Ⓓ The professor states, "Some experts predict that if temperatures in the Arctic rise a few degrees, then lots of permafrost will melt. This could change the landscape. The melting would cause erosion and landslide. There's also lots of organic matter frozen in the ground. If large areas of permafrost thaw, this matter will decay and release methane gas into the atmosphere. This would be an alarming event because it could make the temperature rise even more. That would result in more thawing, which could have global implications." He therefore believes it would cause problems around the world.

2 Ⓑ When the professor remarks, "You thought that out rather well, Sue," he means that the student figured out the answer to her own question, so he did not have to answer it for her.

D

| Script |

Listen to part of a lecture in an astronomy class.

W Professor: Dark areas on the sun's surface frequently appear. These sunspots, as we call them, are so large that they are sometimes bigger than the planets in the solar system. The reason for their dark color is that they're cooler than the rest of the sun's surface. You see, uh, the temperature of a large sunspot is around 3,800 degrees Kelvin whereas the surrounding surface may be about 5,800 degrees Kelvin. Sunspots may appear alone, in pairs, or in groups connected to one another.

Structurally, a sunspot has an outer rim and an inner region. The outer rim is lighter in color and is called the penumbra. The inner darker part is called the umbra. The main differences between them are their temperatures and magnetic fields. 🎧² The penumbra is hotter and has a weaker magnetic field while the umbra is cooler and has a stronger magnetic field. Magnetism plays a role in the formation of sunspots, and the region above a sunspot has a much stronger magnetic field than the rest of the sun's surface. **The theory on sunspot formation accepted by most people is that fluctuations in magnetic forces** eventually becomes too great, so the region of greater magnetism pushes to the surface and forms a sunspot.

Be aware that sunspots aren't permanent. Their formation can take several days or weeks, and then they may last for a few more weeks or even months. Nobody knows why some last longer than others. What we do know is that sunspots tend to grow greater in number every eleven years. This is called the sunspot cycle. The peak sunspot activity time is called the solar maximum and the time with the least activity the solar minimum. The sunspot cycle isn't, uh, isn't a perfect cycle as some sunspots from one cycle continue to exist when the next cycle begins. In other words, there's almost always some sunspot activity on the sun. Most sunspots appear near the sun's northern and southern poles and then move toward its equator before disappearing.

Interestingly, sunspots affect our lives here on the Earth. Their intense magnetic activity helps create solar flares and coronal mass ejections. Coronal mass ejections are the spewing into space of massive amounts of plasma and magnetism from the sun. Both solar flares and coronal mass ejections can cause magnetic storms. These storms, in turn, can cause disruptions to the Earth's magnetic field.

M Student: Wasn't it a solar flare that caused the power failures and communication problems last month?

W: Now that the data has been examined, I'd say you're correct, David. Like most of you, I wasn't pleased about having no electricity and being unable to use my cell phone for several hours that day. Hopefully, people now realize the importance of tracking sunspots and the intense magnetic activity they cause. In the future, we need more advance warnings of large magnetic storms to avoid similar problems.

Answer Explanations

1 Ⓒ The professor says, "Like most of you, I wasn't pleased about having no electricity and being unable to use my cell phone for several hours that day. Hopefully, people now realize the importance of tracking sunspots and the intense magnetic activity they cause. In the future, we need more advance warnings of large magnetic storms to avoid similar problems."

2 Ⓓ When the professor points out that the theory is "accepted by most people," she is indicating that it is possible that sunspots form for another reason. She may not necessarily believe the other reason, but she is implying that it could be true.

Practice with Long Passages   p. 128

A

Answers

1 Ⓐ   2 Fact: ③ Not a Fact: ①, ②, ④   3 Ⓑ

Script

Listen to part of a conversation between a student and a professor.

M Student: Professor Young, um, d-d-d-do you mind if I, uh, if I speak with you about my grade for a moment?

W Professor: Not at all. Please come in and have a seat . . .

M: Thank you.

W: Um, I'm sorry to say this, but I'm afraid I don't know your name. I do recognize you from my Economics 105 class though.

M: Thanks for remembering me. My name's Jason Wilcox, and I'm a sophomore. I'm here because, well, uh . . . I got a C+ on the most recent exam, and I only got a B- on the paper you returned to us today. I was, you know, sort of hoping to get a higher grade, but that didn't happen.

W: 🎧³ All right. Would you like to know how to improve your grade?

M: Yes, absolutely. I also wonder um . . . can I do an extra assignment or something to help my grade?

W: **We can discuss that in a bit.** But let's focus on your performance first.

M: Sure. So . . . what do you think I should do?

W: First of all, one reason I remember you from class is that I have noticed you don't always take notes. You need to be sure to take comprehensive notes since I lecture on material that is not covered in the book. In other words, merely studying the book isn't going to provide you with all the knowledge you need to get an A in my class.

M: Yes, ma'am. I think I finally realized that. Up to now, I've only been reading the assigned material. However, I did a good job taking notes today. And I asked one of my classmates to lend me his notes from our previous classes, so I'll get access to them.

W: Is he a good student?

M: Yes, ma'am. He got a ninety-six on the exam and takes really well-organized notes.

W: Great. Definitely be sure to use his notes then. Now, um, another thing you can do is review your notes after each class. Many students fail to do that, so they forget what they learned in class.

M: Yeah, I'm guilty of not doing that. The only time I look at any notes I ever take is right before an exam when I'm studying.

W: That's a habit you must change. And that is something

which won't require a tremendous amount of time either. Just spend, uh, a quarter of an hour or so reviewing everything. Then, you'll find that you can remember everything much better when it's test time.

M: I hope so. I'll start doing that today.

Answer Explanations

1 Ⓐ The student complains, "I'm here because, well, uh . . . I got a C+ on the most recent exam, and I only got a B- on the paper you returned to us today. I was, you know, sort of hoping to get a higher grade, but that didn't happen."

2 Fact: ③   Not a Fact: ①, ②, ④
First, the student comments, "The only time I look at any notes I ever take is right before an exam when I'm studying." In addition, he does not take comprehensive notes. The professor states, "One reason I remember you from class is that I have noticed you don't always take notes." He does not ask question in class either. There is no mention of that in the conversation. And it is not true that he does not read the assigned material. Instead, he states, "I've only been reading the assigned material."

3 Ⓑ When the student asks about doing an extra assignment, the professor states, "We can discuss that in a bit." She is indicating that she does not want to talk about that topic, so she is implying that she wants to discuss something else.

Dictation

M: My name's Jason Wilcox, and I'm a <u>sophomore</u>. I'm here because, well, uh . . . I got a C+ on the most <u>recent</u> exam, and I only got a B- on the <u>paper</u> you returned to us today. I was, you know, <u>sort of</u> hoping to get a higher grade, but that <u>didn't happen</u>.

W: All right. Would you like to know <u>how to improve</u> your grade?

M: Yes, absolutely. I also <u>wonder</u> um . . . can I do an <u>extra</u> assignment or something to help my grade?

W: We can <u>discuss</u> that in a bit. But let's <u>focus on</u> your performance first.

M: Sure. So . . . what <u>do you think</u> I should do?

B

Answers   1 Ⓑ   2 Ⓑ   3 Ⓐ   4 Ⓒ

| Script |

Listen to part of a lecture in an economics class.

M1 Professor: One of the oldest types of economic activities is banking. The basic purpose of a bank is to serve as a safe place for people to keep their money. When civilization

first began, there wasn't any money, and people mostly bartered for the things they wanted. The main medium of bartering was grain, so it was, naturally, highly valued. Gradually, people started using money in the guise of metal coins. Copper, silver, and gold were the primary metals used to mint coins. Having lots of grain or numerous coins at one's home could attract thieves, so people frequently stored their valuables in safe places.

Initially, the two most common storage sites were temples and palaces. Both had sound structures as well as guards to protect the priests and rulers. The temples and palaces charged small storage fees for the grain or coins. Typically, it was a small percentage of the grain or coins being stored. Soon, temples and palaces started making profits from their activities, so they were able to loan grain and coins to those in need of them. These loans had to be repaid with interest. And that was the beginning of banking.

W Student: That's fascinating. When did people first start doing that? And how long ago did they do this? Around a few centuries ago?

M1: Actually, it started much further in the past. There's evidence of precious metal and grain storage in temples and palaces as well as loans being made in ancient Mesopotamia and Egypt. When exactly it started is harder to determine. However, this type of banking was taking place at least as early as, uh, as 1750 B.C.

M2 Student: How do you know the exact date?

M1: That's the year King Hammurabi, the Babylonian ruler, made what is now known as Hammurabi's Code. There are laws in it related to banking. So, logically, we can surmise that since the code includes several laws regarding banking, the practice must have been well established by that time. There's also evidence that certain families back then were in the business of making loans and storing grain and coins for fees.

Centuries later, the tradition of temples being centers of banking was continued by Greece and Rome. But there were also private individuals who set up structures to store coins. By that time, coins had become more common, and the Greek city-states, Roman Republic, and Roman Empire engaged in the large-scale minting of coins. In Rome, foreigners had to exchange their coins for Roman ones in order to do business. Often, coin exchange centers were established near markets. Of course, people still bartered, but using coins was much easier than moving around large amounts of bulky grain.

Now, uh, let's jump ahead a few centuries. After the fall of Rome in the fifth century, dark times were ahead for Europe, and banking there waned for centuries. Trade in grain and other goods became common again. There were also changes in banking due to religious restrictions on it. Both Christian and Islamic beliefs banned the charging of interest for loans. However, the Jewish faith permitted it.

So during the Middle Ages, Jewish bankers became well established in Europe and the Middle East. They often ran merchant banks, which were large trading houses for grain and other goods.

🎧4 When the Crusades began at the end of the eleventh century, everything changed. The European Crusaders needed plenty of coins to buy goods and services as their armies sailed or marched to the Middle East. This led to two religious orders, uh, called the Templars and the Hospitallers, getting involved in banking. **Their contribution to banking was rather brilliant, uh, I'd say.** If a person deposited money in one of their hundreds of castles, that individual received a deposit note. Then, the person could show the note at another castle and receive the same amount of coinage.

Answer Explanations

1 Ⓑ The professor mostly talks about how banking originated.

2 Ⓑ When the professor talks about banking in ancient times, the female student responds, "That's fascinating," so she clearly finds it very interesting.

3 Ⓐ The professor talks about how people in both Mesopotamia and the Roman Empire used grain to barter with for goods.

4 Ⓒ When the professor says, "Their contribution to banking was rather brilliant," he is praising the European religious orders for their idea related to banking.

Dictation

❶ Initially, the two most common storage sites were temples and palaces. Both had sound structures as well as guards to protect the priests and rulers.

❷ There's also evidence that certain families back then were in the business of making loans and storing grain and coins for fees.

❸ Their contribution to banking was rather brilliant, uh, I'd say.

Answers

PART 1

| 1 Ⓑ | 2 Ⓐ | 3 ①, ③ | 4 Ⓓ | 5 Ⓐ |
| 6 Ⓒ | 7 Ⓓ | 8 Ⓒ | 9 Ⓒ | 10 Ⓑ |

11 Fact: ②, ③, ④ Not a Fact: ① 12 Ⓐ 13 Ⓑ

14 Ⓐ

PART 2

| 1 Ⓓ | 2 Ⓑ | 3 Ⓐ | 4 Ⓑ | 5 Ⓑ |
| 6 Ⓓ | 7 Ⓐ | 8 Ⓒ | | |

9 Owl: ③ Eagle: ① Hawk: ②, ④

PART 1

Conversation [1–4]

| Script |

Listen to part of a conversation between a student and a professor.

M1 Professor: Good afternoon, Jason. Are you here to continue our discussion from this morning's class?

M2 Student: Good afternoon, sir. I'd love to keep chatting about it as it was quite an interesting topic. But, um, I've got to attend a physics class in about ten minutes. Perhaps we can discuss the matter another time.

M1: I look forward to the opportunity. It's always a pleasure to hear an opinion different from mine, especially if the person I'm debating has a good handle on the facts.

M2: I enjoyed it myself, too.

M1: So what brings you here if you're not coming to discuss the early Roman Empire?

M2: I wonder if you can do a favor for me. Do you think you could write a letter of recommendation for me by this time next week?

M1: That won't be a problem. But, um . . . what do you need one for? You're not a senior yet, so this can't be for graduate school.

M2: It's for an internship I'm applying for. I'm hoping to do it this summer. I just found out about it, and I need to have all of my materials submitted by the end of next week.

M1: An internship? But I thought you were planning to do an independent research project under my direction during the summer session. 🎧4 Have you decided to give up that goal?

M2: No, sir. Not at all. This internship is actually connected to the research I hope to be doing.

M1: **Really? I'm intrigued.**

M2: Yeah, it's actually pretty interesting. It's not a business internship or something like that which I'm applying for. Instead, it's for a position at the Posey Museum. I'd be working with the curator and a few of the museum's researchers on some items that were recently donated to the museum's collection.

M1: Should I assume that these items are related to the ancient world?

M2: That's correct, sir. I don't remember the donor's name, but he had a huge collection of ancient Roman pottery, armor, coins, and other items. He gave the museum all of the items a couple of months ago, so they're busy trying to catalog everything.

M1: That's the kind of work you'd be doing if you got the internship?

M2: Yes, sir. The only drawback is that it's an unpaid position. I was hoping to get a job to earn some money for my senior year this summer. But I don't think that will be possible if I do the internship.

M1: So will you still be doing the research project?

M2: Yes. Even if I get the internship, I'll be able to conduct the research during my down time. And if I don't get the position, I'll have plenty of time even if I get a part-time job.

M1: It sounds like you have this all figured out. I'll make sure to write you a glowing recommendation. I'll also give a call to Mr. Wilson at the museum.

M2: You know him?

M1: He calls me to ask about various items from time to time. We've had a working relationship for more than, oh, at least fifteen years now. I wouldn't say that he's my friend. But we definitely get along well with each other.

M2: I had no idea.

Answer Explanations

1 Understanding Attitude Question

Ⓑ The professor is going to supervise the student as he does an independent research project. The professor also remarks, "It sounds like you have this all figured out. I'll make sure to write you a glowing recommendation." So he clearly believes the student is knowledgeable.

2 Detail Question

Ⓐ About the internship, the student states, "The only drawback is that it's an unpaid position."

3 Detail Question

1, 3 The professor tells the student, "I'll make sure to write you a glowing recommendation. I'll also give a call to Mr. Wilson at the museum."

4 Understanding Attitude Question

Ⓓ When the professor says, "I'm intrigued," after the student mentions the internship, he is implying that he would like the student to provide more details about it.

| Script |

Listen to part of a lecture in an economics class.

M Professor: The years after the Civil War ended in 1865 were difficult ones for the Southern states which had joined the Confederacy. Many towns and cities had been destroyed in the fighting, and farms and businesses were gone, too. As a result, the economic base was ruined. And let's not forget that slavery had ended, which caused economic problems for the large plantation owners. To make matters worse, many hundreds of thousands of Southerners had been killed or badly wounded in the fighting, which resulted in severe labor shortages. To overcome these issues, the Union government came up with a plan to rebuild the South's economy. Known as Reconstruction, it lasted from 1865 to 1877, when the last Union soldiers finally departed the South.

The first step taken during Reconstruction was to create a plan to readmit the Confederate states into the Union. To do that, each state had to ratify three amendments to the U.S. Constitution. These amendments, by the way, were the thirteenth, fourteenth, and fifteenth ones. They abolished slavery, made all freed slaves American citizens, and gave all free male slaves the right to vote. One by one, the Confederate states approved the amendments. The first was Tennessee in 1866. By 1870, all of the states had done so and had rejoined the Union. As a result, freed slaves became citizens and were equal in legal status to their former masters. This actually helped the South economically as many freed slaves strove to make new lives for themselves as farmers, merchants, and business owners.

W Student: How did the Southerners react to Reconstruction?

M: Most of them despised it and regarded it as a plot to destroy their lives. And it really was harsh on them. Yet they had little choice but to go along. After all, they had been defeated militarily, and Union soldiers were occupying the South. In fact, in 1867, a series of acts, uh, called the Reconstruction Acts, was passed. These laws called for the continued military occupation of the South. The soldiers would stay there for another ten years and would enforce the will of the Union politicians. This created long-lasting feelings of bitterness that still exist in the present. Many Southerners believed the Northerners who came down to their lands were oppressing them in numerous ways, among them economically. It would, in fact, be many years until the South's economy started to recover.

Here's an example of what I'm talking about. During the war, countless roads, railroads, and even towns were destroyed. There was an effort to rebuild the South, but many of the men the Union sent there to organize the work sought to make themselves wealthy at the expense of Southerners. Others followed these officials as they sought economic opportunities in the chaos that frequently follows wars. These men were, simply put, corrupt individuals. Southerners insulted these Northerners by calling them carpetbaggers. They got the name because they often carried their belongings in bags designed to carry carpets. There was widespread resentment against carpetbaggers since so many of them were only looking out for themselves. There were violent confrontations at times. And it wasn't just Northerners who were corrupt. Many Southern politicians and merchants made efforts to line their pockets. Naturally, these people's actions slowed efforts to rebuild the South and therefore caused harm to the economy. Yet despite the corruption, more railroads and roads were built than had existed before the war. They connected the South to more areas. The improved transportation thus helped boost the economy.

Another problematic area was in agriculture. Because of the labor shortage, both freed slaves and white men alike could bargain for higher wages to work on farms. ∩9 But most wanted their own land. Union laws gave free land to former slaves. They could also buy land or work as tenant farmers or sharecroppers. **Er, I see some confused looks on your faces.** Since you may not know, tenant farmers paid rent on their land and kept all their crops. Sharecroppers, however, borrowed seeds and tools from landowners. They worked the land and then shared the crops with whoever owned the land.

Of course, there were problems. Sometimes crops failed, or other misfortunes occurred. The tenant farmers and sharecroppers had to borrow more and thus went into debt. Many farmers—both black and white—got so deeply in debt that they never escaped from it. Part of the problem was the lack of markets for their crops. While those growing tobacco and sugarcane could find markets, cotton farmers couldn't. During the war, the Union blocked Southern ports. As a result, the big textile businesses in Britain and elsewhere had to search for new cotton sources. They continued using them after the war. So the Southern farmers couldn't rely upon their old buyers.

Reconstruction was a difficult and unfortunate period for the South, but the South did manage to recover economically. Here's what happened that started to turn things around . . .

Answer Explanations

5 Gist-Content Question

Ⓐ During the lecture, the professor mostly talks about how Reconstruction affected the South after the Civil War.

6 Understanding Attitude Question

Ⓒ The professor says, "And it really was harsh on them," and then he gives examples of how Reconstruction was

a difficult time for the South.

7 Detail Question

Ⓓ The professor lectures, "Many of the men the Union sent there to organize the work sought to make themselves wealthy at the expense of Southerners. Others followed these officials as they sought economic opportunities in the chaos that frequently follows wars. These men were, simply put, corrupt individuals. Southerners insulted these Northerners by calling them carpetbaggers. They got the name because they often carried their belongings in bags designed to carry carpets. There was widespread resentment against carpetbaggers since so many of them were only looking out for themselves."

8 Making Inferences Question

Ⓒ The professor implies that cotton farmers in the South made more money before the Civil War than after it in commenting, "While those growing tobacco and sugarcane could find markets, cotton farmers couldn't. During the war, the Union blocked Southern ports. As a result, the big textile businesses in Britain and elsewhere had to search for new cotton sources. They continued using them after the war. So the Southern farmers couldn't rely upon their old buyers."

9 Understanding Attitude Question

Ⓒ When the professor says, "Er, I can see some confused looks on your faces," after he mentions a couple of terms, it can be inferred that he will define the terms that he just used.

Lecture #2 [10-14]

| Script |

Listen to part of a lecture in a history class.

W Professor: Timbuktu in Mali was once one of the greatest cities in northwestern Africa. It's located near the Niger River and is considered a gateway to the Sahara since it sits near the desert's edge. Nowadays, this proximity is worrisome since the desert is slowly encroaching on the city. ∩14 The possibility of desertification is of great concern because of the potential loss of thousands of manuscripts stored in the city. These are original works based on the Islamic religion. You see, um, at one point in the past, Timbuktu was a great center of Islamic learning. **But I'm getting ahead of myself.** So let's go back to the beginning.

The city was established as a temporary trading post on a caravan route in Africa. Salt can be found in abundance nearby, and this highly valued trade good made merchants rich. The market in Timbuktu also had vendors who traded gold, cattle, and grain. By the twelfth century, there was a more permanent settlement there. It was centered on the central market, which still dominates the city. It was then that Timbuktu became a place noted for its Islamic scholarship. Muslims carried the Islamic faith with them as they moved across the Middle East, Africa, and Europe. However, in North Africa, their movement was slowed by the Saharan sands. Timbuktu, however, had a good source of water and was on established trade routes. It therefore served as a waypoint for the spread of Islam to sub-Saharan Africa.

The heyday of this activity came in the fifteenth and sixteenth centuries. Muslims in Timbuktu established a major university and dozens of smaller schools there. At one point, almost 25,000 students were studying in Timbuktu. Three large and impressive mosques, which still stand today, were erected there, too. Located on the edge of a desert, Timbuktu lacked building materials. Thus large parts of the city, including the schools and mosques, were built with timber frames plastered with mud to make walls and roofs. Baked hard in the sun, these wood and mud structures have stood the test of time.

By the end of the sixteenth century, Timbuktu had expanded to more than 100,000 people. This included numerous scholars, who came from as far away as Cairo, Mecca, and Baghdad to study and live there. Oh, I should remind you that at that time, the Islamic world was fairly advanced in certain fields of scholarship. People living under Islamic rule were highly knowledgeable in astronomy, medicine, mathematics, science, and other fields. Large amounts of this knowledge were taken to Timbuktu in manuscripts that were stored there. These manuscripts also included details about the history of the rise of Islam.

Unfortunately, Timbuktu was located in the middle of many warring factions. So it didn't remain a center of scholarship for long.

M Student: What happened?

W: Well, in the fourteenth century, the African empire of Mali took over the city and seized control of its trade. Soon afterward, the Songhai tribe conquered the region and made Timbuktu part of its expanding empire. Later, in 1591, the Moroccans defeated the Songhai and took over the city. The Moroccans subsequently drove out many scholars. They said the academics were disloyal to the new region. That act began the slow intellectual and economic decline of Timbuktu. Yes?

M: If the Moroccans drove the scholars out, what did they think of their manuscripts? They must have destroyed some.

W: That's a perceptive observation. It's known that some manuscripts were destroyed then, but we don't know how many. Nor do we know how many there were at the city's peak. What we do know, however, is that somewhere around 700,000 manuscripts have survived. But that leads to another problem.

These manuscripts used to belong to large collections in mosques and schools. But many are in private hands,

uh, owned by Timbuktu's residents. This is a major concern. It's possible that many of the owners will sell the manuscripts to private collectors, so they'll never be seen again. As a result, some organizations are raising funds to purchase the manuscripts and collections.

M: What do you think should be done with the manuscripts, Professor?

W: Hmm . . . Many believe the manuscripts should stay in Timbuktu. I can understand how they feel. These people say the manuscript collections would attract scholars and tourists to a city in desperate need of an economic revival. Those opposed to it say that the slowly expanding Saharan sands will one day engulf the city. They don't want to risk exposing the manuscripts to a situation in which they could be lost forever. And let's not forget that many manuscripts are in poor condition. Any rough handling could cause them literally to fall apart. As for me, well, I think the manuscripts should be photographed, scanned, and put on the Internet for all to see and study. So the originals might not survive much longer, but at least records of them will still exist.

Answer Explanations

10 Understanding Organization Question

Ⓑ The professor points out that the market in Timbuktu is a major feature there in saying, "It was centered on the central market, which still dominates the city."

11 Detail Question

Fact: ②, ③, ④   Not a Fact: ①
The professor says, "Timbuktu was a great center of Islamic learning." She also mentions, "The city was established as a temporary trading post on a caravan route in Africa," and, "It's located near the Niger River and is considered a gateway to the Sahara since it sits near the desert's edge." Finally, she adds, "At one point, almost 25,000 students were studying in Timbuktu." However, it is not true that Timbuktu served as the capital of the Mali Empire for a time. The professor only comments, "Well, in the fourteenth century, the African empire of Mali took over the city and seized control of its trade."

12 Understanding Function Question

Ⓐ The professor comments, "Later, in 1591, the Moroccans defeated the Songhai and took over the city. The Moroccans subsequently drove out many scholars. They said the academics were disloyal to the new region. That act began the slow intellectual and economic decline of Timbuktu."

13 Detail Question

Ⓑ The professor states, "As for me, well, I think the manuscripts should be photographed, scanned, and put on the Internet for all to see and study. So the originals might not survive much longer, but at least records of them will still exist."

14 Understanding Attitude Question

Ⓐ When the professor remarks, "But I'm getting ahead of myself," she means that she is going to talk about a subject but does not want to discuss it quite yet.

PART 2

Conversation [1–4]

| Script |

Listen to part of a conversation between a student and a librarian.

M Librarian: Hello there. You look as if you are having a tough time with the library computer system. I know it can be a bit user unfriendly at times. Is there anything I can help you find?

W Student: Oh, hello. Thanks for the offer, but that's all right. I guess I'm just a bit frustrated because all of the books I'm looking for have already been checked out.

M: That happens sometimes. Would you mind telling me what kinds of books you're looking for? Perhaps I can help you find some related material.

W: The books I need are for a class in the Archaeology Department that I'm taking. It's on Egyptian archaeology. The class is really interesting, but the professor highly recommends that we do a lot of reading for it. Uh, I mean reading that isn't in the textbook.

M: I suppose that some other students in your class must have gotten here first and checked out the books the professor wants you to read.

W: Yeah, that's probably what happened.

M: If you want, I can put a recall on the books for you, and whoever borrowed them will have to return them within two weeks. Then, only you will be permitted to check them out. Would you like for me to do that?

W: No, that's all right. Two weeks will be a bit too late for me.

M: Could I see the list of books that you're looking for?

W: Sure. Here you are.

M: Hmm . . . You know, some of these books are pretty old. That means that the copyrights on them have expired.

W: Um . . . okay? What's the importance of that?

M: It means that some of these books may be available either for free or for very low prices as e-books. 🎧4 Have you ever read an e-book?

W: I'm something of a traditionalist, so I haven't done that before. **However, there's a first time for everything.**

M: That's a good attitude to have. Here, uh, let me borrow your pen, please . . . Okay, this is the URL of one popular online seller of e-books. Why don't you go online and try to find the books? I know for a fact that this one, um, here . . . on your list is available for just ninety-nine cents.

W: Excuse me? Ninety-nine cents? Seriously?

M: Sure. Since it's no longer protected by copyright, anyone can publish it. You'll probably find most of these other books available for the same price, um, or even less.

W: Hey, that's pretty cool. I guess that I can build up an impressive online library.

M: Are you an Archaeology major?

W: That's right. I hope to become a professional archaeologist in the future.

M: Then you should definitely do that. A lot of outstanding books in the field were written more than a hundred years ago, and you can acquire them all cheaply. That beats having to check out used bookstores for what you need, doesn't it?

W: It sure does. Thanks a lot for your help. I really appreciate it. I'm going to take a look at that website you told me about and start ordering books. Who knows? Maybe I'll get a nice collection of reference materials for twenty dollars or so.

Answer Explanations

1 Gist-Content Question

Ⓓ The student remarks, "I guess I'm just a bit frustrated because all of the books I'm looking for have already been checked out."

2 Gist-Purpose Question

Ⓑ Regarding copyrights, the librarian states, "You know, some of these books are pretty old. That means that the copyrights on them have expired." Then, he adds, "It means that some of these books may be available either for free or for very low prices as e-books."

3 Connecting Content Question

Ⓐ The librarian states, "Okay, this is the URL of one popular online seller of e-books. Why don't you go online and try to find the books? I know for a fact that this one, um, here . . . on your list is available for just ninety-nine cents." Therefore, the likely outcome of the student visiting the website the librarian tells her about is that she will be able to acquire some material that her professor wants her to read for the class.

4 Understanding Attitude Question

Ⓑ She student indicates that she has never read an e-book before. But then she states, "However, there's a first time for everything." By that, she means that she is willing to read an e-book.

| Script |

Listen to part of a lecture in a zoology class.

M Professor: Most birds consume all kinds of food, including seeds, fruit, nectar, insects, and worms. Some, on the other hand, eat larger animals, such as, uh, mice, rabbits, and other birds. These birds are active hunters, so we call them birds of prey. Examples of them are the owl, the eagle, and the hawk. Each species has its own hunting methods. Some overlap while others are unique to the species. I'd like to go over them with you now.

Most species of owls are nocturnal hunters, so they primarily search for food at night. Owls normally consume small mammals, including rats, mice, chipmunks, and rabbits. Some species also hunt small birds and fish. Owls have several adaptations that allow them to hunt prey. Their feathers are designed for silent flight, which allows them to fly quietly toward their prey, often before the animals even know they are being hunted. Owls also have large eyes. They have particularly large retinas, giving them superior vision at night. Their ears also help them since they are not symmetrical. This means the left and right ears aren't perfectly placed so that they match on each side but are instead in slightly different positions. As a result, sound reaches each ear at a different time. Owls can use the difference in time to pinpoint the direction where a noise came from. Finally, their talons and beaks are designed for crushing and ripping prey they catch.

Owls usually hunt by employing a wait-and-see style that lets them be highly effective hunters. Here's what they do . . . They sit silently, often in trees, and listen for prey. Upon detecting a sound, they silently fly toward it and use their eyes to find the animal. Then, they swiftly attack, gripping the prey in their talons and then killing it by tearing its flesh with their sharp beak. The prey is either eaten where it was killed or gets carried off to the owl's nest.

W Student: Are all owls night hunters? I heard that some of them hunt during the day. Is that true?

M: It is indeed. Some hunt while the sun is up. Those owls often have feather colors which aid them in hiding, uh, like a sort of camouflage. The snowy owl, for example, has bright white plumage that permits it to blend in with its winter environment.

Let's examine eagles next. They eat a wide range of animals, including small and medium-sized mammals, many types of snakes and lizards, fish, and other birds. Eagle hunting methods vary from species to species. But there are some common factors. Let's see . . . Most hunt in the daytime. They typically fly high above the ground and use their sharp eyesight to find prey on the ground, in the sky, or in the water. After sighting it, eagles swiftly fly to the prey and strike it with their sharp, strong talons. They don't normally eat their prey where they catch it. Most eagles carry it to a higher perch, such as their nest, where they can kill and consume the animal at their leisure. The eyesight of eagles is key to their hunting prowess. Bald eagles, for instance, have eyes that are five times as sharp as those of humans and can spot small mammals on the ground more than a kilometer and a half away.

Some eagles have varying attack methods though. Golden eagles specialize in different attack styles for different types of prey. Ornithologists have identified seven of these styles, which depend on the prey being hunted and the terrain. Let me tell you about two of them. When hunting birds, golden eagles attack from above, and they only hunt birds slower than they are, such as geese. They strike hard and knock the bird away from its flock. For ground attacks on animals such as rats or squirrels, golden eagles fly very low—below the horizon—so they blend into the background. They glide silently and, at the last moment, flare their wings and strike.

Okay, last are hawks. They're medium-sized birds of prey that feed on a wide variety of small mammals, birds, fish, and reptiles. Like eagles, hawks have superior eyesight, permitting them to see prey from a great distance. Observers have noticed that hawks typically hunt in one of four ways. Sometimes they hunt from a perch such as a tree, building, or fence post. They spot their prey and then glide in to strike while grasping the animals with their sharp talons. Sometimes hawks hunt from the ground if they know where a mammal's den is. They wait by the entrance and then strike when the mammal appears. Hawks also attack while flying high or low. They typically dive almost vertically from directly above the prey. Or, uh, they may glide in slowly, depending on where the prey is. Vertical dives end with a hard impact, with both hawks and prey on the ground. They kill the animal and then usually consume it on the spot.

Answer Explanations

5 Understanding Attitude Question

Ⓑ The professor remarks, "Owls usually hunt by employing a wait-and-see style that lets them be highly effective hunters."

6 Gist-Purpose Question

Ⓓ The professor comments, "The eyesight of eagles is key to their hunting prowess. Bald eagles, for instance, have eyes that are five times as sharp as those of humans and can spot small mammals on the ground more than a kilometer and a half away."

7 Connecting Content Question

Ⓐ The professor says, "When hunting birds, golden eagles attack from above, and they only hunt birds slower than they are, such as geese. They strike hard and knock the bird away from its flock." It is therefore likely that a golden eagle will attack a goose from above if it sees one.

8 Understanding Organization Question

ⓒ During the lecture, the professor separately discusses the hunting methods of three species of birds.

9 Connecting Content Question

Owl: ③   Eagle: ①   Hawk: ②, ④

About the owl, the professor says, "Most species of owls are nocturnal hunters, so they primarily search for food at night." Regarding the eagle, the professor notes, "They don't normally eat their prey where they catch it. Most eagles carry it to a higher perch, such as their nest, where they can kill and consume the animal at their leisure." As for the hawk, the professor remarks, "Sometimes hawks hunt from the ground if they know where a mammal's den is. They wait by the entrance and then strike when the mammal appears." The professor also states, "Observers have noticed that hawks typically hunt in one of four ways."

Vocabulary Review

Answers

A
1	symmetrical	2	amendment	3	drop-off
4	waned	5	rim		

B
1	b	2	a	3	a	4	b	5	b
6	b	7	a	8	b	9	a	10	a

64

Chapter 07 | Understanding Organization

Practice with Short Passages

p. 146

A

Answers 1 Ⓐ 2 Ⓑ

| Script |

Listen to part of a conversation between a student and a professor.

M Student: Pardon me, but would you happen to be Professor Alderson?

W Professor: That's me. What can I help you with today, young man?

M: Er . . . I was hoping to be able to sign up for your Astronomy 309 class. Does there happen to be enough room in the class for me to do that?

W: Yes, there's still space available in the class. But, uh . . . you realize this is already the third week of the semester, don't you? We've already met several times, so you're going to be way behind the other students.

M: Yes, ma'am, I completely understand that I'll need to work twice as hard as everyone else to catch up. Fortunately, my roommate is taking the class. So, uh, I can borrow his notes and speak with him if there's something I don't understand.

W: Who's your roommate?

M: His name is Dwight Arnold.

W: Oh, okay. Dwight's taken a couple of classes with me before. He's gotten good grades in them, so you can trust whatever information he tells you.

M: That's great to know. Thank you.

W: I suppose I can let you in the class, but you really are going to have to put a great deal of effort into it. We've got a test coming up next week, and you won't be exempt from it.

M: That's fine with me, ma'am. I'll study to the best of my ability. Uh, I've got the form for adding a class here. Do you think you can sign it now?

W: Why not? Let me find a pen.

Answer Explanations

1 Ⓐ About Dwight Arnold, the student mentions, "Fortunately, my roommate is taking the class. So, uh, I can borrow his notes and speak with him if there's something I don't understand."

2 Ⓑ The professor tells the student that he is not exempt from taking the test, so she mentions it to let the student

know that he has to take the test.

B

Answers 1 Ⓐ 2 Ⓑ

| Script |

Listen to part of a lecture in a history class.

M Professor: The first successful English colony in North America was Jamestown. A group of English investors calling themselves the Virginia Company sponsored it. King James I gave them a charter with rights to explore and settle in the New World. The company's main objective was to establish England as a power in the New World to counter the growing Spanish, French, and Portuguese colonies. Its members also wanted to find a route to the Far East through or around the New World and to convert the natives to Christianity.

On December 6, 1606, 105 men sailed from England on three ships. The ships arrived off the American coast in April 1607, and, on May 14, the colonists decided to settle at a site they named Jamestown in honor of King James. The site was located up a river which they called the James River. They then constructed a fort on a peninsula. The colonists selected the site because it would be easy to defend and also because the river water was deep enough for oceangoing ships to anchor nearby. A third factor was that there were no native tribes living on the peninsula. The colonists began . . . Ah, do you have a question?

W Student: You said there were no natives there, but I thought plenty of them lived in the region the colonists selected.

M: Oh, yes, there were many natives nearby, but there weren't any on the exact site that was picked. You see, uh, the land there wasn't suitable for farming. It was swampy, and the soil was too poor to grow anything. Another negative factor was that the water wasn't very fresh due to the salt water flowing upriver from the nearby ocean. In addition, the place had numerous insects, especially mosquitoes, because of the swamps. So the natives avoided it.

These problems I mentioned would plague the colonists. However, they initially seemed satisfied with the site. So they erected a fort with wooden walls. It was shaped like a triangle, and, at each point of the triangle, they built a bulwark. These were raised platforms upon which they placed cannons to defend the fort. Inside the fort itself, they constructed several buildings.

The colonists completed the fort on June 15, 1607. Soon afterward, the ships left for England to pick up more

Chapter 07   65

supplies and people. It was only after the ships left that it became apparent that the colonists had chosen a poor site for their settlement. People fell ill from drinking the brackish river water. Others died of fever, possibly due to mosquito-borne diseases. Food supplies began to run out, and hunger became an additional problem. All these woes were compounded by two other factors. First, the colonists were mostly upper-class Englishmen who had no skills at farming or heavy labor. Second, they had built their fort in the middle of a region with roughly 15,000 natives led by a powerful chief named Powhatan. As we shall see, hard times lay ahead for the colonists.

Answer Explanations

1 Ⓐ The professor tells the students about the settling of Jamestown in chronological order.

2 Ⓑ The professor remarks, "Food supplies began to run out, and hunger became an additional problem. All these woes were compounded by two other factors. First, the colonists were mostly upper-class Englishmen who had no skills at farming or heavy labor."

C

Answers   1 Ⓑ   2 Ⓑ

| Script |

Listen to part of a lecture in an archaeology class.

W Professor: Most of you are likely familiar with the cave paintings discovered in European caves. However, you may not know that they aren't the only ancient cave paintings that have been found. On the island of Sulawesi in Indonesia is a town called Moras. There are hundreds of paintings in a series of caves located near it. They were discovered more than fifty years ago but weren't intensively studied until recently.

Let me show you some pictures while I lecture. Look at the screen, please. Many of the paintings depict animals like this one . . . This one here . . . looks like the modern-day pig-like babirusa. Close to many of the animal paintings are stencils of human hands . . . Most of the paintings were done in charcoal . . . or ochre, a reddish material that prehistoric people used to make pigment for artworks. The big question archaeologists are trying to answer is when the paintings were made. Originally, it was believed they couldn't be more than 10,000 years old because the heat and humidity in the tropics would destroy anything older. However, in the past few years, radiocarbon dating tests have been done on the Moras cave paintings. Fourteen paintings in different caves were tested. The results concluded that the paintings are between 17,000 and 40,000 years old.

M Student: Does that mean the scientists are not sure about the exact dates? Or does it mean the paintings were made

at different times?

W: Ah, good question, Marcus. What I mean is that each sample was dated at a different time, so it's highly likely that the paintings were made at separate times. And before you question the results, the scientists are confident in the numbers because they used uranium to date the paintings. You see, uh, they first noticed lumps under the paintings. Here's a picture . . . The lumps are called cave popcorn and are made by dripping calcite that hardens. Calcite, if you don't know, is the substance that forms stalagmites and stalactites in caves. The cave dwellers painted over the calcite lumps . . . so we know the samples didn't gain any more calcite after they were painted over. What's more important is that calcite lumps contain uranium. We know the half-life of uranium, so we can accurately estimate the ages of the paintings. Here are two examples. One animal painting . . . uh, this one . . . was made 35,400 years ago while one of the hand stencils . . . was made 39,900 years ago. That makes them two of the oldest cave paintings ever discovered.

The dating of these paintings also raises new questions about early humans. We know humans came from Africa and spread around the world. What's uncertain is how and where they learned cave painting. They might have learned it in Africa and taken that knowledge with them. Or different branches of humanity may have independently learned cave painting. We just don't know yet. Now, uh, back to the Moras paintings . . .

Answer Explanations

1 Ⓑ The professor shows pictures of the cave paintings to the students and lectures to them at the same time.

2 Ⓑ The professor states, "Calcite, if you don't know, is the substance that forms stalagmites and stalactites in caves. The cave dwellers painted over the calcite lumps . . . so we know the samples didn't gain any more calcite after they were painted over. What's more important is that calcite lumps contain uranium. We know the half-life of uranium, so we can accurately estimate the ages of the paintings."

D

Answers   1 Ⓑ   2 Ⓐ

| Script |

Listen to part of a lecture in an anthropology class.

M Professor: The ancestors of the Dravidian people were most likely the founders of the Indus River Valley civilization, which thrived around 4,000 years ago in land located in modern-day Pakistan and India. Today, their descendants, the Dravidians, comprise a large segment of the Indian population and a smaller part of the Pakistani one. In case you're curious, about twenty-eight percent of

Indians are Dravidians. Most of them live in the southern part of the country. Compared to the majority of the Indian population, Dravidians are darker skinned and speak different dialects. In the Dravidian group, there are several subgroups, uh, based mainly on their languages and cultural and religious beliefs.

The modern Dravidians probably came from a northern farming tribe that, um, over centuries, developed a large civilization in the Indus Valley. The Indus civilization lasted from roughly 2600 B.C. to 1900 B.C., and its decline is usually blamed on a long drought. Archaeologists have studied the remnants of this civilization to attempt to uncover its origins and to determine who its people were. The major obstacle is a lack of understanding of the Indus people's writing. Today, we're pretty certain there's a connection with the Dravidian language group. From this evidence, we can conclude that the ancestors of the modern Dravidian people built the Indus Valley civilization.

I should, however, point out that there is not total agreement on this. Some academics believe the Indus writing isn't writing at all. Instead, they claim it's comprised of symbols representing different things and therefore isn't an alphabet and isn't even like Egyptian hieroglyphics. They believe the writing might have been like the European heraldic symbols used to represent families. A second opinion is that the writing is of an Indo-European language, like most of the modern languages of northern India. Finally, a third group of experts believe the Indus writing is the ancient form of the Dravidian language family.

Deciding which theory is correct is difficult. We have no translations in other languages to compare the Indus script. So there's no Rosetta Stone with three languages describing the same thing. We also don't know what language the Indus people spoke. The final problem is that virtually all of the extant texts are very short, so we're dealing with a small amount of material.

However, some experts have learned a great deal about the inscriptions that have been found at Indus dig sites. They've found patterns which make it likely that it's a form of writing. They say it's based on the idea that pictures represent words or parts of words, like Egyptian hieroglyphics. Further studies have shown a connection between some words in this language and some words in the language of modern-day Dravidians. Again, let me stress that not everyone agrees with these conclusions. Some believe that the Indus people's roots are connected to people living in Pakistan or northern India. Hopefully, future research will let us read the entire Indus script and reach a definitive answer.

Answer Explanations

1 Ⓑ During the lecture, the professor talks about some theories about the Dravidians that are based on language.

2 Ⓐ The professor makes a comparison in stating, "Some academics believe the Indus writing isn't writing at all. Instead, they claim it's comprised of symbols representing different things and therefore isn't an alphabet and isn't even like Egyptian hieroglyphics."

Practice with Long Passages
p. 150

A

Answers

1 Ⓓ   2 Ⓑ   3 Ⓐ, Ⓒ
4 Mass Education before 1819: ②, ③
   Mass Education after 1819: ①, ④

Script

Listen to part of a lecture in an education class.

W Professor: In our last class, one of you inquired about the education system used in our country. You asked where it came from. Well, I'll tell you about that today. The current education systems in countries around the world are based on the Prussian model developed in the nineteenth century. A three-tiered system that evolved in Prussia eventually became the modern-day elementary, middle, and high school systems. This model placed groups of children in a classroom with one teacher providing instruction. The model emphasized discipline, rote learning, and conformity to a national standard. It also stressed that children should be taught in such a way that would, uh, that would benefit the state. This model led to the mass education of the nineteenth century that has continued to modern times.

The system got its start under the rule of King Frederick the Great of Prussia. Frederick was a product of the Enlightenment and was keenly interested in education reform. In 1763, he enacted a law calling for universal education for all children between the ages of five and twelve. Reading and writing were the main subjects, and some emphasis was placed on religious studies and the arts. The state provided some funding for schools, but most were privately run. After this basic education, children could proceed to secondary school, which prepared them to enter the more difficult gymnasium. Now, uh, don't misunderstand. The gymnasium wasn't a physical education center like you may be thinking. It was a common term in Europe for a university preparation school, uh, much like high school is today. Starting with secondary school, students had to pass difficult exams to be permitted to study at the next level.

Despite being a compulsory system, not everyone attended the schools. Many poor and rural families resisted as they wanted their children to help on the farm or to learn a trade which would benefit the family. Many nobles also opposed mass education. They feared that giving the masses the ability to read and think would lead to revolution."

M Student: Who paid? Was it the families or the state?

W: The lowest level was usually free because the state provided funding. However, the second and third tiers cost families money as most of those schools were privately run and received little or no compensation from the government. Attending university cost people as well. This, obviously, was a hindrance to mass education since not everyone could afford to pay the required fees.

Anyway, the three-tiered structure was utilized until Napoleon soundly defeated Prussia in battle in 1806. Many Prussians came to believe that they had lost because the common soldiers were thinking too much and weren't disciplined enough to obey their orders. Thereafter, educators started changing Prussian education. This was done to produce highly disciplined children who would fit into their proper places in the state.

This idea fit the trend of rising nationalism in Europe that had been unleashed by the French Revolution and Napoleon's wars. There was also a belief in John Locke's idea that the mind of a child was a blank slate needing to be filled. Based on all this, a new form of education was introduced in 1819. It was still a three-tiered system. But it was more rigid and left little room for flexibility in teaching. Instructors were trained and had to earn a certificate from the state noting that they had passed a course on teaching. They had to follow a strict curriculum, too. Many teachers became advocates of German nationalism and had a strong influence on the futures of their students.

The Prussian model was often called a factory model of education. The schools were like factories while the teachers were like assembly line workers, producing the same product year after year. Now, uh, let's look at how it spread to other countries, including the United States.

Answer Explanations

1 Ⓓ The professor mentions the role of the king in establishing Prussian mass education in stating, "The system got its start under the rule of King Frederick the Great of Prussia. Frederick was a product of the Enlightenment and was keenly interested in education reform. In 1763, he enacted a law calling for universal education for all children between the ages of five and twelve."

2 Ⓑ The professor wants to make sure the students do not misinterpret her comments when she lectures, "After this basic education, children could proceed to secondary school, which prepared them to enter the more difficult gymnasium. Now, uh, don't misunderstand.

The gymnasium wasn't a physical education center like you may be thinking. It was a common term in Europe for a university preparation school, uh, much like high school is today."

3 Ⓐ, Ⓒ The professor states, "Many poor and rural families resisted as they wanted their children to help on the farm or to learn a trade which would benefit the family. Many nobles also opposed mass education. They feared that giving the masses the ability to read and think would lead to revolution."

4 Mass Education before 1819: ②, ③
Mass Education after 1819: ①, ④
Regarding mass education before 1819, the professor says, "Reading and writing were the main subjects, and some emphasis was placed on religious studies and the arts," and, "Starting with secondary school, students had to pass difficult exams to be permitted to study at the next level." As for mass education after 1819, the professor remarks, "Instructors were trained and had to earn a certificate from the state noting that they had passed a course on teaching," and, "Many teachers became advocates of German nationalism and had a strong influence on the futures of their students."

Dictation

❶ The system got its start under the rule of King Frederick the Great of Prussia.

❷ Now, uh, don't misunderstand. The gymnasium wasn't a physical education center like you may be thinking.

❸ Many teachers became advocates of German nationalism and had a strong influence on the futures of their students.

B

Answers   1 Ⓓ   2 Ⓐ, Ⓒ   3 Ⓑ   4 Ⓐ

Script

Listen to part of a lecture in a chemistry class.

M1 Professor: Chemists classify heavy metals in several ways, none of which agrees with each other. For example, um, some classifications are based on density, others on atomic number, and others on atomic weight. And a few scientists classify them according to their chemical reactions. So as you can imagine, there's a certain amount of confusion. Yet I believe it's safe to say that a heavy metal is a metal with a high density, a high atomic weight, and a high atomic number. This definition includes most of the elements we have discovered. Some are naturally occurring while scientists have produced others, such as plutonium, through artificial means.

W Student: I'm sorry, but did you just say that plutonium is an artificial element? I thought it appears in nature.

M1: Ah, good catch, Mary. Plutonium does appear in extremely miniscule amounts in nature. But it's most efficiently produced in nuclear reactors, so we often consider it an artificial element.

Now, uh, the interaction of heavy metals and living organisms is an area of great interest these days. Some heavy metals can benefit living creatures while others are highly toxic or are so radioactive that they can be fatal. Among the good heavy metals are iron, zinc, cobalt, copper, and magnesium. They, uh, and others, play helpful roles in the functions of the body. They're beneficial in small amounts but may be toxic in high quantities. As a general rule, most people get sufficient amounts of heavy metals in their daily diets. For instance, iron can be obtained by eating meat, beans, and fish.

Nevertheless, most heavy metals aren't good for living creatures. Five of the worst are arsenic, cadmium, lead, mercury, and chromium. All of them have been linked to severe health issues. Let's see, uh . . . Cadmium can be absorbed into the lungs and then gets lodged in the liver, kidneys, and pancreas. It has been linked to cancer in all of those organs. Lead is another potential killer. It's heavily used in various industries. Lead concentrates in the bones of living creatures. In humans, it has been linked to severe mental problems, such as anxiety, depression, attention deficit disorder, and even Alzheimer's and Parkinson's. Lead is especially dangerous to young children and unborn babies as it has been linked to some developmental disorders. Mercury poisoning has been an issue for fish for years. Runoff from industries gets into water sources and contaminates fish. It concentrates in the nervous systems of organisms. Mercury can increase the risk of heart disease and damages the immune system in humans, too.

Most people aren't directly exposed to toxic heavy metals unless they smoke. Instead, people are normally exposed to them indirectly through the air, water, or food. Heavy metals can be found in these environments, and it's often difficult to remove them.

M2 Student: Why doesn't the government just ban the use of those harmful heavy metals?

M1: Well, it's not as easy as you may think. Heavy metals have numerous uses in a wide variety of industries, so it would be practically impossible to make them illegal to use. Plus, in some cases, banning them wouldn't lead to any positive results. The reason is that some places around the world have already suffered extensive damage from heavy metals. And let's not forget that there are natural ways for heavy metals to enter the environment.

M2: There are? Like what?

M1: Well, mercury can be emitted as a gas when volcanoes erupt. It can then combine with clouds and fall as rain, where it enters the water supply. So I don't think it's fair

to blame government inactivity on this problem. Now, I think this is a good time to examine some ways that people can rid their bodies of heavy metals.

Answer Explanations

1 (D) The student comments, "I'm sorry, but did you just say that plutonium is an artificial element? I thought it appears in nature." She asks the professor about plutonium because she is checking on a statement that he made and which she thought was not true.

2 (A), (C) About cadmium, the professor remarks, "Cadmium can be absorbed into the lungs and then gets lodged in the liver, kidneys, and pancreas. It has been linked to cancer in all of those organs." As for mercury, he notes, "Mercury poisoning has been an issue for fish for years. Runoff from industries gets into water sources and contaminates fish. It concentrates in the nervous systems of organisms. Mercury can increase the risk of heart disease and damages the immune system in humans, too." So he compares that type of harm they can do and the parts of the body in which they are found.

3 (B) The professor says, "Plus, in some cases, banning them wouldn't lead to any positive results. The reason is that some places around the world have already suffered extensive damage from heavy metals."

4 (A) During his lecture, the professor first defines what heavy metals are and then discusses how they can affect people.

Dictation

❶ For example, um, <u>some</u> classifications are based on density, <u>others</u> on atomic number, and <u>others</u> on atomic weight.

❷ I'm sorry, but did you <u>just say that</u> plutonium is an artificial element? I <u>thought</u> it appears in nature.

❸ Well, it's not <u>as easy as</u> you may think. Heavy metals have <u>numerous</u> uses in a wide variety of industries, so it would be <u>practically</u> impossible to make them <u>illegal</u> to use.

Answers

PART 1

1 Ⓐ	2 Ⓑ	3 Ⓒ	4 Ⓑ	5 Ⓑ
6 Ⓒ	7 Horns: ② Antlers: ①, ③, ④		8 Ⓑ	
9 Ⓐ	10 Ⓐ	11 Ⓒ	12 Ⓐ	13 Ⓓ
14 Ⓑ				

PART 2

1 Ⓒ	2 Ⓑ	3 Ⓐ	4 Ⓒ	5 Ⓓ
6 Ⓓ	7 ①, ④			
8 Vorticism: ③ Futurism: ①, ②, ④				9 Ⓑ

PART 1

Conversation [1-4]

| Script |

Listen to part of a conversation between a student and a Drama Department employee.

W Student: Hello. Are you Mr. Dupree? Ms. Sullivan in the Drama Department office told me that I should speak with you about something.

M Drama Department Employee: Yes, I'm Bruce Dupree. Is there something that I can help you with?

W: I sure hope so. My name is Anita Thorpe. I'm the president of the drama club here on campus. Each spring, we give a performance on the stage in McMurdo Theater.

M: Yes, I've worked at the school for nearly a decade, so I'm familiar with the performances. I even remember seeing one of them a few years back.

W: That's good news. I'm glad you're familiar with what we do.

M: So, uh, what does this have to do with me?

W: Well . . . we're going to be giving a performance next Thursday night, but there are a few problems with the stage which have to be fixed before then. Ms. Sullivan mentioned that you are the person who is responsible for making repairs.

M: That's right. It's my job to handle any problems. Wait a minute. ∩4 What exactly is wrong with the stage? There was a performance at the theater about, uh, five weeks ago, but none of the performers complained about anything at that time.

W: **They didn't?** That's weird. There are actually several problems which are in need of repairing before we can perform.

M: Like what?

W: The main problem is the squeaking noise the stage makes at times.

M: Squeaking noise?

W: Yeah, I think it does that because of the wood. There are a couple of places where, uh, if you step on the wood, it makes a loud, er, squeaking noise. Do you think you can repair that?

M: Ah, I know what you're talking about. There's a spot right near the front of the stage in the center, and there's another spot beside the exit on the left in the back part of the stage, right?

W: Yeah, that's exactly where the problems are. You can fix that, can't you?

M: No. Sorry, but that would involve replacing the wood in the stage. Actually, I'm a bit surprised you were not aware of that problem already. It's been an issue for years. People have asked me to have it fixed for quite a while, but the school won't come up with the money to allow me to repair the stage. You're just going to have to do what all of the other performers have done over the years.

W: What's that?

M: Simple. They remember where the stage makes noise, and they make sure not to step on the floor in those places. You'll just have to tell all of the actors what to do. It shouldn't be too hard. So, uh, what else is wrong with the stage?

W: The curtains are another big problem. We can get them to open, but they won't close.

M: Oh, that's not good. That's happened in the past, and it's a huge problem for me to repair. I'd better get to the theater right now so that I can get to work on it.

W: All right. I'll go along with you because we're going to start rehearsals in a few minutes.

Answer Explanations

1 Detail Question

Ⓐ The student tells the man, "We're going to be giving a performance next Thursday night."

2 Understanding Organization Question

Ⓑ The student comments, "The curtains are another big problem. We can get them to open, but they won't close."

3 Making Inferences Question

Ⓒ The man says that he will go to the theater, and then the student responds, "I'll go along with you because we're going to start rehearsals in a few minutes."

4 Understanding Function Question

Ⓑ When the man says that nobody complained about any problems five weeks ago, the student responds, "They didn't?" She is clearly surprised by his remark since she states that the theater has several problems.

| Script |

Listen to part of a lecture in a zoology class.

W Professor: Two other types of appendages that mammals have are horns and antlers. There are many types of each one, and they're all used for similar purposes. But let me make one thing clear to you: Horns and antlers are not the same. They have some major differences. Included among them are, um, how long they last, how they grow, and what they're made from. Yet they also have similarities, including how many there are, where on the body they're found, and what they're used for.

First, I think I should cover which species have horns and which have antlers. Horns are typical of the Bovidae family of mammals. It includes cattle, water buffalo, musk oxen, sheep, gazelles, antelopes, and goats. Males always have horns, and females of many species do as well. The horns of males tend to be larger and stronger than those of females though. Antlers, meanwhile, are typical of the Cervidae family of mammals, which includes deer, moose, elk, and caribou. All males of these species grow antlers. However, only female caribou have them. Horns and antlers both grow in pairs in the front of the head, uh, usually right above the eyes. Horns come in many shapes, lengths, and styles, but antlers have similar structures for all species. The main antler characteristic is branches, uh, like on trees. Horns, however, have no branches.

Okay, uh, let's learn what they're made from. Horns have a bony center that's covered by a substance called keratin. This is a protein found in the skin of many species of animals. So be aware that horns are not just made of bone. Please note that unlike antlers, horns are permanent and grow as the animals reach adulthood. Horns begin as bony knobs under the skin. They grow from the skin, not the skull. Later, the horns fuse with the skull through strong connective tissue. In some species, horns only grow to certain lengths, but they never stop growing in others.

M Student: Excuse me, but what about the rhino? You said that horns have a bony center, but I remember reading somewhere that rhino horns don't have that.

W: Well, rhinos have hornlike structures, but they are made of only keratin and lack a bony center. So, while they are not truly horns as I have defined them, it is common to say that rhinos have horns.

All right, let's look at antlers. They're much different from horns because they grow and fall off every year. They are attached to support structures called pedicels, which are connected to the skull. Antler growth is regulated by hormones in the body. Hormone levels in the animals' bodies increase in spring, which prompts the antlers to begin growing. At first, the antlers are rather weak, but they gradually become stronger. They grow a soft hair

covering called velvet. The velvet contains nerves as well as blood vessels, which provide nutrients to the antlers as they grow. The antlers continue growing in summer. Then, in fall, the velvet dies, so the mammals rub it off on trees. As they do that, their antlers become shiny and take on a wood-like appearance. Soon, the hormone levels in their bodies decrease, and the support structures of their antlers weaken. Eventually, their antlers break off, uh, only to regrow when spring returns.

One major function of horns and antlers concerns the leadership of a herd. The largest male with the strongest horns or antlers dominates a herd. Males clash violently for this right since the one that wins gets to mate with the females. Mating is the prime driving force for most species as it allows them to pass their genes on to future generations. Clashes between males happen during the mating season. Males make aggressive displays and then fight one another. They charge and clash heavily with their horns or antlers. Some even attempt to stab their opponents to give them nasty wounds. Eventually, one of them backs away and gives up the fight, leaving the victor to mate with the females. Ah, I should also mention that some zoologists believe that females are naturally more attracted to males with the largest sets of horns or antlers.

Females of many species have horns, but they aren't used for mating rituals. They are normally straighter and thinner than those of males. This makes them ideal for defense against predators. Ah, be aware that all species with horns and antlers use them to defend themselves and their young when necessary. The Cape buffalo of Africa actually charges predators. It has two curved horns that it uses to attack and kill predators, even large male lions, which get too close to its young. Musk oxen are another type of animals that use their horns effectively. They put their young in the center of a large group and then turn outward to display their horns menacingly if wolves or other predators are nearby.

Answer Explanations

5 Making Inferences Question

Ⓑ The professor states, "Antlers, meanwhile, are typical of the Cervidae family of mammals, which includes deer, moose, elk, and caribou. All males of these species grow antlers. However, only female caribou have them." So it can be inferred that female deer have no antlers.

6 Understanding Function Question

Ⓒ The professor tells the students about rhino horns after a student asks a question about them.

7 Connecting Content Question

Horns: ② Antlers: ①, ③, ④

About horns, the professor states, "Males always have horns, and females of many species do as well." As for antlers, the professor remarks, "Eventually, their antlers break off, uh, only to regrow when spring returns," and,

"They grow a soft hair covering called velvet. The velvet contains nerves as well as blood vessels, which provide nutrients to the antlers as they grow." The professor also comments, "The main antler characteristic is branches, uh, like on trees."

8 Detail Question

Ⓑ The professor remarks, "Females of many species have horns, but they aren't used for mating rituals. They are normally straighter and thinner than those of males."

9 Understanding Organization Question

Ⓐ The professor compares and contrasts horns and antlers throughout her entire lecture.

Lecture #2 [10–14]

| Script |

Listen to part of a lecture in a physics class.

M Professor: 🎧13 One of the keenest scientific minds of the nineteenth century belonged to Britain's William Thomson. Has anyone ever heard of him . . . ? Hmm . . . **Just as I had expected.** In that case, have you ever heard of Lord Kelvin . . . ? Good. That's the name William Thomson is mostly known by today, so that's what we'll use in this class. Kelvin was a mathematician and physicist. Most of his work was in the fields of electricity and thermodynamics. He also played roles in the development of the telegraph and in the making of suitable instruments for sea navigation. Today, he's best known for giving his name to the Kelvin temperature scale.

Kelvin was born in Belfast in the northern part of Ireland in 1824. His father was a professor of mathematics at Glasgow University in Scotland. Kelvin was an outstanding student and began studying university-level material at the age of ten. He wrote his first scientific paper when he was sixteen. From 1841 to 1845, he studied at Cambridge and became a full-time professor at Glasgow University when he was twenty-two. He would hold that position for fifty-three years. At Glasgow, he led the Physics Department and established the school's first scientific laboratory.

Early on, Kelvin was interested in thermodynamics. A major theory then was that molecules would stop moving at the temperature called absolute zero. Kelvin believed it would be useful to have a more precise temperature scale to define absolute zero. In 1848, he wrote a paper describing his thoughts on that scale. It begins with zero, a temperature equal to absolute zero. This is minus 273 degrees on the Celsius scale. Today, we call his creation the Kelvin scale. And please note that we don't use the word "degree" with it. We simply say that something is, uh, 105 Kelvin. Or you could just use the letter K, um, as in ninety-three K. There are no negatives on the scale either as the lowest temperature is zero K.

You should be aware that thus far, we have not been able to attain absolute zero and make molecules stop moving. So zero K is merely theoretical at this time. And we don't usually use it for everyday activities like measuring the temperature. Instead, the Kelvin scale is customarily used in physics and for calculating the temperatures of stars. I don't want to go into detail on that today, but we basically do it by examining the colors of stars and then estimating their temperatures in Kelvin.

While studying temperatures in the early 1850s, Kelvin defined the second law of thermodynamics. It states that heat does not transfer from a colder body to a hotter one. This means that energy does not move from low-temperature objects to higher-temperature ones. This is one of the limitations modern refrigerators and air conditioners must overcome to run properly. There's no, uh, no spontaneous flowing of cold air to hot areas, so they must use engines to overcome that fact.

In the mid-1850s, Kelvin took a break from his laboratory experiments. He was asked to join the Atlantic Telegraph Company, which wanted to lay an underwater telegraph cable between North America and Britain. One of the difficulties the company was experiencing was in detecting electric currents in the long cable. They couldn't read messages if they were unable to detect electric current pulses in Morse code. Kelvin subsequently invented a device called a mirror galvanometer. He patented it in 1858.

Kelvin's mirror galvanometer used a small mirror suspended on a silken thread. On the back of the mirror were some small magnets. The mirror itself was suspended inside a wire coil. When even the slightest bit of electricity passed through the coil, it created a magnetic field. This, in turn, attracted the magnets on the mirror. The mirror moved, and a light source reflected off the mirror. The light struck a scale, which a telegraph operator could see at his station. If the light moved one way, it indicated a dot in Morse code. And if the light moved the other way, it was a dash. This reflected the different strengths of the currents being sent through the cable when the operator at the other end was sending either short dots or long dashes.

🎧14 **Now, uh, there's not too much time left.** But I think I should mention just one more area of Kelvin's work before we continue talking about him on Thursday. Kelvin was an avid sailor and therefore had an interest in marine instruments. He invented an improved compass, an astronomical clock that showed the positions of the sun, moon, and stars, and a sounding device. It enabled sailors to know the depth of the water that was under their ships. All three inventions contributed to the improving of maritime safety.

Okay, be sure to read the rest of chapter three by our next class. See you then.

10 Gist-Content Question

Ⓐ The professor focuses on the scientific achievements of Lord Kelvin in his lecture.

11 Understanding Organization Question

Ⓒ The professor explains how absolute zero applies to the Kelvin scale in stating, "In 1848, he wrote a paper describing his thoughts on that scale. It begins with zero, a temperature equal to absolute zero. This is minus 273 degrees on the Celsius scale. Today, we call his creation the Kelvin scale."

12 Detail Question

Ⓐ The professor comments, "When even the slightest bit of electricity passed through the coil, it created a magnetic field. This, in turn, attracted the magnets on the mirror. The mirror moved, and a light source reflected off the mirror. The light struck a scale, which a telegraph operator could see at his station."

13 Understanding Function Question

Ⓓ When the professor states, "Just as I had expected," after asking a question to which he got no answer, he is indicating that he believed no students would recognize the name that he mentioned.

14 Making Inferences Question

Ⓑ When the professor says, "Now, uh, there's not too much time left," he means that the class is almost over, so he is implying that he is going to let the students leave soon.

PART 2

Conversation [1-4]

| Script |

Listen to part of a conversation between a student and a professor.

M Student: Professor Carter, I wonder if I could talk to you for a minute. It's about the research paper topic that you assigned me.

W Professor: Yes, David? Which topic were you assigned?

M: I'm supposed to do a report on squid.

W: Ah, marvelous. You'll have a great time doing research on that animal. It happens to be one of my favorites in the entire animal kingdom.

M: But, uh, actually . . . I was hoping you'd allow me to change topics. I mean, um, I don't know anything about squid.

W: Well, that's why you're at college, David: to get an education. You're supposed to be taking this class to learn new things, not to go over information you already know. Tell me . . . What do you know about squid?

M: Er . . . I know people eat them a lot. And, uh . . . they shoot out ink sometimes when they're trying to escape from predators.

W: All right, that's a good start. Now, let me tell you a few more things about squid so that you can see how fascinating they are.

M: Sure.

W: First, there are more than 300 species, and they range in size from a few centimeters in length to nearly fifteen meters long.

M: Woah, I had no idea they could get that big.

W: That's the giant squid. Sperm whales often dive deep beneath the ocean to feed on it. However, giant squid are fierce fighters. Well, um, we think they are. Nobody has actually seen a fight in person, but we've seen scars on the heads of various sperm whales. Giant squid can clearly inflict a great amount of damage.

M: Hey, uh, if they get that big, does it mean that those stories about giant squid attacking and sinking ships are really true?

W: I doubt it. I don't believe giant squid are big enough to sink a large ship. But I suppose they could pull a small boat under the water. I'm not sure if that has ever happened though.

M: Okay, what else can you tell me?

W: Some squid are able to change colors. Some can even become transparent. So you tell me . . . What's the importance of this skill?

M: Hmm . . . I would say that it's a form of camouflage. You just mentioned that some animals hunt squid, so I assume they use this for defensive purposes. And, um . . . are squid carnivorous?

W: Yes.

M: So I guess they could use camouflage to disguise themselves while hunting. If prey animals can't see them, then they must be pretty effective hunters.

W: That's right. Well done, David. Now, I'm going to tell you one more important thing about squid: they are quite intelligent. Along with octopuses, they're the smartest invertebrates we know of. They're capable of using tactics when they hunt. And scientists in laboratories have done experiments with squid in which they have shown a remarkable degree of problem-solving abilities.

M: Really? That sounds cool. What kinds of problems can they solve?

W: I'm going to leave that up to you to find out. Why don't you write your paper about squid intelligence and how it benefits them when they're hunting? You seem sufficiently interested in the topic now, so I think you can write a good paper on it.

1 Gist-Content Question

Ⓒ The student tells the professor, "I was hoping you'd allow me to change topics. I mean, um, I don't know anything about squid."

2 Understanding Function Question

Ⓑ The professor is trying to find out how much the student knows about squid when he says, "Well, that's why you're at college, David: to get an education. You're supposed to be taking this class to learn new things, not to go over information you already know. Tell me . . . What do you know about squid?"

3 Understanding Organization Question

Ⓐ The professor focuses on how well some squid can fight when he remarks, "Sperm whales often dive deep beneath the ocean to feed on it. However, giant squid are fierce fighters. Well, um, we think they are. Nobody has actually seen a fight in person, but we've seen scars on the heads of various sperm whales. Giant squid can clearly inflict a great amount of damage."

4 Detail Question

Ⓒ The professor says, "Why don't you write your paper about squid intelligence and how it benefits them when they're hunting? You seem sufficiently interested in the topic now, so I think you can write a good paper on it."

Lecture [5–9]

| Script |

Listen to part of a lecture in an art history class.

M Professor: Two distinct art movements in the early twentieth century were Vorticism and Futurism. Both movements were influenced by Cubism. They were attempting to move away from the standard artistic ideas of landscapes and portraits by making something a bit more radical. Although both were international in flavor, the Futurist movement was centered in Italy whereas the Vorticist movement had its home in Britain, particularly London. Another key difference is that Futurism lasted longer than Vorticism. Finally, while Vorticism was mainly concerned with art and literature, the Futurist movement encompassed art, literature, music, dance, film, and architecture.

First, I'm going to go into detail on the origins and history of Vorticism. Then, I'll do the same with Futurism. Okay . . . Vorticism began in London in 1914. However, its roots go back further to Cubism and were also influenced somewhat by the emerging Futurist movement. Vorticism's founder was British artist Wyndham Lewis. He and those who joined him were rebelling against the plain, common art forms that British art critics adored at that time. Instead, the Vorticists wanted to shake up the establishment with art featuring bold colors, radical angles, and geometric shapes with harsh lines. They created paintings, sculptures, and drawings to fit this mood, which they called Vorticism.

W Student: Pardon me, Professor Meadows, but I don't know what that word means.

M: Ah, yes, that's perfectly understandable. Basically, it's a term that describes the art form. Let's look at some examples on the screen. Here's Wyndham Lewis's 1915 painting called *Workshop* . . . Notice the radical angles . . . the sharp lines . . . the abstractness of the entire work. The influence of Cubism is easy to see. Here's the cover of *Blast* magazine, the literary arm of Vorticism. Again, there are sharp angles . . . and a whirling mass of shapes and forms . . . This all suggested a whirlpool, like an eddy in water, or a vortex, to American poet Ezra Pound. He was living in London in 1914 and was friends with Wyndham Lewis. Pound saw many of the early works of the movement and coined the term Vorticism to describe it.

Vorticism didn't last very long. Lewis and his followers printed the first issue of *Blast* in July 1914. In it, they expressed their ideas for the new movement. While it was a radical departure from the norm, it didn't attract very much attention. An exhibition followed in 1915, and there was a second edition of *Blast* printed. After that, the movement basically died out. The main reason was the start of World War One. Several members of the movement joined the military, including Lewis, and some were killed during the war. The rest were repelled by the violence of the war, and most moved away from radical art forms. By the time the war ended in 1918, Vorticism as a movement was over.

Let's move on to Futurism . . . As its name suggests, the members of this movement were focused on the future. It began in Milan, Italy, in 1909. The movement's founder was Filippo Marinetti, a poet. He published a manifesto in an Italian magazine describing his ideas for Futurism. His writing received widespread notice, and many artists were attracted to his ideas. His main idea was to conduct a rebellion against the art forms of the past, uh, against what he called the old canvases in old museums. He felt that the art establishment held contempt for emerging art forms like Cubism. Marinetti's idea was to embrace the machines, the devices of the future.

The result was an explosion of ideas for the future. Many Futurist works of art showed urban landscapes and machines such as cars, trains, and airplanes, and they used vivid colors and radical lines. One key theme was to show dynamism. By this, I mean that Futurists wanted to portray movement in their works. They weren't interested in stillness, like the old landscapes and portraits showed. Instead, they were all about moving ahead to embrace the future. One example is this 1910 painting *The City Rises* by Umberto Boccioni . . . Here it is . . . Its centerpiece is the construction of Milan's new power station. Notice the frenzy of movement of men and horses trying to move equipment and material for the power plant.

Futurism came in two waves. The first was from 1909 to 1914. Then, World War One interrupted most of the movement. But it didn't die. It was revived after the war, and the second generation of Futurists carried on their founder's ideas. The Futurists published more manifestos expressing their ideas, so, as a result, the movement spread across Europe and went to North America. It also began encompassing more than just art. Other mediums, such as literature, film, and music, were affected by it. Now, let me show you some of the art that was created during the second generation.

Answer Explanations

5 Gist-Content Question

ⓓ The lecture is almost entirely about two art movements, Vorticism and Futurism, that were influenced by Cubism.

6 Understanding Organization Question

ⓓ The professor talks about Ezra Pound to state that he came up with the name Vorticism. He says, "This all suggested a whirlpool, like an eddy in water, or a vortex, to American poet Ezra Pound. He was living in London in 1914 and was friends with Wyndham Lewis. Pound saw many of the early works of the movement and coined the term Vorticism to describe it."

7 Detail Question

☐1, ☐4 About the reasons Vorticism died out as a movement, the professor comments, "Several members of the movement joined the military, including Lewis, and some were killed during the war. The rest were repelled by the violence of the war, and most moved away from radical art forms. By the time the war ended in 1918, Vorticism as a movement was over."

8 Connecting Content Question

Vorticism: ☐3 Futurism: ☐1, ☐2, ☐4
About Vorticism, the professor notes, "The Vorticists wanted to shake up the establishment with art featuring bold colors, radical angles, and geometric shapes with harsh lines." As for Futurism, the professor states, "One key theme was to show dynamism," and, "Futurism came in two waves. The first was from 1909 to 1914. Then, World War One interrupted most of the movement. But it didn't die. It was revived after the war, and the second generation of Futurists carried on their founder's ideas." He also says, "The Futurist movement encompassed art, literature, music, dance, film, and architecture."

9 Understanding Organization Question

ⓑ During his lecture, the professor first talks about Vorticism and then covers Futurism.

Vocabulary Review   p. 164

Answers

A
1	banned	2	brackish	3	stab
4	obstacles	5	confident		

B
1 a	2 b	3 b	4 b	5 a
6 a	7 a	8 b	9 b	10 a

Practice with Short Passages
p. 168

A

Answers 1 Ⓑ 2 Ⓐ

| Script |

Listen to part of a conversation between a student and a professor.

M Student: Professor Humphries, I'm so sorry I was late for class today.

W Professor: That's all right, Ted. I've gotten quite used to it this semester. What's your excuse this time?

M: Er . . . Well, as you know, we had a paper due today, so I had to print it before class. Unfortunately, my printer ran out of toner in the middle of printing it. So, um, I had to run to the store to get some. After everything was finished, I ran to class.

W: Hmm . . . I believe you used a printer problem as an excuse for our first paper, which you also turned in late, Ted.

M: Yeah, uh . . . Sorry about that. I'll make sure it doesn't happen again for the final one of the semester.

W: That's good to hear. Um . . . I know you're only a freshman, so you aren't really used to college life yet. But I think you need to change how you're doing things.

M: What do you mean?

W: Well, college isn't like high school. You probably received good grades in high school but didn't have to work very hard. Am I right?

M: Yes, ma'am. That's essentially what happened.

W: Okay, but college is different. If you put in the same amount of work that you did while you were in high school, you're going to get very poor grades. In fact, you'll likely fail out of school. It's much harder here, so you need to do your best at all times.

M: I will. Thanks for encouraging me.

Answer Explanations

1 Ⓑ First, the student tells the professor why he is submitting his paper late. Then, the professor says, "I believe you used a printer problem as an excuse for our first paper, which you also turned in late, Ted." After that, the student mentions, "I'll make sure it doesn't happen again for the final one of the semester." So it can be inferred that the students must write three papers for the professor's class.

2 Ⓐ First, the professor comments, "You probably received good grades in high school but didn't have to work very hard." Then, she says, "Okay, but college is different. If you put in the same amount of work that you did while you were in high school, you're going to get very poor grades. In fact, you'll likely fail out of school. It's much harder here." So she compares the difficult level between high school and college.

B

Answers 1 Ⓒ 2 Phobos: 1, 3 Deimos: 2, 4

| Script |

Listen to part of a lecture in an astronomy class.

M Professor: Mars has two moons, named Phobos and Deimos. American astronomer Asaph Hall discovered both of them in 1877. If you're curious about the odd names, they're named after the sons of the Greek god of war, Ares. Phobos represented fear while Deimos represented panic. Mars itself was named after the Roman god of war, so I suppose it's somewhat strange that Greek names were used for its moons.

The moons of Mars are among the smallest in the solar system. Phobos is only twenty-two kilometers in diameter. Deimos is even smaller, having a diameter of only twelve and a half kilometers. Their small sizes account for the reason they weren't discovered until the late 1800s. Other moons, like Europa and Io, which orbit Jupiter, were discovered in the early 1600s. But they, of course, are much larger. Phobos and Deimos are also very close to Mars, so they were subjected to the glare of sunlight reflected from Mars, and that made it difficult to spot them with telescopes.

Now, uh, let me provide you with a few details regarding each of them . . . Phobos is closer to Mars than its little brother. It's 9,377 kilometers away from Mars whereas Deimos is 23,460 kilometers away from the planet. As you'd expect, Phobos orbits Mars faster than Deimos. It takes only eight hours to make one orbit, but Deimos requires around thirty hours. Phobos orbits faster around Mars than the planet itself rotates on its own axis. A day on Mars is a bit more than twenty-four hours, so Phobos orbits it three times in a single Martian day. Deimos, on the other hand, takes more than one Martian day to complete an orbit of the planet.

Both moons are locked in a position so that only one side of them faces Mars all the time. In that regard, they're like Earth's moon. They also have very circular orbits with hardly any deviation in them. Phobos and Deimos are oddly shaped, making them more like asteroids than the spherical moons most planets have. They also have a similar composition as they're made mainly from a form of carbon that's similar to the type found in asteroids.

In fact, as you may have guessed, many astronomers believe the two moons are asteroids which broke off from the asteroid belt between Mars and Jupiter. At some time in the past, they were captured by Mars's gravitational field. Of course, that's just a theory because we don't know enough about them yet. All of our data for them is based on observations since nobody has landed any probes on their surfaces. There were plans to do that in the past, but the missions either failed to be completed or didn't reach the moons after being launched.

Answer Explanations

1 Ⓒ The professor says, "Mars has two moons, named Phobos and Deimos. American astronomer Asaph Hall discovered both of them in 1877." Later, he mentions, "Other moons, like Europa and Io, which orbit Jupiter, were discovered in the early 1600s."

2 Phobos: ①, ③ Deimos: ②, ④
About Phobos, the professor says, "Phobos is closer to Mars than its little brother," and, "Phobos is only twenty-two kilometers in diameter. Deimos is even smaller." Regarding Deimos, the professor remarks, "Phobos orbits Mars faster than Deimos. It takes only eight hours to make one orbit, but Deimos requires around thirty hours." He also notes, "Deimos is even smaller, having a diameter of only twelve and a half kilometers."

C

Answers 1 Ⓓ 2 Ⓑ

| Script |

Listen to part of a lecture in a botany class.

W Professor: Not all soil is the same. The composition of soil depends upon a number of factors, all of which can influence how, uh, how plants grow. One of the more crucial factors is acidity. Soil acidity is a measure of the concentration of hydrogen ions in the soil. We use the pH scale to measure it. The scale symbol is written as a lower-case p and a capital H. The pH scale goes from zero to fourteen, with the lower number representing a higher level of acidity. Seven is neutral on the pH scale, and above that number is soil that's more alkaline. Let me give you a few examples so that you'll understand how it works. Vinegar scores a three on the pH scale while potatoes are around six, and lime is twelve.

The question I want to examine is this . . . How does acidity affect plant growth? And the answer . . . Well, it depends on the plant being affected. Some plants thrive in acidic soil while others don't. First, you should understand that most of a plant's minerals and nutrients

are derived from the soil. There are seventeen essential nutrients and minerals plants need. Fourteen of them are found in soil. Most plants do well in soil with an acidity of six or seven on the pH scale. Phosphorous, for instance, is more readily soluble to plants if the pH is around six. Soil with a low pH usually means it has high concentrations of iron, aluminum, and manganese, which are toxic to many plants. However, some plants can grow in such soil. Conifer trees . . . uh, like pine trees . . . have a high tolerance for acidic soil as do azaleas and rhododendrons.

The main causes of soil acidity are related to natural processes. Heavy rains can leech from the soil basic elements such as calcium, magnesium, potassium, and sodium, all of which plants need. But the rainwater may leave behind elements which can increase the soil's acidity. A second cause of soil acidity is carbon dioxide from plant matter that's decomposing. As plant matter rots and breaks down, it mixes with water in the soil and forms carbon dioxide. This increases the acidity level of the soil. Decaying plant matter can also create strong organic and inorganic acids.

M Student: Is it possible to make soil less acidic?

W: Sure. If you have a garden with soil that has high acid levels, just sprinkle some lime on it. Uh, I don't mean the fruit by the way. I'm talking about the calcium compound. Lime does wonders because it raises the alkaline level by replacing hydrogen ions. It also adds two beneficial nutrients, calcium and magnesium, to the soil. But remember that some plants need acidic soil, so make sure you understand which plants need lime and which don't before using it.

Answer Explanations

1 Ⓓ The professor states, "Soil with a low pH usually means it has high concentrations of iron, aluminum, and manganese, which are toxic to many plants. However, some plants can grow in such soil. Conifer trees . . . uh, like pine trees . . . have a high tolerance for acidic soil as do azaleas and rhododendrons." Then, the professor mentions, "If you have a garden with soil that has high acid levels, just sprinkle some lime on it. Uh, I don't mean the fruit by the way. I'm talking about the calcium compound. Lime does wonders because it raises the alkaline level by replacing hydrogen ions." It can therefore be concluded that by sprinkling lime around a pine tree, the tree will not grow very well.

2 Ⓑ The professor remarks, "Lime does wonders because it raises the alkaline level by replacing hydrogen ions. It also adds two beneficial nutrients, calcium and magnesium, to the soil." Since lime has a high pH level and adds calcium to the soil, it can be inferred that calcium also has a high pH level.

D

| Script |

Listen to part of a lecture in a zoology class.

M Professor: One of the largest mammals in North America is the bear. The black bear and the grizzly bear are two of the largest bears. Comparing the two, we can observe both similarities and differences. The main similarities are their diets and mating habits while the main differences are related to their appearances.

We'll look at their differences first. Grizzly bears tend to be larger than black bears. This isn't always the case though as male black bears can be larger than female grizzly bears. The faces of the two species are also different. When looked at in profile, a black bear has a straight face whereas a grizzly's face is indented. This is called a dish-shaped face. A grizzly has a longer nose than a black bear and also has a humped shoulder, something the black bear lacks. A grizzly bear's ears are short and rounded while the black bear's ears are taller and slightly more pointed. A grizzly has longer front claws, too. A grizzly's claws are five to ten centimeters long, but a black bear's are fewer than five centimeters in length. Both, of course, are long enough to do serious harm to any animals they strike. Oh, a grizzly's claws are straighter than a black bear's as well. If you ever find bear tracks in the woods, you can see another difference. A black bear's tracks show the toes are more arched while the grizzly's toes form a straighter line. Now, let's look at their diets.

W Student: Excuse me, but you didn't mention their fur coloring.

M: I was saving that for their similarities. You see, many people believe the bears' fur colorings are different, but they're actually rather close in color. The black bear does tend to be darker than the grizzly, but some can also be brown, uh, like the grizzly. And some grizzlies are very dark. So fur coloring is not the best way to tell them apart.

As for their diets, both are omnivores, which means that they consume vegetation and meat. They prefer to eat grass, sedges, mosses, berries, and roots. Up to ninety percent of a bear's diet is vegetation. Of course, they eat fish and attack and eat deer, caribou, and elk if they have the opportunity. They also eat dead animals at times. Both species hibernate in early winter, so they consume lots of food in fall to create fat that can be stored for the winter.

Both bears mate in spring and early summer. Their offspring are usually born in their dens during the winter months. The only major difference in their mating habits is that the black bear mates in its third year while the grizzly doesn't mate until it is four years old. Cubs of both species stay with their mothers for two or three years. Mother bears are fiercely protective of their young and will attack if they sense someone or something is potentially harmful to their offspring.

Answer Explanations

1 Black Bear: ☐1, ☐3 Grizzly Bear: ☐2, ☐4
About the black bear, the professor comments, "A grizzly's claws are five to ten centimeters long, but a black bear's are fewer than five centimeters in length," and adds, "A black bear has a straight face." As for the grizzly bear, the professor lectures, "The grizzly doesn't mate until it is four years old," and says, "Grizzly bears tend to be larger than black bears."

2 ⓑ The professor states, "As for their diets, both are omnivores, which means that they consume vegetation and meat. They prefer to eat grass, sedges, mosses, berries, and roots. Up to ninety percent of a bear's diet is vegetation. Of course, they eat fish and attack and eat deer, caribou, and elk if they have the opportunity. They also eat dead animals at times."

Practice with Long Passages p. 172

A

| Script |

Listen to part of a conversation between a student and a student activities office employee.

M Student Activities Office Employee: Hi. Do you need some assistance with something?

W Student: Yes, sir. I do, but I'm not sure if this is the place where I need to be.

M: Why don't you tell me what you want? Then, I can tell you if you can have your question answered here or somewhere else.

W: Okay, great. Thanks. Um . . . I'm thinking of joining a club on campus, but, uh, I'm not really sure if I should or not. I've heard that it's a good idea to participate in extracurricular activities. But . . . uh, I don't want to be involved in a club which meets so often that I can't study enough.

M: You've definitely come to the right place as we are responsible for all of the university-sanctioned clubs on campus. Okay, now, can I assume that you're a freshman?

W: Yes, sir. That's correct.

M: All right, in that case, you definitely don't want to get involved in certain extracurricular activities because they will consume a large amount of your time. For instance, uh, writing for the student newspaper is extremely intensive, and intramural sports are as well. Intramural teams may play two games a week, and some of them even have practices.

W: Wow, that's a lot of time. That's too bad since I enjoy soccer, but I don't want to play if I won't have time to study. What about other clubs?

M: Hmm . . . It mostly depends on the club. There are some clubs that meet once a week for an hour or so while there are others that might only meet once every two weeks.

W: That sounds intriguing. Do you happen to know which clubs meet less often?

M: Sure. I've got a sheet listing everything right here. Look here . . . The hiking club meets once a week on Saturday, but its members may hike for several hours at a time.

W: I'll pass. I'm not into that kind of physical activity. What else is there?

M: Let's see . . . How about the chess club, the computer club, or the history club? Each of them only meets once every two weeks.

W: I love computers. When does that club meet again?

M: You're in luck. Its members are getting together tonight, so you can attend the meeting and sign up.

W: Excellent. What time and where?

Answer Explanations

1 Ⓓ The student tells the man, "I'm thinking of joining a club on campus, but, uh, I'm not really sure if I should or not."

2 Ⓐ First, the man says, "Writing for the student newspaper is extremely intensive." Then, he comments, "How about the chess club, the computer club, or the history club? Each of them only meets once every two weeks"

3 Ⓑ About the computer club, the student remarks, "I love computers. When does that club meet again?"

Dictation

M: There are <u>some</u> clubs that meet once a week for an hour or so <u>while</u> there are <u>others</u> that might only meet once <u>every</u> two weeks.

W: That sounds <u>intriguing</u>. Do you happen to know which clubs meet <u>less often</u>?

M: Sure. I've got a sheet <u>listing</u> everything right here. Look here . . . The hiking club meets <u>once a week</u> on Saturday, but its members may hike for several hours at a time.

W: I'll <u>pass</u>. I'm not into that kind of physical activity. <u>What else</u> is there?

M: Let's see . . . <u>How about</u> the chess club, the computer

club, or the history club? <u>Each of them</u> only meets once every two weeks.

W: I love computers. When does that club meet again?

M: You're <u>in luck</u>. Its members are getting together tonight, so you can attend the meeting and <u>sign up</u>

B

Answers

1 Ⓐ   2 Cloud-to-Ground Lightning: ③
Internal Cloud Lightning: ①, ④   Ball Lightning: ②
3 Ⓒ   4 Ⓐ

| Script |

Listen to part of a lecture in a meteorology class.

M Professor: So that's how lightning forms. Questions . . . ? No, okay, then please look at these pictures of lightning on the screen. Look here . . . here . . . here . . . and here . . . Notice that the lightning looks different in each picture. The reason is simple: Not all lightning is the same. Lightning is classified according to which direction it travels, its location in the sky, and the shape and branching of its bolts.

Lightning frequently travels from clouds to the ground and from the ground to clouds. Lightning moving from clouds to the ground is positively charged while lightning moving from the ground to clouds is negatively charged. There are more ground-to-cloud lightning strikes than there are cloud-to-ground strikes. These lightning strikes happen too fast to tell where they originated from, but we know they came from the ground because of the extra lightning branches they sprout. Ground-to-cloud strikes have lots of branching bolts at low altitudes, and, uh, the branching seems to extend toward the ground. As for cloud-to-ground strikes, there's hardly any branching at all. Instead, it typically appears as one huge bolt. Oh, there's another type of ground-to-cloud lightning. It originates from tall objects, so it doesn't appear to come from the ground. Skyscrapers and steel towers can serve as origin points for this type of lightning.

W Student: Which of those types of lightning is the most common?

M: None of them. The most common type of lightning is internal cloud lightning. This happens when a bolt travels from one cloud to another. It's also called sheet lightning because when it strikes, it seems to light up entire clouds, uh, as if they were white bedsheets. However, we usually don't see this kind of lightning except when it illuminates clouds.

All right, so those are the main types. But there are some other, um, more unusual ones. Look at this short video . . . It's anvil crawler lightning. Note how slowly it moves . . . It strikes in a horizontal direction, and the many branches it sprouts are formed in the direction it moves. Anvil crawler lightning occurs at high altitudes and produces soft, rolling thunder. It's sometimes visible at far distances when it lights up the sky, but we don't see the actual bolts. We often call it heat lightning.

A rarer form of lightning is called a bolt from the blue. This occurs when lightning appears to come from a clear sky. Actually, it comes from a distant cloud to a place where there are no clouds at all. It typically originates at the top of thunderstorms and travels downward, uh, but mostly horizontally, a great distance before striking the ground. Some of these bolts have been recorded hitting the ground more than fifteen kilometers from the nearest storm.

Look at this . . . and this . . . The first is bead lightning while the second is ball lightning. Both are rare and get their names from the shapes of their bolts. Bead lightning is a regular bolt that breaks up into small pieces or beads as it cools. It's uncommon to observe since it happens so swiftly. Ball lightning is extremely rare. It consists of spheres of electrical discharge floating along during thunderstorms. Many people have observed it, but there are few good pictures of it. And there is thus far no scientific explanation for it.

🎧4 Finally, there are two types of lightning rarely seen from the ground but which are sometimes observed by airline pilots. They shoot out from the tops of thunderstorms and are called sprites or jets. They come in red . . . and blue colors . . . **Nice, aren't they?** The red ones are fast and hard to see with the naked eye while the blue ones last longer and are commonly observed.

Answer Explanations

1 Ⓐ During the lecture, the professor talks about several types of lightning individually.

2 Cloud-to-Ground Lightning: ③
Internal Cloud Lightning: ①, ④ Ball Lightning: ②
About cloud-to-ground lightning, the professor says, "As for cloud-to-ground strikes, there's hardly any branching at all. Instead, it typically appears as one huge bolt." Regarding internal cloud lightning, he remarks, "It's also called sheet lightning because when it strikes, it seems to light up entire clouds, uh, as if they were white bedsheets," and, "The most common type of lightning is internal cloud lightning." As for ball lightning, he remarks, "And there is thus far no scientific explanation for it."

3 Ⓒ The professor describes what both anvil crawler lightning and bead lightning look at in the sky.

4 Ⓐ When the professor says, "Nice, isn't it?" with regard to the lightning he is looking at, he is indicating that he thinks the lightning looks impressive.

iBT Practice Test
p. 176

Answers

PART 1

1 Ⓓ 2 Ⓐ 3 Tutor: ②, ③ Study Group: ①, ④
4 Ⓑ 5 Ⓒ 6 Colonies in Spain: ①, ④
Carthage: ②, ③ 7 ①, ④ 8 Ⓒ 9 Ⓑ
10 Ⓑ 11 Ⓐ 12 String Instrument: ④
Wind Instrument: ①, ② Percussion Instrument: ③
13 Ⓓ 14 Ⓐ

PART 2

1 Ⓓ 2 Ⓐ 3 Ⓒ 4 Ⓓ 5 ①, ③
6 Ⓑ 7 Ⓐ 8 Ⓑ 9 Ⓓ

PART 1

Conversation [1-4]

| Script |

Listen to part of a conversation between a student and a professor.

M1 Professor: So, Marco, you e-mailed me last night and asked to have a meeting with me. Why don't you tell me what's on your mind?

M2 Student: Um, I'm really sorry to say this, but let me be frank . . . I'm thinking about dropping this class, Professor Reed.

M1: Dropping the class? B-b-b-b-but . . . but the semester is more than halfway finished. If you drop the class now, think of all the time you will have wasted. You should consider as well that the fact you took this class and then dropped it later will be noted on your transcript. That won't look good at all.

M2: Yes, sir, I am aware of both of the points you're making. But I need to tell you that the material we're covering has become much too difficult for me. I simply don't understand what we're doing in the class or the labs each week. I'm really worried that my grade on the final exam is going to be poor, and that will negatively affect my overall GPA.

M1: Okay, hold on a minute. You're concerned because you don't understand the material?

M2: Yes, sir. For the past, uh, two weeks or so, I've been totally lost in the class.

M1: Have you tried speaking with your teaching assistant? You know, um, asking whoever is assigned to you for some extra help.

M2: I spoke with my TA, but he didn't really seem interested in helping me.

M1: Who's your TA?

M2: Um . . . I think his name is Dave. I don't remember his last name though.

M1: David Parker. Okay, I've heard similar complaints about him in the past. It sounds like the two of us need to have a bit of a chat. He's got to take better care of the students in the class.

M2: Er . . . but if you tell him I was the student who complained, that could harm my grade. I mean, uh, he's the one who grades my tests and papers, right?

M1: Not anymore. I'll take care of them from now on. Now, let me ask a question . . . If you get some help on the material we're studying, will you stay in the class?

M2: Absolutely, sir. I need to take this class for my major. I really don't want to drop it and have to take it again next semester.

M1: Excellent. Then let me propose two solutions. First, you can obtain the services of a tutor from the tutoring office. Second, you can join a study group.

M2: Which would you recommend?

M1: Well, they both have advantages and disadvantages. If you use a tutor, for instance, you'll get all of your questions answered since you'll be learning one on one. However, the tutor might not always be available to meet when you have free time.

M2: And what about the study group?

M1: There are usually ten or so students in each study group. They're led by a grad student in this department. So you'll study with your classmates. Of course, not all of them are serious about studying, so you might not learn at a very fast pace depending upon the study group you join.

M2: Hmm . . . I think a study group is the better option for me. But, uh, I have no idea how I can join one.

Answer Explanations

1 Gist-Content Question

Ⓓ The student declares, "But I need to tell you that the material we're covering has become much too difficult for me. I simply don't understand what we're doing in the class or the labs each week."

2 Understanding Attitude Question

Ⓐ The professor says that he has heard complaints about David Parker before. Then, he remarks, "It sounds like the two of us need to have a bit of a chat. He's got to take better care of the students in the class." So he believes David Parker is doing a poor job as a teaching assistant.

3 Connecting Content Question

Tutor: ②, ③   Study Group: ①, ④

About tutors, the professor mentions, "If you use a tutor, for instance, you'll get all of your questions answered since you'll be learning one on one. However, the tutor might not always be available to meet when you have free time." And about study groups, the professor notes, "They're led by a grad student in this department. So you'll study with your classmates. Of course, not all of them are serious about studying, so you might not learn at a very fast pace depending upon the study group you join."

4 Making Inferences Question

Ⓑ The student remarks that he wants to join a study group but then says, "But, uh, I have no idea how I can join one." It is therefore likely that the professor will explain to the student what he needs to do.

Lecture #1 [5-9]

| Script |

Listen to part of a lecture in a history class.

M Professor: After becoming established as a major power in the eastern Mediterranean region, Phoenicia began expanding by founding colonies. Most of them were on the coast of North Africa and in parts of southern Europe. They also expanded onto some major islands in the Mediterranean, including Sicily and Crete. The Phoenicians, as you can imagine, were excellent shipbuilders and sailors. They even sailed out of the Mediterranean Sea and set up colonies on the Atlantic coasts of Spain and Morocco. Perhaps their largest and best-known colony was Carthage, um, in North Africa where Tunisia is presently located.

Historians believe this began around 1100 B.C. The Phoenicians had been trading with people in Greece and Egypt and then started moving further west. A large amount of their trade was in fish, salt, dyes, and textiles, especially wool. Then, they discovered silver, gold, and tin in distant Spain and had to find a way to ship everything home safely. They began setting up waypoints along the route. At first, these were simple trading outposts as the Phoenicians had no intention of establishing colonies. But, uh, as time passed, the outposts grew in size and importance. Within a few centuries, Phoenicia had colonies across the Mediterranean. Carthage, which would become their largest colony, was founded in 814 B.C.

These colonies quickly became powerful and stopped taking orders from the homeland. That's why we don't speak of the Phoenician Empire like we do about the Roman Empire or Alexander the Great's empire. At first, each colony paid tribute in goods to the homeland, but there was no central control. In time, the colonies became self-governing entities. This actually became necessary since the Babylonians and then, uh, later, Alexander defeated and captured the Phoenician homeland. It, by the way, was located where Lebanon and Israel are today. Although Phoenicia was conquered, its colonies thrived. In fact, many modern-day cities are located on the sites of Phoenician colonies. These include Genoa, Italy, and Marseilles, France.

Now, uh, I mentioned that the Phoenicians had colonies in Carthage and Spain. Well, there were a few differences between them. Carthage's wealth was based primarily on trade since it, being on the edge of a vast desert, had few resources of its own. The Spanish colonies' wealth, however, was based on mineral deposits and other natural resources. What else . . . ? Ah, yes. Carthage was a large, unified colony that encompassed many former Phoenician colonies while the small Spanish colonies were independent of one another. The Spanish colonies were, for the most part, on the coast of Spain or on the island off its southern shores. As a result, they didn't control much land in Spain's interior. The colonists in Spain were content to live that way though. That enabled them to become wealthy and to avoid aggressive conflicts.

Carthage, on the other hand, was extremely aggressive. Over time, it took control of all the Phoenician colonies in North Africa. Soon, it ruled nearly the entire North African coast, uh, with the exception of Egypt. It established a powerful navy and made a push for island colonies. Carthage soon gained control of Malta, Sardinia, some of the Phoenician colonies in Spain, and half of Sicily. This led to several wars with Greece for control of Sicily. The Greeks had moved south and west toward Sicily and the Italian mainland, so both sides frequently clashed. Carthage, however, suffered a setback in one of its wars against Greece as they both competed for control of Sicily. As a result, Carthage's power weakened, so in 410 B.C., some Spanish colonies that had been founded by Carthaginian settlers declared their independence. This resulted in the reduction of Carthage's supply of silver, tin, gold, and copper. Carthage was unable to deal with the Spanish colonies for a while since it was deeply involved in wars first with Greece and later with Rome.

W Student: Who won the war in Sicily? Did Carthage win?

M: Actually, I'd say nobody emerged victorious. The two sides fought for more than a century. Each won and lost various battles. The main outcome was that Carthage successfully prevented the Greeks from taking complete control of Sicily. Carthage also stopped the Greeks from advancing further south or west.

Later, in 264 B.C., Carthage and Rome clashed in the first of the famous Punic Wars. After the First Punic War ended, Carthage decided to deal with its rebellious Spanish colonies once and for all. An expedition there was led by Hamilcar Barca, the father of the famous Hannibal, who accompanied his father there. Hamilcar's army invaded southern Spain in 237 B.C. and easily overran the colonies. Hamilcar and his family controlled most of southern Spain after defeating many tribes and securing the mines in the region. Unfortunately for them, those conquests were lost during the Second Punic War from 218 to 201 B.C. Now, I think it's time to backtrack and go into detail on the First Punic War.

Answer Explanations

5 Gist-Content Question

Ⓒ The professor lectures on the colonies of the Phoenician Empire for the most part.

6 Connecting Content Question

Colonies in Spain: 1, 4   Carthage: 2, 3

About the colonies in Spain, the professor says, "The small Spanish colonies were independent of one another," and, "The Spanish colonies' wealth, however, was based on mineral deposits and other natural resources." As for Carthage, the professor remarks, "Carthage's wealth was based primarily on trade," and, "Carthage soon gained control of Malta, Sardinia, some of the Phoenician colonies in Spain, and half of Sicily."

7 Detail Question

1, 4 The professor tells the students, "Actually, I'd say nobody emerged victorious. The two sides fought for more than a century. Each won and lost various battles. The main outcome was that Carthage successfully prevented the Greeks from taking complete control of Sicily." There is no mention in the passage of Carthage losing control of several islands due to the fighting in Sicily. And it lost access to valuable minerals in Spain, not Sicily.

8 Understanding Organization Question

Ⓒ The professor mentions Hamilcar Barca to discuss his role in Carthage's wars.

9 Making Inferences Question

Ⓑ At the end of the lecture, the professor states, "Now, I think it's time to backtrack and go into detail on the First Punic War."

Lecture #2 [10-14]

| Script |

Listen to part of a lecture in a musicology class.

W Professor: Music has been around for as long as humans were able to make noises with their mouths and beat sticks on pieces of wood. Interestingly, many modern percussion, string, and wind instruments have ancestors that look familiar. I'd like to look at some now and then discuss the nature of music in the ancient world.

String instruments are among the oldest and most common types of musical instruments. We have some fragments of them, and there are references to them in paintings and texts from Mesopotamia, Egypt, Greece, and Rome. The most common string instrument was the lyre. Ancient lyres were string instruments that produced sound when a person plucked their strings. The sound was amplified by passing the strings over a sound box made either of a large turtle shell or of wood. Wooden boxes produced better sound quality, so it's believed that the more professional musicians used wooden boxed lyres. Look up here at the screen. Here are some pictures of ancient lyres . . . here . . . and here . . . and here are some that have survived to present day . . . Here's another one . . . and another. While they're different in various ways, you can see they all have the basic string and sound box configuration. As you can see . . . most lyres had seven strings . . . but some had more . . . or fewer . . .

A second significant stringed instrument was the harp . . . While similar to the lyre, the harp differs in the way it creates sound. A harp's strings are directly attached to the body of the instrument, and the strings' vibrations produce most of the sound. See here . . . A lyre's strings pass over a bridge on the sound box, and the vibrations make sounds with the assistance of the sound box, uh, sort of like a modern guitar. Speaking of modern guitars, an instrument that was somewhat similar to it was the cithara. It was a Greek instrument similar to a lyre. It was large and had a wooden sound box and seven strings. Here's a picture . . . The strings were often wound around wooden pegs on a cross bar at the top just like the guitar.

Wind instruments were the next most common ancient musical instruments. A common one was the pipe . . . or flute . . . They were ubiquitous as archaeologists have found examples of pipes in almost every ancient society and even at some prehistoric sites. One type of pipe was a hollowed-out wooden stick or a length of bone with strategically placed holes. When covered in certain ways, pipes produced various sounds. In many images from ancient times, we can see musicians blowing two pipes at the same time . . . Pretty neat, huh . . . ? In Greece, this instrument was known as the aulos. Other pipes had rows of hollowed-out tubes grouped together. Every tube produced various sounds because each of them had a different length. The panpipe, uh, here . . . is a good example of this instrument. In ancient Greece, it was called the syrinx.

Yet another ancient wind instrument was the horn. The first horns were hollowed-out, straight, or curved animal horns. Later ones were cast from brass, usually with bell-shaped ends similar to the ones modern brass instruments

have. But these ancient horns had no keys like today's trumpets and tubas. Numerous ancient societies made brass wind instruments. They were especially popular in Greece and Rome. Ancient musicians couldn't produce a wide variety of sounds with their instruments though, so they weren't often used to perform musical pieces.

There was a final common type of instrument. Percussion instruments, such as drums . . . tambourines . . . cymbals . . . and castanets . . . were common. Drums have been around since prehistoric times. Beating a stick on a hollow log may have been the first drum. Later ones used animal skins stretched over wooden or metal frames. Again, each society had its own version, but they all operated on the same principle as modern drums. They, uh, they made sounds through vibrations by striking or shaking objects. Yes, Daniel? Do you have something to add to the class?

M Student: I have a question, ma'am. How do we know what these ancient instruments sounded like?

W: Hmm . . . Well, we can make reproductions, so we know what sounds they were capable of making. But as for what music they played, that's more troublesome. Sadly, few pieces of ancient music have made it to modern times intact.

We do, however, know a few things about it . . . We know that the character of music in the ancient world was different from today's music. Most music in the past was for formal ceremonies or the battlefield. In the ancient world, musicians usually performed during, hmm . . . during royal processions, funerals, weddings, religious rites, victory marches, and games such as gladiatorial contests. Music was also important in war. Military marches helped soldiers stay in formation while horns and drums were used to signal the movements of soldiers. We have a bit of evidence that early societies used music for entertainment as well. Most of this comes from the Greeks. They used music during theatrical productions, while having poetry readings, and while entertaining guests at their homes.

Answer Explanations

10 Detail Question

Ⓑ The professor comments, "Speaking of modern guitars, an instrument that was somewhat similar to it was the cithara. It was a Greek instrument similar to a lyre."

11 Connecting Content Question

Ⓐ The professor says, "In Greece, this instrument was known as the aulos," and, "The panpipe, uh, here . . . is a good example of this instrument. In ancient Greece, it was called the syrinx."

12 Connecting Content Question

String Instrument: ④ Wind Instrument: ①, ②
Percussion Instrument: ③
About string instruments, the professor notes, "The sound

was amplified by passing the strings over a sound box made either of a large turtle shell or of wood." Regarding wind instruments, the professor notes, "Numerous ancient societies made brass wind instruments. They were especially popular in Greece and Rome." Then, she comments, "One type of pipe was a hollowed-out wooden stick or a length of bone with strategically placed holes." As for percussion instruments, the professor states, "Later ones used animal skins stretched over wooden or metal frames."

13 Making Inferences Question

Ⓓ The professor remarks, "Most music in the past was for formal ceremonies or the battlefield. In the ancient world, musicians usually performed during, hmm . . . during royal processions, funerals, weddings, religious rites, victory marches, and games such as gladiatorial contests. Music was also important in war. Military marches helped soldiers stay in formation while horns and drums were used to signal the movements of soldiers. We have a bit of evidence that early societies used music for entertainment as well." So it can be inferred that few people listened to music for enjoyment during ancient times.

14 Understanding Organization Question

Ⓐ During her lecture, the professor describes some different types of instruments and explains what they were used for.

PART 2

Conversation [1–4]

| Script |

Listen to part of a conversation between a student and a professor.

M Professor: Thank you for being patient enough to wait outside my office for a while, Rhoda. That was an important call from the dean of students, so I had to take it. But it went a lot longer than I had expected it to. The dean had a few important things he really wanted to talk to me about.

W Student: It's no problem at all. I just did some reading while I was waiting for you to finish your phone call.

M: That's great. So, um, please come in and have a seat. There's something that's pretty important about which I need to speak to you.

W: Yes, sir.

M: Rhoda . . . you've missed the last five classes in a row. Now, uh, I don't take attendance, so you won't lose any points for missing class. But I highly suggest that you attend every class. I mean, uh, your midterm exam grade wasn't very good. And now you're missing lots of classes. I would really hate to see you fail my class this semester.

W: Yes, sir. I understand. I'll do my best to attend class from now on.

M: That's good. But, er . . . do you mind telling me why you've been missing classes? It's an afternoon class, so you can't be sleeping in. I understand when students miss my 8:30 AM class. Some of them stay up really late studying and simply can't wake up and make it to class that early. But that's just not a plausible excuse for missing a class that begins at 3:00 in the afternoon.

W: Well, uh . . . I've been going downtown a lot lately. So I've been leaving around 2:30 or so each afternoon. And, um, that's why I haven't been able to go to any of your classes the past couple of weeks.

M: Going downtown? What are you doing there? Just hanging out with friends or something?

W: Not exactly.

M: Then what's going on? You should be on campus attending classes, you know.

W: Do you know the Richmond Shakespeare Theater?

M: Of course. I attend all of its performances each year . . . Wait a minute. You aren't working as a stagehand there, are you? That's just not a legitimate excuse.

W: No, sir. Actually, I'm playing the role of Viola in this year's production of *Twelfth Night*. So, uh, I've been rehearsing every day since opening night is this Friday. We want to make sure we all know our lines because this is the first performance of the year.

M: You have one of the main roles in the play?

W: Uh . . . Yes, I guess.

M: Okay. This is something that you should have told me about. I thought you were just skipping classes. But I guess since you're a Drama major, I understand why you aren't attending my History classes. Hmm . . . Well, you still have to do all of the work. You're not excused from that. And please make sure you get notes from someone in the class.

W: Thanks for understanding, sir.

M: And be sure to submit all of your assignments on time. There's a paper due next week. Are you aware of that?

W: Yes, one of my friends told me. I'm about halfway done so far.

M: Great. Then, uh, I guess I'll see you on Friday night.

Answer Explanations

1 Gist-Purpose Question

Ⓓ First, the professor says, "There's something that's pretty important about which I need to speak to you." Then, he adds, "Do you mind telling me why you've been missing classes?"

2 Understanding Function Question

Ⓐ The professor remarks, "I understand when students

miss my 8:30 AM class. Some of them stay up really late studying and simply can't wake up and make it to class that early. But that's just not a plausible excuse for missing a class that begins at 3:00 in the afternoon."

3 **Detail Question**

Ⓒ The professor instructs the student, "And be sure to submit all of your assignments on time. There's a paper due next week."

4 **Connecting Content Question**

Ⓓ About the Richmond Shakespeare Theater, the professor tells the student, "I attend all of its performances each year." Then, the student says, "Actually, I'm playing the role of Viola in this year's production of *Twelfth Night*. So, uh, I've been rehearsing every day since opening night is this Friday." Finally, the professor remarks, "Then, uh, I guess I'll see you on Friday night." So it can be inferred that the professor will see *Twelfth Night* performed at the theater on Friday.

Lecture [5-9]

| Script |

Listen to part of a lecture in an astronomy class.

M Professor: It isn't just the planets and their moons that orbit the sun. In the solar system, numerous other bodies go around the sun. Among the tiniest of them are asteroids. Well, uh, some asteroids are quite big, but the vast majority are very small. Asteroids come in a wide variety of shapes, they have no atmosphere, and they're rocky in nature. Some are free ranging, so, uh, they move on their own through space. 🎧9 But most asteroids lie between the orbits of Mars and Jupiter in the region we call the asteroid belt. There are also others locked into orbits with planets. **Thus far, astronomers have counted approximately a million asteroids, but there are certainly many more out there waiting to be discovered.**

Asteroids range in size from fewer than several meters to hundreds of kilometers in diameter. Some, such as Ceres, are so big that they're now classified as dwarf planets. Outside the dwarf planets, the largest asteroid is Vesta. It's around 530 kilometers in diameter. Most asteroids are irregular in shape, so they aren't spherical like the planets and their moons. In addition, despite being so numerous, the collective mass of all the asteroids discovered thus far is less than that of Earth's moon.

As for their origins . . . we need to go back to the early years of the solar system around 4.6 billion years in the past. At that time, lots of dust and gas were colliding and forming the beginnings of the planets. Some of this material never managed to join with anything else. Nearly all of that material exists between the inner and outer planets. Uh, by that, I mean between the orbits of

Mars and Jupiter. Astronomers theorize that the material was in the process of creating another planet. However, Jupiter formed first, which caused a problem. You see, Jupiter is so massive and its gravity so strong that these two factors prevented the formation of a planet between Mars and Jupiter. Some of the material had already achieved enough mass, however, so the bodies which had formed weren't broken apart by Jupiter's gravity. As a result, Ceres, Vesta, and many other asteroids were large enough not to be affected. But the rest of the material was not able to form anything large and therefore remained small, rocky bodies.

While most of the solar system's asteroids are in the asteroid belt, others are not. There's a special group called Trojan asteroids. These have the same composition as regular asteroids, but they have distinct orbital paths. Trojans are in the same orbital paths as planets. You're probably wondering why they don't crash into any planets. The reason is that they stay in special orbital spots called Lagrange points. Lagrange points are located both in front of and behind planets in places where gravitational forces create regions of stability. So asteroids kind of, um, just float in space and follow their planets around the sun. Most Trojan asteroids follow Jupiter, but a few have been found around other planets. Oh, and just so you know, the orbital points where they are located are named for the astronomer who identified them in the 1700s, Joseph Louis Lagrange.

Asteroids can be classified by their composition. Astronomers have named three main subtypes of asteroids: C, M, and S. C-type asteroids have a high level of carbon and are the most common. M-type asteroids have a high quantity of metallic elements, especially iron and nickel. S-type asteroids have lots of silicate materials. After C-type asteroids, S-type asteroids are the most common while M-type asteroids are the least common.

I should also talk about the usefulness of asteroids and the dangers they pose. Since asteroids are made of material that originally formed the universe, it's possible that we can learn from them. As a result, in recent years, some space probes have been sent to asteroids. In 2005, a Japanese probe landed on an asteroid and returned to the Earth with some material it had collected in 2010. It's also likely that we'll be mining asteroids in the future. But I don't want to discuss that until after the break.

Now, uh, most scientific effort directed toward asteroids is concerned with the danger they pose. The major fear is that a massive asteroid might impact the Earth someday.

W Student: Do you mean like a meteoroid?

M: Not quite. A meteoroid is just a smaller version of an asteroid. One way of looking at it is that if an object has a diameter smaller than one meter, it's a meteoroid. But if it's larger than that, it's an asteroid. Both can be dangerous though. If one comes near Earth, it's called an NEO. That's short for near-Earth object. There's an entire section of NASA that tracks NEOs and gives warnings about any that may come close to Earth. Now, let me talk to you about what could happen if an asteroid actually hit the planet.

Answer Explanations

5 Detail Question

[1], [3] The professor remarks, "You see, Jupiter is so massive and its gravity so strong that these two factors prevented the formation of a planet between Mars and Jupiter."

6 Connecting Content Question

Ⓑ First, the professor states, "But most asteroids lie between the orbits of Mars and Jupiter in the region we call the asteroid belt." Then, he adds, "You see, Jupiter is so massive and its gravity so strong that these two factors prevented the formation of a planet between Mars and Jupiter. Some of the material had already achieved enough mass, however, so the bodies which had formed weren't broken apart by Jupiter's gravity. As a result, Ceres, Vesta, and many other asteroids were large enough not to be affected." By indicating that Vesta is located between the orbits of Mars and Jupiter, the professor implies that it orbits the sun from inside the asteroid belt.

7 Understanding Organization Question

Ⓐ The professor focuses on why Trojan asteroids do not collide with planets when he says, "Trojans are in the same orbital paths as planets. You're probably wondering why they don't crash into any planets. The reason is that they stay in special orbital spots called Lagrange points. Lagrange points are located both in front of and behind planets in places where gravitational forces create regions of stability. So asteroids kind of, um, just float in space and follow their planets around the sun."

8 Connecting Content Question

Ⓑ The professor comments, "A meteoroid is just a smaller version of an asteroid. One way of looking at it is that if an object has a diameter smaller than one meter, it's a meteoroid. But if it's larger than that, it's an asteroid."

9 Understanding Function Question

Ⓓ The professor first states that there are "approximately a million asteroids" that astronomers have counted. Then, he adds, "There are certainly many more out there waiting to be discovered." The professor therefore implies that there are more than a million asteroids in the solar system.

| Vocabulary Review

p. 186

Answers

A
1 sanctioned 2 significant 3 toxic
4 fragments 5 encouraged
B
1 b 2 a 3 a 4 b 5 b
6 a 7 b 8 b 9 a 10 b

Actual Test

Answers

PART 1

1 ⓒ	2 Ⓑ	3 ①, ④	4 Ⓑ	5 Ⓓ
6 Ⓑ	7 Ⓓ	8 ⓒ		

9 Steam Car: ① Electric Car: ④ Gas Car: ②, ③

10 Ⓓ	11 ⓒ	12 ⓒ	13 ⓒ	14 Ⓑ
15 Ⓓ	16 ⓒ			

17 Soviet Space Program: ③, ④
American Space Program: ①, ②

PART 2

1 ⓒ	2 Ⓐ	3 Ⓓ	4 Ⓑ	5 Ⓓ
6 Ⓓ	7 ⓒ	8 Fact: ①, ②, ④ Not a Fact: ③		
9 Ⓑ	10 ②, ④	11 Ⓑ		

PART 1 Conversation   p. 189

| Script |

Listen to part of a conversation between a student and a professor.

M Student: Professor Jackson, I overheard someone in the department office talking a few minutes ago. The person commented that you've got a research project which you're going to be working on this summer. Would you, uh, would you happen to need any assistance on it?

W Professor: Yes, Allen, you're correct. I received a grant from a foundation to do some research. And I'll be working on it this summer as well.

M: That's awesome. Congratulations.

W: Thank you very much. I'm really looking forward to doing the project.

M: So . . . can I help you on it?

W: Don't you even want to know what it's about?

M: Yeah, I guess that would be good to know, wouldn't it? But I pretty much figure that it must be in your area of research, which is what I like. Am I right?

W: You are. I'll be doing research on one of the Native American tribes that lived in this area more than a thousand years ago. You might have heard that a new site was discovered in a farmer's field about half an hour away from here. Apparently, there are numerous artifacts all over the area. Fortunately, the farmer has agreed to give us access to his land to excavate the area.

M: Yeah, I remember reading something about that in the newspaper a month ago. I was wondering if you were going to get involved with the excavating.

W: Yes, I was pleased when I was asked to help on it. Now, it just so happens that I could use an assistant during the summer.

M: Yes?

W: 🎧4 And I believe you would be perfect for the job.

M: Wonderful. I accept.

W: **Sorry, Allen, but it's not as simple as that.**

M: It's not?

W: Sorry, but I have to do this properly. School rules, you know.

M: What do you have to do?

W: First, I have to advertise the position in the school newspaper. Then, I have to look at the applications which are submitted and interview the students who look like they have the potential to be good assistants. Finally, once all of that is done, I can make my selection. Now, you will most likely be the strongest candidate for the position, but you still need to complete an application and be interviewed.

M: Oh, okay. I guess that makes sense.

W: And just so you know, it's a paid position, but the stipend isn't very much. It only pays $500 a month for three months. And you'll have to arrange your own transportation to and from the dig site every day. It's also going to be difficult work. You know how hot it gets here in the summer? Well, you're going to be outside all day long, and you're going to be doing manual labor. 🎧5 Most people can't handle working that hard. Are you up for it?

M: **It's what I've always wanted to do, Professor.** And just so you know, I own a car and live fairly near the dig site, so getting there won't be a problem.

W: That's good to hear. Now, uh, the advertisement will appear in tomorrow's paper, and you'll be able to download an application form from the department's website then. So get your application to me as quickly as you can.

Answer Explanations

1 Gist- Content Question

ⓒ Most of the conversation is about a summer research project that the professor is going to be doing.

2 Making Inferences Question

Ⓑ The professor is talking about a Native American excavation site and conducting a dig for relics, so it can be inferred that she is a professor of archaeology.

3 Detail Question

①, ④ The professor comments, "It's a paid position, but the stipend isn't very much. It only pays $500 a month for three months." She also says, "You're going to be doing manual labor."

4 Understanding Attitude Question

Ⓑ When the professor says, "Sorry, Allen, but it's not as simple as that," after he comments that he will take the job, she is indicating that she has not hired him for the position.

5 Understanding Function Question

Ⓓ When the student responds, "It's what I've always wanted to do, Professor," after the professor asks him if he will be able to working hard, he is indicating that he will be able to do the hard work that will be required.

PART 1 Lecture #1   p. 192

| Script |

Listen to part of a lecture in a history of technology class.

M Professor: For most of history, people have used horses and other animals to travel, to transport loads, and to do other types of work. But the invention of the automobile—the modern car—changed how people lived. Now, uh, you should realize that the development of the automobile took time and advanced with small steps. It's a story which mainly took place in the eighteenth and nineteenth centuries in Europe and the United States. As for who invented it, well, it would be wrong to say that one person was responsible. Instead, several inventors played significant roles in its creation and, uh, later, its mass production.

🎧10 Okay, um, you should know that there were three primary types of early cars. We can describe them based on the power they used. These power supplies were steam, electricity, and gasoline. **Something most of you are likely unaware of is that the earliest cars utilized steam engines.** These were essentially, um, wagons with steam engines attached to them. The best-known steam car was built by Nicolas-Joseph Cugnot, a Frenchman, in 1769. Unfortunately, it, like the tractor he tried making for the French army, wasn't particularly successful. Both had trouble maintaining the steam pressure necessary to propel the machines due to leaks. Thus, they couldn't move much faster than a person walking could. However, they were important steps since they were among the first vehicles to move without animal power.

Later, inventors tried employing electricity as a power source. In Europe and the United States, inventors used electric engines powered by heavy batteries. These designs were more successful than cars with steam engines since they had more power and didn't need to burn fuel. Scottish inventor Robert Anderson is credited with making the first electric car. He did that sometime between 1832 and 1839. Yet his and other inventors' electric cars weren't good enough to replace horses. The biggest complaints were that the batteries were too heavy, didn't have enough power, and required frequent recharging. In addition, there were no recharging stations like there are today, so long trips were simply impossible.

The next step in the production of automobiles was the internal combustion engine. Again, several inventors produced working engines of this type. They utilized a variety of fuels, including coal gas, kerosene, and gasoline. The credit for the design of the modern-day gasoline-powered internal combustion engine goes to German inventor Gottlieb Daimler. He developed his engine in 1885. At the same time, German inventor Karl Benz created a car based on a gasoline engine of his own design. He received a patent for his car in 1886. His car was simple by today's standards. You can see some pictures of it if you look at page, um, page 268 in your books . . . Take a look . . . It had three wheels, so it looked like a tricycle . . . The engine was in the back . . . It also had a bench seat and an open cab . . . The driver controlled it with a long stick, uh, like a joystick in a jet fighter. See how it looks . . . ? Fascinating, isn't it? Benz's car had power and was reliable, yet interest in his invention was lacking. Then, in 1888, his wife took on the role of advertising his car. She and their two sons drove on a long trip between two cities. The subsequent publicity proved to people that the car was capable of replacing the horse. At the Paris World's Fair in 1889, Benz showed off his car to many curious onlookers.

In the next two decades, car manufacturers popped up around the world, and cars became rather popular. Yet they still didn't replace the horse. One reason was that the necessary infrastructure for cars was slow to grow. Roads weren't paved in most places, and cars often broke down on bad roads. Additionally, gas stations were rare because oil companies didn't want to invest in them when there were so few cars around. Plus, inventors were still working on steam and electric cars, so the market was flooded with various types of motor vehicles. Not all were reliable, so there was still a general mistrust of cars. 🎧11 Oh, and let's not forget that cars were expensive, so they were mainly tools and playthings for the wealthy.

W Student: I thought that the Model T and other American cars were both reliable and cheap.

M: **Ah, I haven't gotten to that part of my talk yet.** But I suppose I can mention it now. The turning point for cars came when American Henry Ford started mass-producing gas-powered vehicles. Ford founded his company in 1903. He wanted to reduce the manufacturing costs to reduce the prices of his vehicles. Over time, he developed assembly-line techniques to mass-produce cars. His greatest success came with the Model T car, uh, first made in 1908. It was the first car common workers could afford to buy. Initially, it was priced at around eight hundred dollars. But by the 1920s, the ease and cheapness of manufacturing let Ford sell it for about three hundred dollars.

6 Gist-Content Question

Ⓑ Most of the lecture is about how the automobile was developed over time.

7 Detail Question

Ⓓ The professor comments, "Scottish inventor Robert Anderson is credited with making the first electric car."

8 Understanding Organization Question

Ⓒ The professor says, "You can see some pictures of it if you look at page, um, page 268 in your books . . . Take a look." Then, the professor describes the car.

9 Connecting Content Question

Steam Car: 1 Electric Car: 4 Gas Car: 2, 3
About the steam car, the professor mentions, "They couldn't move much faster than a person walking could." Regarding the electric car, the professor says, "Inventors used electric engines powered by heavy batteries." And as for the gas car, the professor remarks, "The turning point for cars came when American Henry Ford started mass-producing gas-powered vehicles," and, "At the Paris World's Fair in 1889, Benz showed off his car to many curious onlookers."

10 Understanding Attitude Question

Ⓓ In stating, "Something most of you are likely unaware of," the professor is implying that he believes he is stating a little-known fact.

11 Understanding Function Question

Ⓒ The student mentions the Model T as a cheap car, and the professor responds, "I haven't gotten to that part of my talk yet." In saying that, he is indicating that he agrees with the student that the Model T was cheap yet simply hasn't gotten to the point in his lecture where he is ready to discuss it.

PART 1 Lecture #2 — p. 195

| Script |

Listen to part of a lecture in an astronomy class.

W Professor: Soviet cosmonaut Yuri Gagarin became the first human to fly into space on April 12, 1961. The first American to accomplish that feat was Alan Shepard. He did that on May 5, 1961. Prior to those two flights, both countries sent living creatures into space. They used several different species of insects and mammals. The Soviets mostly sent dogs while the Americans preferred to launch monkeys into orbit in the years before the first manned flights.

They did this for one simple reason: No one knew exactly what would happen to a living creature while in outer space. In space, there's no gravity, there are extremely hot and cold temperatures, and radiation presents problems, too. Scientists had some idea how those factors would affect humans, but they weren't sure what would happen. They were also concerned about prolonged periods of weightlessness and how it would affect the bodies of people in orbit. Since no one had ever been in space, it was deemed prudent to test the conditions on animals first before risking sending a human there.

M Student: Excuse me, but where exactly does space begin?

W: The boundary is generally agreed to be about 100 kilometers above sea level. That's where the atmosphere meets space. It is called the Karman Line. That's K-A-R-M-A-N. It's named for Hungarian scientist Theodore von Karman. The first living creatures to cross this boundary were fruit flies, which some American scientists placed onboard a German V-2 rocket in 1947. They survived the flight and were recovered. Next, rhesus monkeys were tested. A monkey named Albert I was placed in a sealed capsule on top of a V-2 rocket on June 11, 1948. However, the rocket never passed the Karman Line. Even worse, Albert I died due to a lack of oxygen during the flight.

On June 14, 1949, another rhesus monkey, named Albert II, was launched on a V-2 rocket. This time, the rocket traveled more than 130 kilometers above the ground. So Albert II was the first mammal to reach space. Sadly, he died on impact with the ground when the capsule's parachute malfunctioned. Further tests with monkeys proved fatal as well since early rockets had numerous problems. Finally, on September 20, 1951, another monkey, named Yorick, survived the flight and landing. Alas, poor Yorick died soon afterward though. Scientists thought the stress on his body during the flight killed him.

Yorick wasn't the first mammal to survive the flight and landing. The Soviets were also busy launching dogs into space. In a series of tests, they launched nine dogs— all females—into space. Three of the dogs made two trips. The first flight was on August 15, 1951. Two dogs named Dezik and Tsygan were launched into space. They survived the flight and impact, becoming the first mammals to do so. They continued to live, unlike Yorick. Other dogs weren't as lucky, but most of the Soviet test dogs lived through their flights. After the successful launch and orbit of the artificial satellite *Sputnik* in 1957, the Soviets hastened to get a man into space before the Americans could. They were ambitious, too. They didn't just want to get a man past the Karman Line. They wanted to make him orbit the planet.

The first step the Soviets took was to put a dog into orbit in a container under a satellite similar to *Sputnik*. They put a female dog named Laika onboard and launched her into orbit on November 3, 1957. The satellite wasn't designed to return to the Earth. In fact, the Soviets were too hasty and designed the container poorly. As a result, Laika died after about two hours, either due to overheating or a lack of oxygen. The Soviets learned from this and took care with the next launch. They designed a strong capsule that would return to the Earth. Two dogs—Strelka and Belka—plus a rabbit, some mice, rats, and fruit flies, were sent into orbit on August 19, 1960. They all successfully returned home and became the first animals to survive an orbital flight.

Meanwhile, the Americans continued testing with monkeys. On May 28, 1959, they launched two monkeys into space on the same rocket. One was a rhesus monkey named Able while the other was a squirrel monkey named Baker. They went up almost 600 kilometers above the surface and traveled nearly 3,000 kilometers before the capsule returned to the Earth. Able and Baker withstood strong g-forces and weightlessness with no negative effects on their bodies as they survived the flight. The next animal into space was a chimpanzee named Ham. During his flight on January 31, 1961, he pulled levers and did other tasks that proved living creatures could work in zero gravity. The success of all these animal flights led the Soviets and Americans to approve manned missions, which would start soon afterward.

Answer Explanations

12 Gist-Content Question

ⓒ The entire lecture is about the various animals that the Soviets and Americans sent into outer space.

13 Gist-Purpose Question

ⓒ About the Karman Line, the professor notes, "The boundary is generally agreed to be about 100 kilometers above sea level. That's where the atmosphere meets space. It is called the Karman Line."

14 Connecting Content Question

ⓑ First, the professor states, "The boundary is generally agreed to be about 100 kilometers above sea level. That's where the atmosphere meets space. It is called the Karman Line." Then, the professor remarks, "On June 14, 1949, another rhesus monkey, named Albert II, was launched on a V-2 rocket. This time, the rocket traveled more than 130 kilometers above the ground." The professor therefore implies that Albert II traveled past the Karman Line.

15 Understanding Organization Question

ⓓ The professor comments, "After the successful launch and orbit of the artificial satellite *Sputnik* in 1957, the Soviets hastened to get a man into space before the Americans could. They were ambitious, too. They didn't just want to get a man past the Karman Line. They wanted to make him orbit the planet."

16 Detail Question

ⓒ About Ham, the professor says, "The next animal into space was a chimpanzee named Ham. During his flight

on January 31, 1961, he pulled levers and did other tasks that proved living creatures could work in zero gravity."

17 Connecting Content Question

Soviet Space Program: ③, ④
American Space Program: ①, ②
About the Soviet space program, the professor states, "The Soviets mostly sent dogs," and, "The Soviets learned from this and took care with the next launch. They designed a strong capsule that would return to the Earth. Two dogs—Strelka and Belka—plus a rabbit, some mice, rats, and fruit flies, were sent into orbit on August 19, 1960. They all successfully returned home and became the first animals to survive an orbital flight." Regarding the American space program, the professor notes, "The first living creatures to cross this boundary were fruit flies, which some American scientists placed onboard a German V-2 rocket in 1947," and she mentions other instances of the Americans sending V-2 rockets into space.

PART 2 Conversation p. 198

| Script |

Listen to part of a conversation between a student and a Registrar's office employee.

M **Registrar's Office Employee:** Hello. If you're next in line, you can come over here, and I can help you.

W **Student:** Thank you, sir.

M: My pleasure. What can I do for you today?

W: I'm planning to withdraw from school, but I don't know what the process is.

M: Okay . . . Can you tell me why you're going to leave? Does this have to do with money, grades or, uh, something else?

W: Neither of those reasons. I'm planning to go abroad to do some volunteer work in Argentina. I'll be away for around six months or so.

M: Ah, so this isn't a permanent withdrawal, right? Do you intend to come back and reenroll once your volunteer service is complete?

W: Yes, that's exactly what I plan to do.

M: And when are you leaving? At the end of the semester?

W: Actually, uh, two days from now.

M: Um . . . we're still in the middle of the semester. Do you realize you're either going to get F's or incompletes in all of your classes if you do that?

W: I spoke with my professors already, and all but one of them agreed to give me an incomplete. Those professors are going to let me complete my coursework when I return next semester. As for the other professor, well, um,

I'm going to drop her class.

M: Okay, that's good. I'm glad you already spoke with them. Now, uh, what you need to do is fill out this form, uh . . . here . . . This is a temporary leave of absence form. 🎧5 Please be sure to fill out every blank on the paper, especially the one explaining why you're going to be away from school. Then, you need to sign the form and get your advisor to sign it, too.

W: Oh . . . **I think that's going to be a problem.**

M: Why do you say that?

W: My advisor just left this morning to attend a conference in New Orleans. He's not going to be back until next week, and, well, I'm going to be gone by then. What happens if I don't bother filling out the form?

M: Nothing good. You'd get all F's in your classes for the semester. As a result, you'd be put on academic probation. And, of course, your GPA would be negatively affected by having so many failing grades. Future employers or graduate schools would notice your poor performance and be less likely to hire you or accept you into their programs.

W: Ugh. You're right. That's not good. Well, what do you recommend that I do? My flight leaves on Saturday, and there's nothing I can do to change it. I can sign the form, of course, but my advisor can't.

M: Okay, here's what I want you to do. You need to go to the dean of students right now and explain the situation to him. He should be able to authorize the head of your department to sign in your advisor's place. So get that person's signature and bring the form back here to me by tomorrow.

W: Is the dean of students in his office?

M: He's always there until six on Wednesdays. I'll call his secretary and explain the situation, so you'll be sure to get in to see him. Now, take this form and get going. You've got to walk halfway across campus to get there.

Answer Explanations

1 **Gist- Content Question**
Ⓒ The student remarks, "I'm planning to withdraw from school, but I don't know what the process is."

2 **Detail Question**
Ⓐ The student says, "I'm planning to go abroad to do some volunteer work in Argentina."

3 **Understanding Function Question**
Ⓓ The student asks, "What happens if I don't bother filling out the form?" Then, the man responds, "You'd get all F's in your classes for the semester."

4 **Making Inferences Question**
Ⓑ The man tells the student that she needs to see the dean of students and then adds, "He's always there until six on Wednesdays. I'll call his secretary and explain the

situation, so you'll be sure to get in to see him. Now, take this form and get going."

5 **Understanding Function Question**
Ⓓ The man tells the student to get her advisor's signature, but then she remarks, "Oh . . . I think that's going to be a problem." When the student says this, she is implying that she cannot get her advisor's signature.

PART 2 Lecture   p. 201

| Script |

Listen to part of a lecture in an architecture class.

W1 Professor: When you think of Roman architecture, I bet one structure comes to most of your minds. Look up here at the screen and see if I'm right . . . Yeah, it's the Colosseum in Rome. It's one of the numerous Roman structures which have survived to modern times and is a popular tourist attraction. Right now, I'd like to provide some background information on the Colosseum, and then I'll discuss it in detail.

The Romans built the Colosseum between 72 and 80 A.D. and then added various modifications at later times. The builders designed it for various entertainment spectacles. It was built with several tiers of seats and eventually included places underground for gladiators and animals to wait before entering the arena. Over several centuries of use, many types of shows were put on there. Most of these spectacles involved violence of some kind. 🎧11 These even included gladiatorial battles involving hundreds of fights and mock battles with ships. Yes, ships. The Colosseum could be filled with water so that ships could float on it. Incredible, huh? **You don't see engineering ability like that these days.**

The structure's original name is the Flavian Amphitheater. It was named for the Flavian Dynasty of Roman emperors who oversaw its construction. Over time, its name changed to the Colosseum. By medieval times, it was generally known by that name. The change was probably due to the huge statue of Emperor Nero that stood nearby the amphitheater. The Romans often called the statue Colossus since it was similar to the fabled statue known as the Colossus of Rhodes. Somehow, the name of the statue began getting used for the arena itself.

Emperor Vespasian . . . here's a picture of him . . . initiated construction on the Colosseum in 72 A.D. He selected a flat area of land which Nero had used to build a lake and gardens on. Workers filled in the lake and destroyed the surrounding structures to make room for the arena. Most amphitheaters in the ancient world were built into hillsides and used the earth as a support for many rows of seats. The Colosseum, however, is a free-standing structure made mainly of stone, brick, and concrete. Remember that the Romans invented concrete and mastered the ability to use it to make solid structures. The fact that the Colosseum is still standing today proves this point.

Um, as I said a moment ago, the builders designed it for public spectacles, so it had several tiers of seats. The Colosseum could hold up to 50,000 spectators. This made it the largest amphitheater in the ancient world. Slaves, many of whom had been captured in wars, did most of the heavy labor. Architects, engineers, and skilled stonecutters did the more complex work. It's estimated that more than 100,000 cubic meters of limestone from nearby quarries was used to construct the Colosseum.

W2 Student: I know it's enormous, but what are its dimensions?

W1: Just a moment . . . I have the figures right here . . . Ah, here they are. The Colosseum is oval in shape so is 188 meters in length on its long axis and 156 meters in length on its shorter axis. It was nearly fifty meters high originally.

Now, uh, what about its design particulars . . . ? The structure has four main levels . . . See them here on the screen . . . The first three have tiers of arches supported by columns like this one . . . Each level uses a different style of column. At the bottom are simple Tuscan columns . . . That's the Roman version of the Greek Doric column. In the second row here . . . are Ionic columns . . . and the third row contains columns in the elaborate Corinthian style . . . The arches on the lower row are slightly higher than those on the top row. The fourth level at the top has small, square windows spaced wider apart than the arches on the other levels. Most of the fourth level is gone now, uh, mainly due to earthquakes. In Roman times, the fourth level had canopies, um, like screens, that were pulled over the stands on hot days to protect spectators from the sun.

Look here . . . The Colosseum has four main entrance arches . . . located at each end of its long and short axis, thereby allowing spectators easy access. The main area floor is seventy-six by forty-four meters in dimension. Originally, it had a simple ground floor covered with sand. But later modifications added a wooden floor supported by posts . . . and then a stone floor supported by posts later . . . These floors were then covered with sand for the events. Under the floors were numerous chambers for gladiators and animals . . . Look at that . . . There were also lifts that could carry men and animals to the arena floors from underground. The floor has long since disappeared, and the underground chambers can be easily seen . . . here . . . and here . . . The floor was surrounded by a three-meter-high wall around its edges. The builders included many elaborate stucco designs . . . paintings . . . and other ornamentation . . . However, much of it disappeared over the centuries. Today, most of the Colosseum is merely the stone, brick, and concrete of the original structure.

6 **Gist-Content Question**

ⒹThe professor focuses on the primary features of the Colosseum in her lecture.

7 **Understanding Function Question**

ⒸThe professor comments, "The change was probably due to the huge statue of Emperor Nero that stood nearby the amphitheater. The Romans often called the statue Colossus since it was similar to the fabled statue known as the Colossus of Rhodes. Somehow, the name of the statue began getting used for the arena itself."

8 **Detail Question**

Fact: 1, 2, 4   Not a Fact: 3
The professor says, "Most amphitheaters in the ancient world were built into hillsides and used the earth as a support for many rows of seats. The Colosseum, however, is a free-standing structure made mainly of stone, brick, and concrete." She also states, "The structure has four main levels . . . See them here on the screen . . . The first three have tiers of arches supported by columns like this one . . . Each level uses a different style of column." Finally, she notes, "The Colosseum could hold up to 50,000 spectators." However, the professor mentions, "The Romans built the Colosseum between 72 and 80 A.D.," so it did not take more than ten years to build the Colosseum.

9 **Understanding Function Question**

ⒷThe professor describes the dimensions of the Colosseum after a student asks, "I know it's enormous, but what are its dimensions?"

10 **Detail Question**

2, 4 The professor remarks, "Under the floors were numerous chambers for gladiators and animals . . . Look at that . . . There were also lifts that could carry men and animals to the arena floors from underground."

11 **Understanding Attitude Question**

ⒷWhen the professor comments, "You don't see engineering ability like that these days," she is indicating that Roman engineering skills were better than those in modern times as she is very impressed by their quality.